REDEFINING DEATH

REDEFINING DEATH

Karen Grandstrand Gervais

YALE UNIVERSITY PRESS
New Haven and London

Designed by Susan P. Fillion and set in Novarese Book
display and Electra text type by The Composing Room of
Michigan. Printed in the United States of America by The
Alpine Press, Stoughton, Mass.

Library of Congress Cataloging-in-Publication Data

Gervais, Karen Grandstrand, 1944–
    Redefining death.

    Bibliography: p.
    Includes index.
    1. Death.   I. Title.
BD444.G44   1986   128'.5   86–10978
ISBN 0–300–03616–7

*The paper in this book meets the guidelines for permanence
and durability of the Committee on Production Guidelines
for Book Longevity of the Council on Library Resources.*

10   9   8   7   6   5   4   3   2

To the memory of my mother and father
Irene Caroline Grandstrand, 1904–75
Charles Marvin Grandstrand, 1904–79
and to
Lourene, beloved aunt
Jerry, beloved husband
Heidi and Kerry, beloved children
Jerry Alan, James, and Cindy, beloved stepchildren

Death is the one great certainty.

President's Commission, *Defining Death*

If technology has blurred the traditional distinction between a man alive and a man dead then there is an urgent and pressing reason to restore clarity.

David Lamb, *Death, Brain Death and Ethics*

In the absence of an understanding, I may owe you, in your extremity, unbounded attention and concern, comfort and livelihood, room and board, and the best medical attention in perpetuity, and feel guilty when I stop to wonder whether you are worth the burden you are putting on me. When it is my turn of course I'll expect the same from you (or from whoever has the corresponding responsibility toward me that I had toward you), feeling a little guilty perhaps but not enough to relinquish my claim. But if we could sit down together at an early age in good health and legislate our relation to each other, specifying the entitlements we wished to obtain between us, recognizing equal likelihood of being beneficiaries or benefactors, we could elect to eschew exorbitant claims.

Thomas C. Schelling, *Choice and Consequence*

Contents

Preface   ix
Acknowledgments   xiii

1. Introduction   1
   The Ambiguous Concept of Human Death   1
   A History of the Problem   6
   A Blueprint   15

2. Concepts and Criteria   18
   The Nature of a Conceptual Problem   21
   The Traditional Criteria and the Brain-death
   *   Criterion*   23

3. Biological Arguments   45
   Lawrence Becker's Organic Definition   46
   David Lamb's Brain-death Definition   62

4. Moral Arguments   75
   The Moralists   79
   Assessments of the Moral Approach   105

5. Ontological Arguments 111

 Green and Wikler's Ontological Argument 113
 Implications of the Ontological Argument 134
 David Lamb Revisited 144

6. Redefining Death 159

 Reconsidering the Meaning of Human Death 162
 Human Death as the Death of the Person 164
 The Ontological Approach to the Conditions of
 Personal Existence 177
 Redefining Death 181

7. Public Policy Considerations 183

 The Theoretical Argument 183
 The Uniform Declaration of Death Act 198
 Recommendations for Policy Change 205

 Notes 217
 References 223
 Index 229

Preface

Since there are many constituencies interested in the issue of redefining death, and therefore several vantage points from which one might approach its perplexities, it is important to outline my purpose at the outset. This book is a philosophical one, born of a sense that there is a disturbing disconnection between theory and practice about declaring death. It is a sustained effort to show that disconnection, and to identify and provide the means to remedy it. Much of this book (in particular chapters 3, 4, and 5) is a critical analysis of the work of others who have contributed significantly to the drifting philosophical discussion surrounding the redefinition debate. I hope that my analysis of their views will provide a forum for discussing the conceptual deficiencies currently so pervasive in the philosophical literature on redefining death. Thus, the analysis forms the backbone of my entire argument.

My medical knowledge is modest, but sufficient to the tasks I undertake here: first, to show that the use of the brain-death and neocortical-death criteria rests on a common conceptual commitment that differs from the concept supporting the traditional heart-and-lung criteria; second, to argue that we ought to abandon our conceptual commitments to the traditional criteria for declaring death; and third, to discuss the public policy readjustments warranted by this conceptual revision and by ethical commitments already central to health care policy making in our society.

The full elaboration of the argument of this book would require an extensive excursis into personal identity theory as well as a discussion of the merits of alternative models of ethical reasoning. With respect to the former, I use the method of counterexample to show that a particular personal identity theory (that espoused by John Perry and appealed to in the work on redefining death by Michael Green and Daniel Wikler) has difficulties that a more modest mentalist view avoids. I point to some of the realities for which such a theory must account and suggest a redesigning of the theory. In the end, I argue that the philosophical direction we must take to vindicate the brain-death and neocortical-death criteria is that of personal identity theory.

With respect to ethical reasoning, this book is not a treatise in theoretical ethics. Some readers may be disappointed that there is not more discussion of theoretical issues. Everyone doing applied ethics suffers under this same burden, of course. Devising an adequate perspective for ethical reflection is a formidible task indeed, one I hope to further in this book. I suggest that a contractual approach to ethical problem solving is the most promising. Such an approach can elicit thoughtful responses to pressing questions from individuals of diverse personal, intellectual, and professional backgrounds. I use the contractual approach at two points: first, to establish the crucial premise that our focus should be on the human as person if we are to define an adequate concept of human death; and second, to support the public policy recommendation I develop in chapter 7.

Medical, legal, and other professionals interested in the redefinition of death may not be altogether comfortable with a substantially philosophical treatment of the issue. I confess that I have taken from their literature only as my general purpose has dictated. That purpose is philosophical. This book provides strong presumptive evidence for the claim that the resolution of complex practical issues requires philosophical analysis and argument, as well as for the claim that philosophical analysis and argument necessarily have practical impact. In a letter to Norman Malcolm, Ludwig Wittgenstein wrote, "What is the use of philosophy . . . if it does not improve your thinking about the important questions of everyday life?" Surely death must be among those questions. While this is a philosophical work, then, it is not on that account for philosophers only. Some practical dilemmas will never be settled without philosophical inquiry. The redefinition of death is such a dilemma, and I hope that this book may help lay it to rest.

Acknowledgments

Acknowledgments for one's first book must extend deeply into one's past, reflecting one's intellectual roots. For me, this is a complex matter. My parents—high school graduates only—provided me with an environment that encouraged me to identify myself as a student. The values they placed on hard work and education have helped to bring about this book. As an Oberlin College student I was influenced by Clyde Holbrook, who praised and fostered my native analytical inclinations, and by Ira Steinberg, who helped me make the difficult leaps from truths gained in analytical work to the drastic changes of life that intellectual honesty demands of us. As a graduate student in philosophy at the University of Minnesota, I began a friendship with Mario del Carril, who contributed significantly to the early stages of my preparation as a philosopher and a teacher.

My graduate school experience led to associations with philosophers who influenced me in important ways. May Brodbeck tempered her dedication to the highest standards of professionalism with a deeply compassionate attitude toward others. She will always remain an example to me. Norman Dahl, my dissertation adviser, helped me to become a more disciplined thinker and writer, and eventually persuaded me to live with the idea that perfection was always at least one more draft away. Late in my graduate school career, Rolf Sartorius turned my philosophical concerns in a specific direction which has had a strong impact on this book. In addition, Rolf has provided the initial advice and guidance that someone new to publishing requires. As a teacher he commits himself to the fullest nurturing of his students' capacities.

Among my colleagues at Illinois Wesleyan University, two have been particularly supportive of my work. My chairperson, L. W. Colter, has read and commented extensively on several chapters of the manuscript. My deepest appreciation must go to Gregory Leyh, a colleague in political science. Greg's meticulous commentary on the manuscript has both challenged and encouraged me; and his willingness to labor over my work, often at the expense of his own projects, has been an inspiring lesson in both collegiality and friendship.

I must also acknowledge Illinois Wesleyan University for granting me sabbatical leaves in 1980–81 and in January 1985, as well as for providing financial support to offset some of the costs of final preparation of the manuscript for publication. For her exacting work in the typing and final preparation of my manuscript, Glenna Schaab has my sincere praise and gratitude.

Finally, my family. The completion of this book was possible because of their willingness to let me pull back from my usual responsibilities, to fill in for me or to muddle along in the interim, so that I could complete a line, a paragraph, a page, or a chapter. This book is as much a result of their commitment and perseverance as it is of mine.

REDEFINING DEATH

chapter 1

Introduction

In the literature on death and dying, two ethical issues loom larger than the rest: how should we define death, and is euthanasia ever justified? This book is about the former question. Euthanasia will be discussed only as a possible response to cases of brain death and persistent vegetative existence.

Any decision concerning the adoption of a particular set of practical criteria or clinical tests to be used in declaring a person dead presupposes the acceptance of particular concepts of death, human death, human being, and person, as well as a view about the proper treatment of former persons. Hence, if we are to set forth complete criteria for declaring death, we must first articulate and defend a framework of concepts providing a context for the use of these criteria. Otherwise, the criteria can never be justified by arguments that tie them to the important conceptual commitments underlying their use.

The Ambiguous Concept of Human Death

The traditional criteria for declaring death (the permanent cessation of heart and lung functioning) are no different from the brain-death criterion (the permanent cessation of brain functioning at all levels) in one respect: the use of either presumes certain truths about the nature of human death, human beings, and persons, and about the treatment of persons and former persons. Until we developed the power to maintain cardiac and respiratory functions mechanically, there was really no need to scrutinize the conceptual underpinnings of our decision to declare a person dead when his heart and lungs ceased functioning: heart and lung failure brought on the failure of all the other major organ systems almost immediately. Hence, the whole individual appeared to die at once. There were no confusions to ponder and dispel. Yet it must be emphasized that there was a decision inherent in the use of even the traditional criteria, for the acceptance of any criterion for declaring death must rest on conceptual commitments of the sort mentioned above.

The point is better conveyed, perhaps, by showing that behind the use of any criterion for declaring death there lies what I shall call a decision of significance, that is, a decision that there is a certain feature (or cluster of features) whose permanent absence constitutes the death of the person. Clearly, the traditional criteria rest on such a decision of significance, since a declaration of death on their basis does not coincide with the complete cessation of the organism's biological activity. Hence, the use of the traditional criteria implies that these particular biological events—the cessation of heart and lung function—have been selected out, endowed with a particular significance. To demonstrate this, consider that each of us is a biological organism with a particular biological history. The biological lifeline of an organism starts at conception: the moment the egg and the sperm unite marks the beginning of the growth and differentiation of a unique organism that was not present before. We may likewise imagine the biological lifeline of an individual, along which we might mark certain events, such as a fractured limb, and processes, such as puberty.

Our particular concern is with the end of a person's life, and our question is about the relationship between biological events or processes and the decision to declare a person dead. Let us assume that it is 1800 and that no artificial support systems are available. The individual represented by our biological lifeline suffers a massive heart attack that leads rapidly to the cessation of heart and lung functioning. Moments later, when the permanent cessation of heart and lung activity are obvious, the individual is declared dead by those attending him. We enter the last event on the lifeline, but it must be noted that the biological activity of the organism has not ceased. Various forms of activity will continue in the body for a considerable period of time; while integrated organic functioning has irreversibly ended, all organic functioning has not. Without an argument distinguishing integrated organismic or biological life from the continuation of some forms of biological activity in the organism, the biological lifeline of the individual cannot be closed off. However, the person's death has been pronounced, and the person (or, more accurately, the person's body) will be ushered out of our arena of interaction forever. Biological cessation per se therefore has no important relationship to the decision to declare a person dead. Such a decision rests on a further decision of significance, perhaps unarticulated and unexamined because of its presumed obviousness, but nevertheless there.

As far as the traditional criteria are concerned, there has apparently been no argument in the matter: the changes brought about when the heart and lungs stopped their functioning were taken as unambiguous signs that what had once been a living person was now a dead person. Even though there has always been an apparent consensus that the traditional criteria are appropriate and adequate to their use, we must nevertheless inquire into the conceptual commitments underlying the choice of heart and lung functions, rather than some other biological functions, as signs of life. The declaration of death is clearly an event, just as the heart attack is an event, but it is not a biological event. It is an action, based on a decision of significance, and is therefore an event that has social, moral, and metaphysical roots and implications. As such, we can expect that compelling social, moral, and metaphysical reasons can be set forth as justification of that action.

There has been some debate over whether death is a process or an event. If it is a process, how are we to settle on a precise time of its occurrence? How are we to force it into the language of events? If it is an event, how do we explain the obvious biological situation that deterioration, destruction, and decay are not isolated events but gradual processes?

Robert S. Morison accuses many who use the word *death* of a version of "the fallacy of misplaced concreteness . . . (i.e., regarding or using an abstraction as if it were a thing)."[1] Morison is most concerned with some of the possible results of this practice: "A particularly frequent hazard is the use of abstractions to introduce artificial discontinuities into what are essentially continuous processes. . . . Clearly we are dealing here with a continuous process of growth and decay. There is no magic moment at which "everything" disappears. Death is no more a single, clearly delimited, momentary phenomenon than is infancy, adolescence, or middle age."[2]

From a biological perspective, Morison is right: if we construe dying and death as deterioration and destruction, they are processes, and depending on their cause, they exhibit different temporal characteristics. But Morison's biological claim is consistent with the metaphysical claim that death is an event in the history of a person that is measured by, but not identical with, the occurrence of a particular biological event or events. Our decision to declare death when a certain biological event or set of events takes place is informed by metaphysical and moral considerations. The death of a person is a metaphysical event with a wide range of moral implications: it erases particular social ties; it radically reconstitutes individuals' relationships, responsibilities, and rights. As a result, there is at least the pragmatic necessity to delimit, in the biological process of death, a single event or cluster of events which will serve as a signal that a particular personal existence has ended, and that the appropriate and necessary social, legal, and moral restructuring may now begin. Clearly, then, any approach to human death that allows us to speak in terms of the moment of death presupposes that one moment in the biological process of the dissolution of an organism has greater significance (for metaphysical and moral reasons) than the others.

For instance, the significance upon which the traditional criteria rest might be fleshed out something like this: when the heart and lungs permanently stop functioning, the individual no longer exhibits awareness or a power of self-direction. These functions never return when they have been absent for a certain length of time. Since the patient will never again be aware and active, loss of heart and lung function may be taken as signs that the person is dead. However, a patient who falls into a state of permanent unawareness and inactivity without losing heart and lung function is still alive. As long as the integrated functioning of the individual's body continues, then, he is alive. The criteria for the death of a person include permanent cessation of heart and lung function. The decision of significance underlying the use of the traditional criteria apparently had to do with the importance of organismic functioning per se: its presence was an adequate sign of life, its absence an adequate sign that death had occurred. In this view, the traditionalist's grounds for assigning significance to the absence of integrated organic functioning appear to be the link between the loss of such functioning and the failure to exhibit awareness and activity. Does this mean that his decision of significance really attaches to loss of awareness and activity? It can be argued that it does only if the traditionalist is willing to question his decision to consider the permanently unaware and inactive individual who breathes spontaneously alive. Since people in our own day seem unwilling to question such a decision, it must be concluded that the traditionalist held a thoroughgoing organismic concept of life and death. Oddly, though, one finds serious disagreement in the literature that discusses the concept of human death underlying the use of the traditional criteria. Some agree that the concept is organismic; others argue that it is brain-centered. The resolution of this disagreement is only one step toward the construction of an adequate conceptual framework to support the use of the traditional criteria and the brain-death criterion. I shall return to this question later in my discussion.

Crucial to my argument thus far are two points: (1) the death of a person does not coincide with the cessation of all biological activity in the organism, or *biological death*, even in the case of the traditional criteria; and (2) the use of any criterion for declaring death rests on a decision of significance, that is, a decision concerning the features that humans must possess to be regarded as living persons rather than dead persons. Since the death of a person does not coincide with biological death, how is the death of a person to be conceptualized—as a biological event, or as a metaphysical and moral one? Should the death of a human being be construed as a biological event, subject to biological inquiry into the permanent change in the status of the organism? Or should it be considered an essentially nonorganismic event in the life of a person, so that personal death will be the irreversible loss of those features we take to be necessary for personal existence?

A History of the Problem

It is now standard medical practice to regard an artificially ventilated, totally brain-dead human body as a dead person, and to declare the person dead once the application of a sufficient set of clinical tests has demonstrated that total brain infarction has occurred. Since the law has taken its cues from medicine in this matter, a brain-death criterion, originally articulated in the 1968 Report of the Ad Hoc Committee of the Harvard Medical School to Examine the Definition of Brain Death, has been incorporated into many state statutes alongside the traditional criteria for declaring death. In states having no brain-death statute, medical practice has been regarded as authoritative: court decisions in such states have upheld declarations of death based on the brain-death criterion precisely because this way of declaring death has become standard medical practice in certain cases. Such a state of affairs is troubling because it sets a poor precedent by treating medical practice as self-justifying in such a matter. Medical expertise has no necessary connection with expertise in the resolution of ethical and metaphysical quandaries—quandaries which pervade the present issue. To remedy the confusions inherent in this situation, the Uniform Declaration of Death Act was issued in 1981 by the President's Commission for the Study of Ethical Problems in Medicine and Biomedical and Behavioral Research.[3] I shall subject this work to extensive critical analysis in the final chapter of this book. At this writing, the commission's recommendation for statutory formulation has been adopted by twenty-two states.

Were we to distinguish between the vegetative and the cognitive capacities of the human brain—capacities centered in the lower and upper parts of the brain, respectively—we might say that when brain death has occurred, the lower brain and brain stem no longer support the vegetative function of respiration (the continuation of which will be sufficient for the maintenance of circulation), and that the permanent destruction of the upper brain has left the patient in a permanently noncognitive state: unconscious, unaware, unthinking. Most of us have no problem with the decision that a person is to be regarded as dead under such circumstances. There has been some dissension in the matter, however.[4] Further, the task of justifying the decision to declare a person dead whose brain is dead is not an easy one; a review of the literature from the eighteen years since the publication of the Harvard committee's report reveals both that there is no single, agreed-upon justification for the use of the brain-death criterion, and that there remain some dissenters. I shall return to these matters in chapter 2.

Our subject has been referred to either as that of defining or as redefining death. These ways of describing the problem obscure more than clarify. In its overt form, the debate over the definition of death is concerned with the criteria in accordance with which a person is to be declared dead: a manifestly medical or scientific matter. The role of the philosopher in such discussions can only be that of exposing fallacious reasoning, not of critiquing sets of criteria.[5] The latter is a task for the medically minded, not the philosophically minded. According to Robert Veatch, the debate over when to declare death has arisen because "technology [now] permits us to treat the body organ by organ, cell by cell, [so that] we are forced to develop a more precise understanding of what it means to call a person dead."[6] At one time, the presence of heart and lung activity was an unambiguous sign of life, and the absence of this activity a sign of death. With resuscitative and support systems that mechanically sustain the respiratory, and consequently the circulatory, functions of the human body, however, things are no longer so clear-cut. In cases of mechanical ventilation, which are becoming increasingly commonplace in this age of intensive care, the patient is permanently unconscious and exhibits no evidence of awareness or rational activity. The brain of such a patient has been deprived of oxygen sufficiently long to bring about death in all its parts: cerebrum, midbrain, and brain stem. Hence, we have the respirator-driven body which has undergone total brain death—the circumstance that initiated the debate over the definition of death. Julius Korein describes this condition, labeling it *brain death*:

Brain death is defined as irreversible destruction of the neuronal contents of the intracranial cavity. This includes both cerebral hemispheres, including cortex and deep structures, as well as the brain stem and the cerebellum. An equivalent term is *total brain infarction* to the first cervical level of the spinal cord. . . . In order to develop appropriate criteria to diagnose brain death, it is not required that every neuron in the brain be destroyed. Rather, it implies that the extent of destruction and consequent irreversible neuronal dysfunction is so great that regardless of any supportive measures, irreversible cardiac arrest and death of the adult human being is inevitable within one week.[7]

As Korein indicates, a central medical problem is to develop criteria for diagnosing brain death. Simply stated, this is the problem of specifying a set of clinical tests adequate to establish conclusively that total brain infarction has occurred. While I do not intend to enter the criteriological debate on the medical or scientific level, the nature of the philosophical void in the literature about the redefinition of death is most easily conveyed through a careful analysis of the keynote medical paper in which the brain-death criterion was first effectively elaborated.

In 1968, the Harvard committee began its report thus: "Our primary purpose is to define irreversible coma as a new criterion for death."[8] Although there is some ambiguity in the report as to what the condition of irreversible coma amounts to, the authors seem to intend that it is synonymous with brain death as defined by Korein. The Harvard committee specifies a set of clinical tests which is, it maintains, sufficient for determining that the entire brain of a patient is dead, or that the patient is in an irreversible coma. The committee recommends that, excluding cases of hypothermia and the presence of central nervous system depressants, death is to be declared when a patient exhibits: (1) unreceptivity and unresponsivity; (2) no movements or breathing; and (3) no reflexes. Procedures for determining these three conditions are described in the committee's report. A fourth condition, taken to have confirmatory value only, is a flat EEG reading.[9]

The Harvard committee's recommendation is that when a patient meets all three tests, death should be declared and then the respirator turned off. The recommended sequence of events is crucial. Now that the committee's proposal has become standard practice in many states—that is, now that brain-dead individuals are declared dead prior to the disconnection of the respirator—we no longer need to appeal to the actual cessation of heart and lung functions in order to pronounce a person dead in every case. While such cessation will still be a sufficient condition for declaring death in normal cases, we now have instructions for a special set of cases, those in which the respirator obscures our vision of death.

It has seemed to many that in adopting the brain-death criterion, we have not redefined death in the sense of having altered our understanding of what death is. We have merely adopted a second way of detecting death's occurrence, for use in cases of respirator dependency only. Indeed, some have said that the Harvard comiteee's report is little more than an addendum to instructions on how to use a respirator, and hence represents no real departure from the traditional criteria.

The Harvard committee carefully circumscribed the application of its report: "We are concerned here only with those comatose individuals who have no discernible central nervous system activity."[10] It is these individuals we are able to declare dead, since the Harvard committee's recommendation has gained wide acceptance. On the medical and scientific levels, controversy has continued over the adequacy and even the conservatism of the committee's criteria to demonstrate total brain infarction. Other criteria or testing procedures have been proposed, the most recent of which assess the absence of cerebral blood flow as an indicator of brain death. The role of the EEG has come into question. But the fundamental recommendation of the committee—that a person has died (and therefore ought to be declared dead) if brain death has occurred—remains substantially unchallenged. To most minds, it seems obvious that the death of a person's brain is the death of the person. Clearly, however, the relation between brain death and the death of the person rests on the sort of decision of significance discussed earlier.

The Harvard report is concerned with irreversible coma, or the cessation of function at cerebral, midbrain, brain-stem, and often spinal levels. The oddity of the report and of much of the debate that followed it is its incompleteness. The Harvard committee's recommendation—that a person is to be declared dead when brain death is demonstrated—is made without the barest indication of the reasoning behind it: Why should we declare a patient dead when he is in a state of irreversible coma? What is the significance of total brain death in assessing a person's life status? The Harvard report achieves an important result on a medical and scientific level, providing us with an adequate set of clinical tests to determine the occurrence of brain death. But it leaves the underlying philosophical issue unaddressed: Why should we take brain death to signal human death? In its overt form, then, the brain-death debate concerns the specification of an adequate set of tests for determining brain death. In its covert form, it raises difficult conceptual questions which were not dealt with at all in the original literature: What is death? What is human death? Is human death the death of the organism, the death of the person, or (perhaps) both? Is the death of a person's brain that person's death? With respect to the last question, apparently no one felt a serious need to argue that we ought to consider the status of the brain in determining whether a declaration of death is appropriate. Many were convinced that the use of the brain-death criterion rests on the same concept of death as the traditional criteria. Oddly enough, however, when arguments in defense of the brain-death criterion did begin to emerge—arguments purporting to establish the continuity between the traditional and the brain-centered criteria—there were two varieties, in disconcerting opposition to one another: one was that we have not departed from a heart-centered concept of death, the other was that we have remained true to our brain-centered concept of death. I shall detail and attempt to resolve this embarrassment in chapter 2.

The Harvard report talks about the death of the brain in all its parts. It has no bearing on a case in which a brain is irreversibly damaged in part only, so it contains no recommendation for patients who are conscious but cannot breathe without a respirator; likewise, it does not consider patients who breathe spontaneously yet are unconscious as a result of irreversible damage to the neocortex, that area of the brain responsible for conscious awareness and thought. Korein differentiates cerebral death from neocortical death, apallic syndrome, and persistent vegetative or noncognitive state: "Strictly speaking, cerebral death is defined as irreversible destruction of both cerebral hemispheres exclusive of the brain stem and cerebellum. . . . Clinical situations arise . . . in which the cerebral hemispheres alone may be involved in the destructive process, but the brain stem is spared. These exceptions may lead to a chronic comatose or noncognitive state which must be considered as another diagnostic category."[11] *Cerebral death*, then, involves the irreversible absence of the cognitive functions, but the spontaneous presence of the vegetative functions, of the brain. The respiration of a patient suffering cerebral death does not require mechanical assistance. From this condition, a further degree of brain destruction must be differentiated: neocortical death. Throughout this book, the situation of neocortical death will be used as the exemplar of the persistent vegetative state. Hence, any arguments for a neocortical-death criterion for declaring death will, ipso facto, favor using the permanent absence of consciousness as our measure of human death. That is, a neocortical-death criterion is one example of a persistent-vegetative-state criterion for declaring death. I argue that such a criterion presupposes the same concept of human death as does the brain-death criterion, and I base my public policy recommendation on it. For the most part, I shall speak of neocortical death throughout my discussion.

> [Neocortical death involves] the destruction of cortical neurons bilaterally while deep structures of the cerebral hemispheres such as the thalamus and basal ganglia may be intact along with the brain stem and cerebellum. . . . [These patients] most often . . . have a limited to complex repertoire of brainstem reflexes, which clearly distinguishes them from patients with other conditions. The term apallic syndrome may be considered as essentially similar to neocortical death, although some investigators contest this.[12]

Neocortical death involves significantly less brain destruction than does cerebral death. However, the effect is essentially the same: the patient is reduced to a persistent noncognitive state and requires no mechanical ventilation.

> [*Persistent vegetative state* or *persistent noncognitive state*] are clinical descriptors of a set of irreversible states. The pathologic substrate involving neural structures is not always clearly

definable. Attempts at classifying these syndromes neu-
ropathologically are represented by the terms *neocortical death*
and *apallic syndrome*. . . . The clinical picture reflects the
destruction of critical elements of the central nervous system,
leaving the patient in an irreversible condition in which there
is no evidence that he or she has any sense of awareness.
Higher functions of the brain are absent, and there is no
purposeful response to external stimuli. . . . The patient is not
a sentient individual. . . . These patients are *not* brain-dead. If
appropriate resuscitative procedures are utilized, these patients
may be maintained in this state for years.

[Apallic syndrome results] from absence or destruction of
the pallium, that is, the neocortical structures of the cerebrum.
This term has its major usage in attempting to give one local-
ization for the complex clinical picture of persistent noncognitive state.[13]

As the discussion of brain death has continued, attention has
focused not only on the absence of a clear and adequate conceptual
foundation for the use of the brain-death criterion, but also on the
possibility that such a criterion is too conservative and ought to be
replaced by a criterion that would indicate persistent vegetative state.
At this time, a neocortical-death criterion is the only likely candi-
date. Any such move requires assurance at both the philosoph-
ical/conceptual and medical/diagnostic levels. Just as for the brain-
death criterion, demanding conceptual and empirical problems
must be resolved. In their discussion of the "critical distinctions"
between brain death and the persistent vegetative state, Ronald
Cranford and Harmon Smith write:

In order to support [the contention that the persistent
vegetative state is sufficient ground for the pronouncement of
death], there must be unequivocal certainty, substantiated by
medical data and experience, empirically verifiable, and
supported by autopsy studies confirming the clinical analysis
(as currently exists, we believe, for the total brain death
concept), that there is no functioning of the cerebral cortex.
Merely a severe degree of dysfunctioning is insufficient

evidence for pronouncing death. From a medical standpoint, such a case may be established for a variant of the persistent vegetative state, viz. "neocortical death."[14]

Given that the redefinition of death poses difficult problems of empirical as well as conceptual justification, the philosopher's role must be twofold: (1) to expose fallacious reasoning on either level; and (2) to examine the conceptual underpinnings of the acceptance of the brain-death criterion, to compare them with those of persistent-vegetative-state criteria like the neocortical-death criterion, and to contribute to the complex philosophical discussions about brain death and persistent vegetative existence. Ultimately, the philosopher's task is to present and justify a decision of significance. The argument I shall press—that the noncognitive status of the patient was the critical element in the Harvard committee's decision to declare death and then turn off the respirator—originated in an insight expressed in an article by J. B. Brierley and others. That article described the condition of neocortical death thus: "'Cortex death,' or preferably 'neocortical death,' implies a persistently isoelectric EEG and the absence of sensory evoked responses in the neocortex, together with the resumption of spontaneous respiration and of certain brainstem reflexes."[15] The dilemma posed by the phenomenon of neocortical death is as follows:

> Once neocortical death has been unequivocally established and the possibility of any recovery of consciousness and intellectual activity thereby excluded, the question must be asked, although the patient breathes spontaneously, is he or she alive? . . . In essence, it seems that a person who resumes spontaneous respiration after cardiac arrest, yet exhibits an isoelectric EEG, is to be regarded as "alive," while another surviving the same accident, also with an isoelectric EEG but whose cardiac function depends upon mechanical ventilation, may be regarded as "dead." Clearly this distinction between "alive" and "dead" attaches cardinal importance to the function of respiration and none to those higher functions of the nervous system that demarcate man from the lower primates and all other vertebrates and invertebrates.[16]

In this passage, the writers indicate puzzlement over the move to a brain-centered criterion on the one hand and the apparent reversion to the heart-and-lung criteria on the other. The puzzlement is well founded, for it seems to rest on an insight into the sort of implicit but unexamined conceptual commitment behind the brain-death criterion put forth by the Harvard committee. The suggestion that neocortical death might be a sufficient condition for declaring death raises a host of empirical questions: Is the neocortex the locus of consciousness, awareness, and thought? If not, then what is the connection between neocortical death and the permanent absence of consciousness? Can the existence of irreversible neocortical destruction be conclusively established? Is an isoelectric EEG an adequate indicator of the death of the neocortex? These are important questions, but they do not lie within the philosopher's scope, since they are medical or scientific in nature. Whether or not we have the answers to these questions, however, there are philosophical questions that must be answered if we are to determine that the death of a person's neocortex is that person's death. These philosophical questions were raised by our adoption of the brain-death criterion and have not yet been put to rest by any of the attempts that have been made to address them systematically. Since we have a moral obligation to be foresightful in matters of human dignity and well-being, we cannot avoid the questions raised by the phenomenon of neocortical death. That matters of human dignity and well-being are raised here seems uncontroversial: the condition of neocortical death has persisted for as long as two-and-a-half years in some instances, and the case of Karen Quinlan (which raised questions about the metaphysical significance of permanent noncognition) has had lasting impact. Moreover, the incidence of persistent vegetative survival can be expected to increase, since such cases frequently result from the intrusion of resuscitative machinery and the temporary use of a respirator. We can expect, as well, that our understanding of the brain and our powers of determining its condition will improve with time. Hence, we must address the question, Is neocortical death the death of the person? And we must relate it to our reasonings about the question, Is brain death the death of the person?

A *Blueprint*

The argument of this book will necessarily be complex. Much of it is developed against the background of my critical analysis of the work of others, but substantial portions consist of my own original argument to establish the full set of claims that must be defended if the use of any criterion for declaring death is to be adequately grounded. In this section, I provide a blueprint for the argument of this book.

In the present chapter, I have shown that certain conceptual issues must be resolved if the use of any criterion for declaring death is to be justified. I shall turn to the brain-death criterion in particular in chapter 2, to determine whether or not its use has been provided an adequate conceptual footing. On the basis of the complex story that emerges in chapter 2, I conclude that no strategy has yet been successful, and I argue finally that the traditional criteria and the brain-death criterion presuppose radically different concepts of human death. Hence, the use of the brain-death criterion must be vindicated separately, with a fully elaborated and defended conceptual scheme which answers the sorts of questions I set out early in this chapter. Finally, I argue that the same conceptual commitments that support the use of the brain-death criterion also support the use of the neocortical-death criterion.

With this critical conceptual structure in place, chapters 3, 4, and 5 present a search for an argument that both incorporates and responds to the conceptual commitments that the brain-death criterion entails. This search becomes an involved one for two reasons: first, because no agreement has emerged on the kind of argument required for this task; and second, because significant problems emerge in the analysis of the best representatives of each kind of argument. There appear to be three chief schools in the debate: those who think that the decision about what constitutes the death of the person is biological in nature, and therefore requires a biological argument in its support; those who consider that we are in the realm of the moral, so that our concern is not so much with what features constitute the death of the person as with the determination of the circumstances under which a person ought to be declared dead; and those who take the problem to be ontological or metaphysical in nature, and hence to require the articulation of an adequate theory of personal identity in its defense.[17] Chapter 3 contains a critical analysis of the biological arguments that have been proffered, chapter 4 of the moral arguments, and chapter 5 of the ontological arguments. I emerge from these chapters with the as yet unsupported view that death ought to be construed as the death of the person (and not of the organism); with the supported claims that the biological and moral approaches are unsuited to the central task; and with the supported view that an ontological argument in the form of a personal identity theory provides an adequate philosophical basis for the truth of the claim that the death of a person's brain is that person's death. I show that the same personal identity theory supports the claim that the death of a person's neocortex is that person's death.

Even if we assume that the particular personal identity theory I set forth in chapter 5 is successful in supporting the use of these criteria, a full defense of their uses is not yet in place. Other difficult questions require resolution as well—questions which I raise throughout the book but leave unanswered until chapter 6. If I had argued in chapter 2 that the brain-death criterion simply reiterates the concept of human death presupposed by the traditional criteria, then much of the argument of chapter 6 would be unnecessary. But since I argued that the brain-death criterion must be supported by a different concept of death, I must show that we ought to reconsider, as well as modify, our concept of human death. Second, since the required reconsideration challenges us to view ourselves in fundamentally different terms (as persons, and no longer as organisms), I must defend this change in orientation toward ourselves. While some writers have recognized the need to defend the choice of perspective on the human (as person or organism) for the purpose of determining what constitutes human death, no one has successfully provided such a defense. I attempt a contractarian strategy to generate this argument, and then seek to construct a philosophical rationale for the fruitfulness of this strategy in general, as well as in this particular case.

Third, since I have established that our focus should be on the human as person and have employed an ontological argument to support the use of a particular criterion for declaring death, I must show that the ontological approach is a better tool than a moral analysis for getting at the conditions of existence and nonexistence of persons. Finally, given the commonality of the conceptual underpinning of the brain-death and neocortical-death criteria, I recommend a public policy that is centered on the concept they share: that human death is the permanent cessation of consciousness.

In both its content and its underlying conceptual framework, my public policy recommendation is so thoroughly at odds with the prevailing public policy statement, the Uniform Declaration of Death Act, that it is essential to take a critical look at the act. The final chapter of this book is reserved for this task. In my preface, I stressed that this book is a philosophical work. But philosophical analysis and argument must at some point merge with practice if they are to help us resolve real-life concerns. It is not enough for the philosopher to argue for a particular theoretical position or to defend a set of meanings for central concepts. While I may convince the reader, in chapter 5, that the death of a person's brain is that person's death, or indeed that the death of a person's upper brain is that person's death, nothing necessarily follows about how death should be declared in our society. Public policies are formulated in response to a variety of pressures, only one of which is the general assumption that an adequate set of clearly defined concepts is a good thing. One among many, this assumption may be accorded a subordinate status in the determination of policy—heretical as this might seem to many philosophers.

The general question that informs my discussion in chapter 7 is this: In a free, pluralistic society where divergent concepts of human death are to be expected and respected, what public policy ought to govern the declaration of human death? After a critical analysis of the document produced by the President's Commission, I examine the strengths and deficiencies of three competing policies. Finally, I provide a contractual argument for a non-consensus-based yet conceptually defensible policy which honors our societal commitment to a principle of toleration.

chapter 2

Concepts and Criteria

A s we have seen, the distinction between the criterion for declaring death and the conceptual basis underlying that criterion is absolutely crucial in any discussion of redefining death. It is generally agreed that the redefinition debate poses an empirical as well as a conceptual problem. The empirical task, a medical and scientific one, is to specify an adequate operational definition of death; that is, to delineate the clinical indicators of the death of a human being, in accordance with which death is to be declared. The conceptual task is to clarify the meaning of our concept of human death, so that we know what we are testing for when we apply a particular criterion or set of clinical tests for declaring death. Articulating the conceptual basis for the use of a particular criterion is a philosophical task, while articulating the criterion itself is a medical and scientific task. The history of the redefinition debate in chapter 1 showed that we now use the brain-death criterion in special cases of respirator dependency. That is, in some cases we declare death when we have established that the total brain of the patient is dead, even though respiration and heartbeat continue. We apply the brain-death criterion instead of the traditional heart-and-lung criteria because an overwhelming number of us believe that the latter would give us a false positive result in a significant number of such cases. While we have not replaced the traditional with the brain-death criterion, we now have an additional test we may use in cases where respirators obscure our vision of death. The brain-death criterion enables us to determine that the individual's brain is dead in all its parts, and we can therefore conclude that the individual is dead, since his respiratory and cardiac functions are merely mechanically sustained.

In chapter 1, I claimed that the landmark document in the redefinition controversy, the Harvard committee report, had a significant shortcoming; while it stated clearly that we should declare someone dead who has undergone brain death, and provided an adequate set of tests for determining when total brain death has occurred, it gave no support for the conclusion that a brain-dead individual is dead. Hence, it failed to provide an adequate conceptual analysis grounding the use of the brain-death criterion. The Harvard committee made, but failed to justify, a decision of significance, a decision that the permanent absence of a certain feature or cluster of features constitutes the death of the person.

There are two interesting conceptual puzzles at the heart of the redefinition debate. The first concerns the concepts of death behind the different criteria for declaring death. What concept of death is presupposed by the traditional criteria, and what by the brain-death criterion? This question is one of the persistent puzzles in the redefinition debate, and will provide the framework of inquiry for this chapter.

The second puzzle, which accounts for the persistence of the brain-death debate for many years, concerns the nature of the concept of human death itself. What kind of concept is it, and to what area of inquiry does it belong? When our concern is with an entity as complex as the human being, should our concept of death focus on our distinguishing or our common capacities among living things? What sort of analysis is required to defend a particular concept of human death?

In 1975, Lawrence C. Becker presented biological arguments purporting to establish the boundaries (the beginning and the end) of the life of the human being. He provided what he took to be persuasive biological considerations in favor of "becoming/being" and "being/has been" boundaries: the former did not coincide with conception, and the latter did not mark the time of complete cessation of biological activity in the human organism. For my purposes, I am interested in his view that there is a way to define the endpoint of a human life "in purely biological terms."[1] In 1978, David Lamb, agreeing with Becker that "a biological definition of death" could be formulated, argued against Becker's definition, in favor of one consistent with the brain-death criterion, which was disallowed by the biological concept of death Becker had articulated.[2] These two attempts to provide a biological definition of death differ in the criterion they recommend for use in declaring a human being dead, but apparently agree on an organismic concept of human death. If this is the correct way to characterize their agreement and disagreement, then either one or both of them must be wrong.

Becker and Lamb both disagree strongly with those who have construed the problem as a moral one, those who ask about the qualitative conditions under which a person ought to be declared dead. I discuss the moral arguments in chapter 4. In 1980, Michael Green and Daniel Wikler argued that neither biological nor moral arguments are sufficient to ground the conclusion "that brain-dead patients are dead," the view they took to be correct.[3] They offer instead a third approach, an ontological argument "having to do with the conditions of existence of persons."[4] We not only have several arguments to assess, but several kinds of arguments. Underlying these different analytical approaches is a fundamental difference in focus—either on the human as organism or on the human as person. This choice of perspective must be justified. I shall not attempt this justification until I have examined the three analytical strategies just described. If we agree that our focus should be on the human as person, and not on the human as organism, then the requisite argument explicating our concept of human death must address the question of what persons are. Some argue that our concept of person is both a moral and a metaphysical one.[5] If this is a correct analysis of the concept of person, then it may be either that both moral and metaphysical (ontological) arguments are needed to clarify our central concepts, or that either type of reasoning may suffice alone. Further on I contend that the ontological approach is the more promising. Before we discuss the first of the two puzzles, however, we should consider what a conceptual problem is, and why such a problem has arisen in connection with the matter of declaring death.

The Nature of a Conceptual Problem

A conceptual problem exists whenever we are not entirely clear about the correct analysis of a concept that we use. Such a problem does not necessarily prevent the concept's use; it may not be necessary for us to be perfectly clear about its meaning, if it has always been obvious when the concept applied. If, for example, my toddler wants me to read to her and approaches me, magazine in hand, saying, "Read book, Mom," she has demonstrated that she has an imprecise concept of book, and no concept of magazine. But since her only desire is that I read to her from the written material she has brought me, it does not matter that her concept of book is not well formed or that she has no concept of magazine. The concept of human death was for a long time a case in point. However, as Leonard Isaacs has written:

> Once supportive technologies were introduced that could artificially maintain a previously "vital" characteristic in the absence of its spontaneous functioning, sophisticated philosophical distinctions had to be made about matters that had formerly remained in comfortable obscurity. The respirator, no less than the physicist's electron microscope, reveals that the philosophical ambiguities had been there all the time.[6]

There is another reason for living with a vaguely defined concept: we may not need to argue about the correct meaning or analysis of a concept with several meanings, if the application of the concept, however analyzed, provides the same result in every case. There is often no pressure to defend or attack the meanings others attach to the same concept. Isaacs exhibits this feature of the concept of human death:

> Another way of examining the problem is to inquire: "What is it that is so essential to human life that its irreversible loss

signifies death?" Is it, for example, the loss of the soul, the stoppage of the respiration of air, the cessation of the flow of blood,
the loss of the capacity for bodily integration, the cessation of
unconsciousness, or the loss of the capacity for social interaction? . . . Until quite recently, all these arguably essential
characteristics were lost at virtually the same time. . . . All the
definitions were satisfied in the same fatal human event. It
was, almost always, perfectly obvious whether or not someone
had died; in cases of doubt, one's response was to summon a
physician, not a philosopher.[7]

We have a conceptual problem to resolve, then, when it is no
longer possible to live with a plurality of meanings or an unclarity of
meaning attached to a particular concept. It will eventually become
important for my toddler to acquire clear concepts of book and
magazine, but until then, a little conceptual ambiguity is certainly
tolerable. The use of mechanical support systems to maintain the
human organism, on the other hand, has made it impossible to
tolerate the ambiguity surrounding the concept of human death any
longer. How did this conceptual ambiguity first exhibit itself? Imagine the following situation: Suppose that someone traditionally
minded has just listened to a news report which stated that an individual has been declared dead, even though his respiration and
heartbeat continue, because he is permanently unconscious, his
respiration is mechanically assisted, and his heart retains its natural
function solely because the respirator is inflating his lungs. After the
initial surprise wears off, the listener might make analytical observa-
tions like, "He understands death differently than I do," or "He
means something different by *dead person* than I do." This is simply
a reflection of the fact that the speaker and the listener hold different
concepts of human death. Since a matter of great practical importance is at stake, it is incumbent upon both parties to analyze the
concept in question and to arrive at an acceptable understanding of
its meaning, perhaps even to offer a new analysis of the concept.
Such was the situation when the Harvard committee issued its proposal for defining death as irreversible coma, or total brain death.
Such is now the case when some suggest that because an individual
is permanently unconscious, although breathing spontaneously, he

is dead. The problem is to clarify our concept of human death in order to determine whether or not individuals in the situation described are to be considered dead or alive. This is an involved issue requiring answers to the questions: What is a human being? What is a person? What is death? Is the death of a human being the same as the death of a person? Should a person be declared dead on the basis of characteristics having to do with his identity as a human being, as a person, or both? A lengthy conceptual argument is necessary to provide an analysis of the concept of human death. First, though, we should determine the extent of the work we must do in this connection, by deciding whether the traditional criteria and the brain-death criterion presuppose different concepts of human death.

The Traditional Criteria and the Brain-death Criterion

The Harvard committee not only set forth the brain-death criterion—the set of tests it deemed sufficient to establish that the entire brain was dead—it also discussed the prevailing legal situation regarding the declaration of death. The most recent edition of *Black's Law Dictionary* at that time defined death thus: "The cessation of life, the ceasing to exist; *defined by physicians* as a total stoppage of the circulation of the blood, and a cessation of the animal and vital functions consequent thereupon, such as respiration, pulsation, etc."[8] In its commentary on this definition, the Harvard committee said: "We suggest that responsible medical opinion is ready to adopt new criteria for pronouncing death to have occurred in an individual sustaining irreversible coma as a result of permanent brain damage."[9] The key words in this passage are "new criteria for pronouncing death." For a particular class of patients—those who have undergone permanent and total brain destruction yet still exhibit cardiac function as a consequence of respirator support—"responsible medical opinion" is prepared to use a different test for declaring death. The test described in the *Black's Law Dictionary* definition, that of permanent circulatory cessation, is no longer to be used in cases of irreversible coma. Instead, the committee proposes a test of brain death to diagnose correctly the status of patients in this class.

This is pretty simple to understand. But the two statements that follow cause some significant difficulties: "[1] If this position is adopted by the medical community, it can form the basis for change in the current legal concept of death. [2] No statutory changes in the law should be necessary since the law treats this question essentially as one of fact to be determined by physicians."[10] Statement 1 indicates that if the medical community does adopt the brain-death criterion in addition to (not in replacement of) the traditional criteria, it can affect the prevailing legal concept of death, which is indisputably cardiac centered. The Harvard committee apparently believes that the brain-death criterion rests on a different concept of death from the traditional; the brain-death criterion is not cardiac centered. It would therefore seem that an amendment to *Black's Law Dictionary* is in order. Delford Stickel identifies two respects in which the common-law statement in *Black's Law Dictionary* is 'obsolete': "First, the critically important brain functions are not specifically mentioned. Secondly and more seriously, circulation and respiration are explicitly stated to be functions that cease prior to death, and two thirds of the statement is devoted to mentioning the circulation twice and to relegating other vital functions to a status subordinate to the circulation."[11] Statement 2 explains that the working of legal statutes will need no alteration, since these laws allow physicians to declare death in accordance with whatever criteria they deem (as a medical community) medically sound and appropriate.

When we look back at the Harvard committee report several years later, the first of the two claims remains extraordinarily interesting; many of those favoring the adoption of the brain-death criterion have defended it by arguing that its adoption represents no change in our concept of death—a contradiction of statement 1—and among those who have argued that no change has taken place, there are divergent definitions of the underlying concept of death. That is, many of those involved in the redefinition debate since 1968 have defended the brain-death criterion by arguing that its adoption entails no change in our concept of death. Such a claim seems to oppose the Harvard committee's understanding of things, but the committee could have been wrong. Whether motivated on political grounds (that is, to hasten and cement acceptance of the brain-death criterion) or inspired by genuine conviction, the new claim states a view shared, and not carefully questioned, by many. Indeed, it is basic to the argument of the President's Commission in support of its Uniform Declaration of Death Act. Eventually, I argue that this claim is false, but that is only part of the story. There are two versions of the claim: that the brain-death criterion entails no change in our heart-centered concept of death; and that it entails no change in our brain-centered concept of death.

I shall attempt to show that neither version of the claim is correct, and to defend the insight of the Harvard committee by arguing that the brain-death criterion entails a change in our concept of death from a cardiac-centered to a consciousness-centered concept. The brain-death criterion does entail a change in our concept of death, for the traditional criteria were based on a heart-centered rather than a brain-centered concept of death. The central curiosity is the opposition between the Harvard committee's statement and the two versions of the claim made in defense of the brain-death criterion. If, in the final analysis, my own claim is defensible, then the committee's insight will be vindicated, and it will be necessary to construct a further defense to justify changing our concept of death to support the brain-death criterion. I hope to provide such a defense, as well as to show that the neocortical-death criterion rests on the same conceptual foundation as the brain-death criterion, and hence is justified by the same argument.

HEART-CENTERED CRITERIA

Robert L. Schwager is among those who believe that the brain-death criterion does not alter our heart-centered concept of death. In "Life, Death, and the Irreversibly Comatose," Schwager is interested in determining "how to conceptualize turning off the respirator" on a decerebrate patient because some people remain unconvinced that such a person is really dead.[12] Such people believe that a decerebrate patient supported by a respirator still possesses spontaneous circulatory functioning; and since such a patient obviously does not pass the cardiac-centered test for death given in the *Black's Law Dictionary* definition, he must be regarded as alive. Schwager responds to two proponents of this view, Martin Halley and William Harvey, by agreeing with their definition of death and then by arguing that this definition is fulfilled by the patient in irreversible coma because circulatory function in such a case is not spontaneous. Halley and Harvey provide a tripartite definition of death, with which Schwager concurs: "Death is irreversible cessation of *all* of the following: (1) total cerebral function, (2) spontaneous function of the respiratory system, and (3) spontaneous function of the circulatory system."[13]

Schwager argues that all three conditions are fulfilled in the case of the patient fulfilling the brain-death criterion, and that such a patient is therefore dead. Contrary to Halley and Harvey, he considers that the decerebrate patient does not have a spontaneously beating heart. The cardiac activity of this patient, although not directly assisted by any mechanical contrivance, is nonspontaneous, since it would cease to function were we to terminate direct mechanical assistance to the lungs provided by the respirator. Schwager writes: "I do not believe that the decerebrate individual has truly spontaneous circulatory function."[14] Schwager's way of putting this is odd; the words "truly spontaneous" suggest a distinction where there is none. A function is either spontaneous or not; we must find a clear and meaningful definition of each, and then decide which term correctly applies to the cardiac function of the decerebrate patient. A great deal depends on this decision; if one is devoted to the cardiac-centered concept of death underlying the traditional criteria, and if it cannot be demonstrated that the decerebrate's heartbeat is nonspontaneous, then one cannot accept the brain-death criterion on the ground that it presupposes the same concept of death as the traditional criteria. It must then rest on a different concept of death. To put the point in stronger terms, if we can successfully argue that the cardiac function of the brain-dead individual is spontaneous, and if it is correct to call the decerebrate patient dead, then we must elaborate a new concept of death that is compatible with the use of the brain-death criterion. Does Schwager convince us that the decerebrate's heartbeat is nonspontaneous? His argument reads:

Consider the following extreme case. It has proved possible to maintain both respiration and circulation in the body of an individual who has been decapitated. Now suppose respiration was maintained by the use of an artificial respirator while no further contrivances were necessary to stimulate cardiovascular function. If such circulatory activity were to count as spontaneous, and thus as a sign of life, we should be forced to say that death has not yet taken place and that the individual, *sans head*, was still alive. But this is absurd. Where there has been an irreversible cessation of natural, spontaneous cerebral and pulmonary function, so that circulatory activity continues only because artificial respiration continues to oxygenate the blood, such circulatory activity is neither truly spontaneous nor a sign of life. Where irreversible cessation of total brain activity has occurred, the absence of "recoverable capacity to breathe by [oneself precludes the existence of] recoverable permanent capacity to circulate [oneself]." Thus circulation is no more spontaneous here than is respiration. This is obscured by our failure to realize that the absence of a direct mechanical aid to circulation, such as a heart-lung machine, does not guarantee the spontaneity of that circulation. And once this is understood, we see that the real upshot of the Harvard Committee's recommendation is not really a new definition of death, but rather "a return to a rather traditionalistic understanding of the procedure for stating that a man has died."[15]

Beginning with a *modus tollens* argument that appeals to our overwhelming inclination to regard a decapitated individual as dead, Schwager implies that cardiac activity in a respirator driven, decapitated body is nonspontaneous. His argument appears to be valid, but is it sound? The argument rests on an assumption with which we have been comfortable in the past: spontaneous circulatory activity is a sign of life.

One is reluctant to give up such an assumption as long as one accepts the definition of death in *Black's Law Dictionary*. Historically, the centrality of the heart in the diagnosis of death is accounted for by the invention of the stethoscope. As the President's Commission notes, this invention "laid to rest public fears of premature burial."[16] The real challenge to Schwager's attempt to prove the heart's function nonspontaneous in the case of brain death stems from the apparent independence of the heart and its functions from those of the lungs and the brain. Cranford and Smith describe the relevant physiological interactions:

> Although spontaneous respiratory function is totally dependent upon the brain and cannot exist without a functioning brain stem, this is not the case with cardiac function. While the heart does receive some degree of neural regulation from the brain, normal cardiac functioning can occur in the presence of total brain destruction. For example, when patients are pronounced dead using accepted criteria for brain death and the respirator is then discontinued, the heart may continue to function for periods of 5–60 minutes.[17]

Among the reasons the heart and its activity have always been considered the central vital agency and function is that cardiac activity has a persistence of its own. Respiratory activity may become grossly intermittent and so give the impression of having ceased, yet the heart will continue beating. Hence, the stoppage of the heart was concluded to be a secure sign that all significant functioning had terminated.

> Unlike the respiratory system, which depends on the neural impulses from the brain, the heart can pump blood without external control. Impulses from brain centers modulate the inherent rate and force of the heart beat but are not required for the heart to contract at a level of function that is ordinarily adequate. Thus, when artificial respiration provides adequate oxygenation and associated medical treatments regulate essential plasma components and blood pressure, an intact heart will continue to beat, despite loss of brain functions.[18]

Paul Ramsey has pointed out that the heart's centrality can be attributed to its unpaired status, as well as to the fact that it "ticks."[19] But certainly the unpaired status of an organ has no essential connection with its centrality. If it did, we would have to assign the liver a share in centrality as well. The persuasive point is the relative independence of the heart and its function from the brain and its function; as we have seen, a similar case could not be made for the lungs and their function. Moreover, the independence of the heart from the lungs and brain is an independence for which there is no correspondence in the case of either the brain or the lungs, so the claim that the heart beats spontaneously, even in the case of brain death, appears to be a fair one.

Now that we can prevent the shutting down of some bodily functions that are associated with death, the assumption that a spontaneously beating heart is a sufficient condition for life requires critical assessment. The fact that we intrude in the dying process in certain ways requires us to draw finer distinctions and to settle on a precise and adequate analysis if we are to treat persons and former persons in a morally appropriate manner. Even if Schwager could argue that cardiac function in the brain dead patient is nonspontaneous, we may argue that the spontaneity/nonspontaneity issue has become a nonissue in our age of machine medicine.

If we assume, along with Schwager, that the mechanically ventilated, decapitated individual is dead, then either circulatory activity is nonspontaneous in such a case (Schwager's view), or circulatory activity is spontaneous but not, because of other features of the situation, to be taken as a sign of life. I argue that there is no good reason to expand our criteria for nonspontaneity to include the further criterion that Schwager's argument urges. That circulatory activity is not always a sign of life can be easily defended by reminding ourselves of the persistence of cardiac activity in the case of a decapitated person. Schwager's reasoning in the argument quoted above is as follows: Spontaneous cardiac activity is a sign of life. Where total brain death has occurred, the lungs have no recoverable capacity to function spontaneously, and so the respirator provides direct mechanical assistance to the lungs. This provides a continuous supply of oxygenated blood to the heart. The heart continues to function because of this ongoing supply of oxygenated blood, even though it receives no direct mechanical assistance. The heart's function depends on the nonspontaneous functioning of the lungs, then. Where total brain death has occurred, the permanent inability to breathe spontaneously prevents spontaneous circulation. Therefore, circulatory function is nonspontaneous in such cases, and the Harvard committee recommendation entails no change in our concept of death, which required the permanent absence of spontaneous cardiac functioning.

Schwager is suggesting that the term *nonspontaneity* does not properly apply to cases of direct mechanical assistance alone; indirect mechanical assistance—that is, dependency on an organ system that is receiving direct mechanical assistance—also legitimates its use in the situation of brain death. Schwager does not commit himself to the claim that an indirectly supported function per se is nonspontaneous. He is claiming only that in the presence of irreversible coma, it is appropriate to extend usage of the term *nonspontaneous* to cover those functions which are indirectly maintained by some mechanical contrivance when the total brain is dead. Is there any need to extend the term in this way, specifying a particular usage of *nonspontaneity* that applies only in cases of brain death? The peculiarity of Schwager's definition of *nonspontaneous* is that it applies to a function because of a dependency relation the function bears to another mechanically supported function. Normally, we refer to a function as nonspontaneous when we provide it with direct mechanical support because any one of these conditions obtains: (1) the portion of the brain controlling that system has been destroyed; (2) the system itself has undergone deterioration so that it will no longer function on its own; or (3) some other system, upon which the system in question depends for its ability to function, has become nonfunctional (for example, the muscles). While one might assume that (1) applies to the heart's functioning in the case of brain death, the last passage quoted from the commission's report renders (1) inapplicable. The heart's beating is therefore not dependent upon the brain's functioning. Instead, Schwager appeals to a dependency relation—the dependency of the heart on the lungs plus the fact of direct mechanical assistance to the lungs—to convince us of the nonspontaneity of the heart's functioning. But such a situation is not included in the list of circumstances under which we normally designate a system's functioning as nonspontaneous. Schwager is recommending an extension of *nonspontaneous* for use only in cases of brain death, and recommending that in such cases there is a fourth condition under which a function is nonspontaneous: in the event of brain death, a system dependent for its functioning on another system requiring direct mechanical assistance (functioning nonspontaneously) is itself nonspontaneous in its function.

One compelling reason to resist extending usage of the term is the independence of the heart from the lungs and brain. The dependency relation Schwager bases his case on is factually in error. Beyond this objection, a further obvious problem with the extended usage is its power to confuse. We have always used *nonspontaneous* to apply only to those functions receiving direct mechanical assistance. In order to ground the claim that our concept of death has not been altered with the use of the brain-death criterion, we must adopt a special new use of the term, a use which applies only in cases of brain death. If some are tempted to go along with this expansion in the meaning of *nonspontaneous*, it might be useful to point out that there is good reason to regard cardiac function as spontaneous until it actually stops (unless of course the heart is being given direct mechanical support). In many instances of dying, the heartbeat is the last function to cease, because cardiac tissue will continue its beating after other organ systems have ceased their function. Even when the brain-death criterion is applied and the respirator is shut off, the heart may continue for a significant time period. Since the heart is not beating with the help of an external mechanism, nor is it dependent on any other system itself dependent on a machine, its function would have to be termed spontaneous. This is not the result Schwager wanted, and it means that there is an important change when we adopt the brain-death criterion: the spontaneity of the heartbeat is no longer taken as a sign of life.

There is a further problem with the addition of Schwager's condition to our list. Suppose we have a patient whose lower brain is irreversibly damaged so that he requires respiratory support to survive. We have duplicated two conditions of the decapitated individual: the relevant portions of the brain are not responsible for the functioning of the heart and lungs, and the heart's functioning is causally dependent on the lungs' mechanically assisted functioning. The relevant difference between this case and that of the decapitated person is the presence of consciousness. Would Schwager say the heart's functioning was spontaneous or nonspontaneous? Presumably, since the heart is not directly supported and the patient is conscious, he would want to maintain that the heart's beating is spontaneous. If the heart's functioning were regarded as nonspontaneous in this case, we would be committed to the untenable result that whenever an essential function is mechanically assisted, all dependent functions (including consciousness itself) become nonspontaneous as well. The only genuine difference between the two cases is the presence of upper brain functioning, and hence consciousness, in the latter. The only condition securing the judgment that this patient is alive, then, is the presence of consciousness. It appears to be irrelevant whether the heart's functioning is spontaneous. In either case the patient would be considered alive. It is only when consciousness is absent that the dependency relation is considered the ground for saying "nonspontaneous, and therefore dead."

I have given reason for resisting this addition to our notion of nonspontaneity, as well as for considering the function in question spontaneous. Schwager is wrong to emphasize the functional dependency relation as he does, for that relation does not mark the crucial difference in the two cases of concern here and hence is not the real basis of our decision to consider the decapitated individual dead and the lower-brain-dead patient alive. It is the consciousness of the latter that grounds a different decision regarding his status. To admit this, though, is to admit that the assumption of spontaneous circulatory activity as a sign of life may no longer apply. The spontaneity/nonspontaneity distinction is not important for Schwager unless brain death is present; he makes no decision about the life status of the patient on the basis of spontaneity or nonspontaneity until brain death is established. It is not clear why Schwager requires this condition. The decision that someone is alive or dead rests on the presence or absence of upper brain functioning in conjunction with mechanically supported respiration. It is the absence of consciousness that is critical in Schwager's decision that cardiac function is nonspontaneous. Looking at the question in this light, we must ask why the permanent absence of consciousness would change the nature of the functioning of an organ system. Schwager never addresses this issue, but he should. What he overlooks is the critical relevance of the absence of upper brain function, and the irrelevance of the nonspontaneity of heart and lung function, in the decision to declare death. I hope to establish that we declare death because of permanent unconsciousness—not because of the death of the upper brain in conjunction with the death of the mid- and lower brain.

Those who are willing to declare the brain-dead patient dead obviously believe that in some cases of mechanical ventilation, a declaration of death is appropriate. All of us believe that some cases of mechanical ventilation do not warrant the declaration of death. Examples of this sort of case might include a patient who is mechanically ventilated because the respiratory center of the brain has been destroyed, or a patient supported by an iron lung because of muscular degeneration. In both cases, the point is the same: since the patient cannot breathe spontaneously yet retains higher brain functions, mechanical ventilation is employed to keep him alive. The need for mechanical ventilation, while regrettable, is certainly undeniable where the capacity for certain functions persists. Not to maintain mechanical ventilation in brain-death cases would seem to require a special rationale, then, for we are not opposed to continuous mechanical ventilation per se. This rationale must refer to the functions persisting in the non-brain-death cases, since the persistence of these functions is the only genuine difference between them and brain-death cases. Why is it acceptable to declare a person dead when a respirator could keep him breathing and circulating blood even though he is in a state of irreversible coma, yet not acceptable to declare another person dead when he is dependent upon mechanical ventilation but has sustained irreversible damage to the lower brain only? The crucial difference is that in the second case the mechanism supports higher brain functioning, thus allowing for awareness and cognition. The reason for declaring death in the case of brain death is that the respirator cannot support upper brain activity, and the patient is therefore permanently unconscious. The nonspontaneity of the lungs' (and possibly of the heart's) functioning is beside the point, as the management of conscious patients shows. Why is the permanent absence of consciousness relevant? Since Schwager never answers this question, he fails to provide adequate support for the claim that cardiac function in a decerebrate patient is nonspontaneous, and thus fails to establish that the brain-death and the traditional criteria rest on a common heart-centered concept of death. I have suggested that the cardiac functioning of the brain-dead patient is better regarded as spontaneous. If this suggestion stands, then a different concept of death must underlie the brain-death criterion. Some, however, have argued that the traditional and the brain-death criteria share a common *brain*-centered concept of death.

BRAIN-CENTERED CRITERIA

Alongside the attempt to defend the brain-death criterion by showing that it affirms the same heart-centered concept of death as the traditional criteria, we find arguments with the same purpose maintaining that the traditional and the brain-death criteria rest on a common brain-centered concept of death. Rather than considering it a "radical departure from our traditional idea of death," Howard Brody describes the brain-death criterion as "a conservative revision necessitated by our modern medical technology." Brody continues:

> The reason heart and lung function become the legal and social standard to determine the time of death, we might argue, is that when one either stopped breathing or suffered cardiac arrest, irreversible loss of total brain function invariably followed within minutes. Today, however, mechanical devices have made it possible to maintain artificially heart and lung function even in the presence of brain death. If we have other tools, such as the Harvard criteria, to tell us what is actually going on with the brain, we should rely on those, and not the artificially maintained heart and lungs, to determine death.
> This argument assumes that heart and lung function are important, not for themselves, but as signs of brain activity. [20]

Brody suggests here that heart and lung function have always been central to the determination of death because of their connection with brain function rather than because of a perception of the intrinsic importance of their own functions. Schwager would argue that the traditional criteria were applied because the functioning of the lungs, and especially of the heart, were seen to be the central life functions, important "for themselves." Which of the two views is the more credible?

Before we possessed sophisticated knowledge of the interactions of the basic systems of the body, the decision that someone was dead could be based only on the cessation of observable functioning. Life persisted, then, as long as the individual respired or had a beating heart. It would seem to be a falsification to attribute to those lacking knowledge of the interactions of the basic bodily systems as well as an understanding of the brain's functioning, the view that the use of the traditional criteria was appropriate because the permanent absence of heart and lung functioning was indication enough of the death of the brain. In their original use, the traditional criteria were based on an organic conception of life and death rooted ultimately in the heart, because of the persistence of the heart's functioning even after respiration had ceased. They were, to use Brody's words, important for themselves.

On the basis of his assumption that the traditional criteria were used as signs that brain death had occurred, Brody goes on to argue that since artificial maintenance systems simply restore heart and lung function in cases of brain death, and since we now have tests for determining whether the brain is dead, the use of the brain-death criterion is simply a more direct test of the brain's status, and hence of death's occurrence. In this argument the traditional and the brain-death criteria become merely alternate tests for death, the concept of which has undergone no change. But the argument flounders if we cannot accept the central claim that the traditional and the brain-death criteria are both brain-centered.

Brody is not the only commentator on the brain-death issue who has argued that the adoption of the brain-death criterion entails no change in our brain-centered concept of death. Julius Korein sets forth the same understanding that the brain has always been viewed as the central vital agency. We have declared people dead based on the traditional criteria because we have known that when the heart stops, all possibility of brain life is lost. Now, in cases where machines impair our understanding of the heart's status and we are able to measure the status of the brain more directly, we can apply our tests to the brain itself. The declaration of death has always been a comment on the status of the brain. Consistent with this claim is the fact that those whose heart or lung function has become permanently nonspontaneous are not declared dead if they are conscious. Korein argues:

> It should be made unmistakably clear that the alternative definition of brain death [occurring in revised state laws concerning the declaration of death] does not replace the classical definition of death but only adds another set of criteria that may be used in the pronouncement of death under highly spec-

ified conditions. These conditions exist in the intensive care unit (ICU), for example, where the technology and specialized personnel for resuscitation, monitoring, and maintenance of life-support systems are available. Furthermore, the reader must be aware that these laws do not represent an intrinsic concept that there are two different kinds of death, in that brain death is actually central to both sets of criteria. If an individual suffers irreversible total circulatory and respiratory failure, death of the brain inevitably follows immediately, certainly within a few minutes if not seconds. It is only with the advent of modern medical advances used in the ICU that we face the relatively infrequent situation in which the brain dies before other systems that are maintained by life-support and resuscitation technology. Therefore, both definitions are actually predicated on an implicit *concept* of brain death.[21]

Korein's argument begins with the assertion that the brain-death criterion is merely a new criterion for use in the "highly specified conditions" we associate with the intensive care unit. Next, Korein asserts that the concept of brain death is central to both the traditional and the brain-death criteria. But does Korein argue for the view of the traditional criteria implied here? He points out that brain death follows immediately upon total respiratory and cardiac failure, but that fact does not legitimate concluding that the traditional criteria are brain-centered, as I have argued in connection with Brody's statement.

How can we account for the appeal of the claim that the brain-death criterion does not alter our brain-centered concept of death? We understand the connections between heart, lung, and brain functioning, and we are predisposed to consider consciousness a clear sign of life. When the brain's capacities for consciousness and for maintaining heart and lung function are destroyed, there is an appropriateness about declaring death that is not present when someone has experienced the death of the lower brain alone. But we look at things with the perspectives gained by the use of iron lungs and respirators. At least one decision has come easily for us: the conscious, respirator-supported patient is alive. The permanently unconscious, respirator-supported patient is dead if it can be demonstrated that the entire brain of this patient is dead. Even though the latter decision has come with relative ease for many, there is a dissenting claim, that the brain-death criterion rests on a different concept of death from the traditional criteria; this claim is discussed in the next section. Representative arguments to demonstrate that the traditional and the brain-death criteria share a common concept of death are clearly unacceptable.

DIFFERING CONCEPTS OF DEATH

There are reasons to be skeptical of any defense of the brain-death criterion on the ground that it reiterates the concept of death presupposed by the traditional criteria. The brain-death criterion is not heart-centered, and the traditional criteria are not brain-centered. Moreover, as discussed in chapter 1, the traditional criteria rest on an organismic concept of human death—one focusing on the integrated functioning of the organism, based on the presence of heart and lung activity. We must now assess arguments that different concepts of death underlie the use of the traditional and the brain-death criteria. Although the brain-death criterion is in general use now, it has not been without its opponents. Some have rejected its use because, among other things, they think it presupposes a new and untenable concept of death.

Lawrence C. Becker, for example, rejects the brain-death criterion on the ground that it departs from the biological concept of death we have always held. Becker associates the following definition of death with the traditional criteria:

A human organism is dead when, for whatever reason, the system of those reciprocally dependent processes which assimilate oxygen, metabolize food, eliminate wastes, and keep the organism in relative homeostasis are arrested in a way which the organism itself cannot reverse. It is the confluence of these and only these conditions which could possibly define organic death, given the nature of human organic function. Loss of consciousness is not death any more than the loss of a limb. The human organism may continue to function as an organic system. [22]

Becker clearly implies that the traditional criteria presuppose that human death is some kind of breakdown in organic function, a breakdown of the system of "reciprocally dependent processes." Brain functions are not included among those processes, however. Becker considers the absence of the brain's ability to function to be as inconsequential to a declaration of death as the loss of a limb. As long as "the system of those reciprocally dependent processes" is functioning—spontaneously or machine-assisted—death has not occurred. The absence of consciousness, and the fact that the brain is entirely and permanently dead, are of no consequence in determining the life status of the patient. Becker's lengthy argument that human organic death is a necessary and sufficient condition for declaring death is discussed in the next chapter. He is unwilling to consider the fact of permanent unconsciousness—indeed the fact of brain death—relevant to the matter of human death. I have argued that the fact of permanent unconsciousness appears to be the real reason that individuals support the use of the brain-death criterion. Becker considers that its adoption involves a dramatically different concept of death, one he rejects with his rejection of the importance of consciousness. In chapter 6, I discuss whether this rejection can be sustained; that is, whether machine medicine necessitates a departure from this focus on the human as organism in a determination of death.

In stark contrast to Becker, others applaud the addition of the brain-death criterion to our criteria for declaring death, seeing it as a necessary redefinition of death—from a cardiac-centered to a consciousness-centered concept—necessitated by our intensive care technology. Without this redefinition, they argue, we make ontologically and morally inappropriate decisions about the treatment of persons and former persons. Robert Veatch has attempted to justify a redefinition of death on moral grounds, to clarify the levels of debate in the redefinition dispute, and to set forth the competing concepts of human death underlying the use of alternative criteria. In *Death, Dying, and the Biological Revolution*, Veatch begins his discussion with a "formal definition of death" and then explains the alternate concepts of human death which one might hold.[23] From these concepts of death, Veatch distinguishes the locus of death, the place in the human body where one applies the criteria for determining death's occurrence. I will concentrate in particular on the distinction Veatch draws between death understood as "the irreversible loss of the flow of vital fluids" and as "the irreversible loss of the capacity for bodily integration" (30–31).

At the highest level of generality, Veatch provides us with "the formal definition of death": "Death means a complete change in the status of a living entity characterized by the irreversible loss of those characteristics that are essentially significant to it" (25). Such a definition is formal because it makes no specific commitment of content. It is up to us to decide what sort of "complete change in status" is at issue here, as well as which "characteristics . . . are essentially significant to" a particular entity, if we are to apply this definition. Since the particular entity we are focusing on is the human being, the definition requires that we decide which characteristics are essentially significant to the human being, such that their loss constitutes a complete change in his status. There is a serious disagreement centering on just this matter: some, like Lawrence Becker, believe that the "essentially significant" characteristics are tied to the integrated organismic functioning of the human being; others, to the distinctively personal existence of the human being. Since different concepts of human death rest on incompatible choices of "essentially significant characteristics," the choice itself will require justification. I address this complexity in chapter 6.

Having provided his formal definition, Veatch goes on to discuss four different concepts of human death. He begins with the most widely, firmly held concept: "What the traditional concept of death centered on was not the heart and lungs as such, but the flow of vital fluids, that is, the breath and the blood. . . . According to this view the human organism, like other living organisms, dies when there is an irreversible cessation of the flow of these fluids" (30). Veatch does not say that this concept underlies the use of the traditional criteria, but it becomes clear that he thinks it does as he continues his discussion of loci and criteria. Veatch delineates three more concepts of death. Since some hold that what is essentially significant to the human is the possession of an immortal soul, their concept of death is "the irreversible loss of the soul from the body" (31). Responding to both these concepts, Veatch says that the creation of support mechanisms has necessitated a "reexamination of the concept of death" (32). In articulating a third concept of death, "the irreversible loss of the capacity for bodily integration," Veatch agrees with the Harvard committee's belief that it was altering the traditionally held concept of death by recommending a shift to a neurological criterion. Veatch writes:

> It is not the collection of physical tissues called the brain, but rather their functions—consciousness; motor control; sensory feeling; ability to reason; control over bodily functions including respiration and circulation; major integrating reflexes controlling blood pressure, ion levels, and pupil size; and so forth—which are given essential significance by those who advocate adoption of a new concept of death or clarification of the old one. In short they see the body's capacity for integrating its functions as the essentially significant indication of life (36–37).

Veatch is correct that a brain-centered concept of death centers on the importance of the functions of the brain. Further, a concept of death that stresses the relevance of the neurologically based integrating capacities of the human body is a clear departure from the traditional concept, which considered certain nonneurological functions to be the sine qua non of life. The neurological concept Veatch has introduced grounds the use of criteria that measure the capacity for certain types of neurological functioning. The absence of the brain's ability to support respiration and heartbeat is different from the absence of the heart's functioning; we are taking a different kind of absence of functioning as significant in the decision about declaring death. Veatch goes on:

> There appear to be two general aspects to this concept of what is essentially significant: first, a capacity for integrating one's internal bodily environment . . . and, secondly, a capacity for integrating one's self, including one's body, with the social environment through consciousness which permits interaction with other persons. Clearly these taken together offer a more profound understanding of the nature of man than does the simple flow of bodily fluids (37–38).

Here, then, is Veatch's defense of the new concept over the old: it provides "a more profound understanding of the nature of man," and it "seems much more meaningful and plausible" because "it is a much more accurate description of the essential significance of man and of what is lost at the time of death" (38). But Veatch is begging the question, for he has yet to provide a defense of any enumeration of the essentially significant human characteristics. In Veatch's favor, we can agree that the irreversible flow of vital fluids, as a concept of human death, is impoverished alongside the concept of the irreversible loss of the capacity for bodily integration—particularly as Veatch clarifies all that is involved in such integration. The fourth competing concept of human death, "the irreversible loss of the capacity for social interaction," is the one Veatch espouses; it is discussed in chapter 4, on the moralists' contributions to the redefinition debate. This fourth concept differs from the neurological concept by centering solely on the brain's capacity for consciousness and for integrating the self with the social environment. It obviously narrows the notion of what is essentially significant to the human, and hence represents a different concept of death.

> Thus a fourth concept of death is the irreversible loss of the capacity for consciousness or social integration. This view of the nature of man places even more emphasis on social character. Even, given a hypothetical human being with the full capacity for integration of bodily function, if he had irreversibly lost the capacity for consciousness and social interaction, he would have lost the essential character of humanness and, according to this definition, the person would be dead (39).

From formal definition of death and concept of human death, Veatch distinguishes a third tier of concern in the redefinition debate—the locus of death.

> Differing concepts of death will lead us to look at different body functions and structures in order to diagnose the death of the person as a whole. This task can be undertaken only after the conceptual question is resolved, if what we really want to know is where to look to determine if a person is dead rather

than where to look to determine simply if the person has irreversibly lost the capacity for vital fluid flow or bodily integration or social interaction (43).

The loci involved in the determination of death understood as the permanent cessation of vital fluid flow are the heart and lungs, while the locus of integrating capacity is the brain: "The brain's highly complex circuitry provides the minimal essentials for the body's real integrating capacity" (45). The criteria for declaring death are the medical tests we apply to a particular locus. We have already described the tests corresponding to the two concepts of death we are examining in this chapter.

Veatch considers, then, that the traditional criteria rest on a concept of death that answers the question, "What characteristics are essentially significant to the human being?" That answer differs substantively from the answer that results from the concept underlying the brain-death criterion. While Veatch does not do so, it is useful to indicate the points at which the two criteria clearly diverge. Unlike the traditional criteria, the brain-death criterion is based on the beliefs that the continuation of respiration and circulation are no longer unambiguous signs of life, so organismic functioning per se is no longer a clear sign of life; and that the irreversible loss of the capacity for consciousness is directly pertinent to the decision that someone has died. The traditional criteria rest on the notion that continued integrated organic functioning, associated with the continuation of heart and lung function, is what is essentially significant to the human being, such that its absence constitutes death. By contrast, the brain-death criterion rests on the view that consciousness is the essentially significant characteristic of the human being, since it is only when consciousness is permanently absent that we discount the relevance of mechanically maintained respiration.

I will examine Veatch's moral defense of the use of the brain-death and the neocortical-death criteria in chapter 4, but it should be noted here that Veatch performed an important service to the redefinition debate when he distinguished the various levels of the debate and elaborated the four competing concepts of human death.

H. T. Engelhardt, Jr., reiterates Veatch's position: "The older definition of death measured the point at which organismic death occurred, when there was a complete cessation of vital functions. The life of the human organism was taken as a necessary condition for being a person, and, therefore, such a definition allowed one to identify cases in which humans ceased to be persons."[24] Here Engelhardt indicates that organismic functioning was considered essentially significant to the existence of the human being, or "a necessary condition for being a person." Engelhardt then sets forth his understanding of the concept of death underlying the brain-death criterion:

> The brain-oriented concept of death is more directly concerned with human *personal* life. It makes three presuppositions: (1) that being a person involves more than mere vegetative life, (2) that merely vegetative life may have value but it has no rights, (3) that a sensory-motor organ such as the brain is a necessary condition for the possibility of experience and action in the world, that is, for being a person living in the world. Thus in the absence of the possibility of brain-function, one has the absence of the possibility of personal life—that is, the person is dead (272).

The persistence of vegetative or organic functioning, while a necessary condition for the life of a person, is not a sufficient condition for it. Engelhardt thinks that the brain-death criterion entails a distinction between the human as organism and the human as person, and that we should declare death when it is concluded that the features of persons are now permanently absent: "The brain-oriented concept of death is of philosophical significance, for, among other things, it implies a distinction between human biological life and human personal life, between the life of a human organism and the life of a human person" (272–73). This concept implies the organism/person distinction because it implies that death is to be declared even though organismic functioning persists. It is, then, an overruling of the significance of vegetative or organismic functioning that would be detected by the application of the traditional criteria. "In the case of the definition of death, one is saying that even though genetic continuity, organic function, and reproductive capability may extend beyond brain death, personal life does not. Sentience in an appropriate embodiment is a necessary condition for being a person.

One, thus, finds that persons die when this embodiment is undermined" (275).

Such arguments leave us with a clear sense that the traditional and the brain-death criteria have no concept of death in common. This situation exacerbates the problem of justifying the use of the brain-death criterion, as well as any criterion resting on a different concept of human death, for we no longer have the security born of the claim that we are merely updating our tests for the same underlying phenomenon. It is clear that we are not doing this when we use the brain-death criterion, since by its use we are asking about the possibility of certain kinds of neurological functioning; we are not asking if the heart and lungs are still functioning. Since we do not declare death when the lower brain alone can no longer support respiration and circulation, but only when the upper brain is also permanently destroyed, the permanent absence of consciousness has an undeniable and crucial bearing on the decision to declare death. If the source of organismic functioning per se is of no consequence in a decision that someone is dead or alive—as the use of the brain-death criterion implies—then consciousness has become, with the adoption of that criterion, the sine qua non of human life. If this view can be justified, it will be only a short step to justifying the use of a neocortical-death criterion, since we have already adopted the concept of death it presupposes when we adopted the brain-death criterion. I will turn to these matters in chapter 6.

chapter 3

Biological Arguments

This chapter examines the first of the three competing kinds of analyses of the concept of human death. A careful review of these three analytical strategies is essential if we are to understand the nature of the concept of human death itself. The essential disagreement among the competing analytical approaches has to do with the concept of human being. The biological arguments construe the human being as a particular kind of organism, whose life status is measured by determining whether the capacity for integrated organismic functioning persists. The moral arguments (with the exception of Hans Jonas's view) and the ontological approach construe the human being as a person, whose life status is measured by determining the quality of life remaining for an individual (the moral argument), or the continuation or permanent absence of the conditions necessary for personal identity (the ontological argument). Since the moral and ontological approaches rest on a fundamentally different way of regarding the human being—a way which is a clear departure from tradition—that way must be defended. If it can be, we can then argue that the fundamental perspective should be on the human as person. In the next three chapters, I refer to the chief disputants in the debate as the biologists, the moralists, and the ontologists. I adopt these labels for convenience only; none of these terms designates a unified view, only a particular way of analyzing the concept of human death and of attempting to defend a particular criterion for declaring death. Within each group are differing answers to our central questions. I begin with the divergent biological arguments of Lawrence C. Becker and David Lamb, arguments that were described briefly in the last chapter.

The biologists have claimed that it is possible to put forth a strictly biological definition of death. They assume that death is essentially a biological phenomenon, and that the effort by moralists to define human death fails because it confuses a quality-of-life issue with a definitional problem. The moralist asks: Is the quality of life of the brain-dead individual so low that he is really dead? The biologist claims that such a question gets us nowhere in determining whether a human being is living or dead; how much quality a life has for its possessor has nothing to do with whether life is still present.

Setting aside for a moment the question of the kind of argument required to disambiguate the concept of death, it must be noted that our motivation for resolving this difficulty may be entirely unlike that of the argument we require in order to resolve it. That is, there are weighty moral reasons for addressing the question of when a person is to be considered dead. These may be patient-centered as well as other-centered reasons. This does not necessarily mean, however, that the concept of human death should be clarified on the basis of moral analysis.

Lawrence Becker's Organic Definition

In "Human Being: The Boundaries of the Concept," Becker attempts to overturn two views: "(1) There is no decisive way to define, in purely biological terms, either the point at which human life begins, or the point at which it ends. (2) In any case, if the end points are going to be used as moral divides, they should be defined in terms of morally relevant characteristics, not purely biological ones."[1] Since Becker gives scant insight into what has been thought to recommend these two views, we should first expand them and clarify the positions that underlie them. They derive from a related perspective, which assumes that death is a complex biological process and that while there may be good reasons for designating a moment in that process as the time of death, such a choice cannot be made on biological grounds. Instead, the choice must be informed by social and moral, and possibly ontological, considerations. This argument leads very easily to the second claim—that since the line we draw will determine how someone is treated, only moral reasons will suffice in deciding where to draw the being/has been boundary on the biological lifeline.

The argument as thus expanded has both explanatory and logical force. It gives us a reason for thinking that biological arguments are totally inappropriate to our task, and it suggests a link between the first and second claims. As it stands, however, the second is not entailed by the first; one could agree with the first yet take exception to the second, as Green and Wikler do in their ontological argument in support of the brain-death criterion.

Becker espouses and develops a complex view in his article. He writes: "My purpose is to attack both of these propositions by proposing what I take to be decisive biological definitions of the boundaries and by giving reasons for thinking that, for moral theory, such biological definitions are preferable to 'morally relevant' ones"(335).

THE METAMORPHIC DEFINITION

In the first part of his article, Becker argues for a metamorphic definition of the becoming/being boundary. He likens human development between conception and birth to metamorphic development, and draws the becoming/being boundary at the earliest point in fetal development at which generative differentiation may have been completed. While I am not concerned with the particular becoming/being boundary Becker specifies, I am concerned with his assumptions that the boundary-drawing process itself is a biological task and that his boundary between becoming and being can be defended because of its usefulness in settling the sorts of moral questions that can arise in relation to someone's death—in cases of homicide, for example. What is the connection between biological line-drawing and moral choice and action? If the former is to help settle nagging questions about serious moral matters such as homicide, then one would hope that the boundary could be supported by persuasive moral considerations.

Why is the completion of generative differentiation elected as a biological "event" of such significance that it is conceptualized as the becoming/being boundary? Becker invokes an analogy between the metamorphosis of a butterfly and the development of a human fetus; "human generative development sits comfortably as a *type* of metamorphosis" (342). This is an interesting analogy. We may have a boundary, but to label it the becoming/being boundary is a value-laden choice, given the uses to which such a line will be put. It is not similarly value-laden in the case of the butterfly; no decisions about how butterflies are treated hinge on it, and the treatment of butterflies is not, in general, a moral concern. We should therefore be cautious about the uses to which we put the analogy.

It is clear that Becker also espouses the becoming/being boundary because it is useful in cases where we require the drawing of a boundary—for example, to settle questions of homicide. But surely this is a moral rather than a biological reason to prefer this boundary-drawing over some other. All Becker seems to offer is an interesting biological mapping of human development and decline. He defends his choice of boundaries against the charge of arbitrariness not by arguing that it is nonarbitrary, but by arguing that other boundary choices *are* arbitrary, or for other reasons unacceptable.

In response to the suggestion that there is no good reason to draw any becoming/being boundary in the prenatal phase of human development, Becker appeals to the twinning phenomenon:

> The empirical error in the life-cycle definition utterly destroys its plausibility as an account of the becoming/being boundary. Monozygotic twinning can occur any time from the two-cell stage to about the fourteenth day after conception. And it is thought that most such twinning is not genetically determined. What this means is that one cannot say at conception, even given complete knowledge of the genetic makeup of the conceptus, how many humans will develop from it. It surely will not do, therefore, to say that the process of becoming *a* human being ends at conception (339–40).

If Becker's twinning argument does not succeed, he will have failed to provide any compelling reason for looking beyond conception for the becoming/being boundary, for he argues persuasively against all the other obvious options between conception and birth.

A plausible refutation of his appeal to twinning as a ground for not drawing his becoming/being boundary at conception is as follows: In every case, conception generates one human being (not a human becoming); and in some cases an additional human being is generated when twinning occurs. What we are able to detect at the time the egg and the sperm unite cannot be considered proof that something either does or does not exist. Our detection problem is an epistemological one which Becker mistakenly accords ontological authority. There is nothing in principle different in saying, "Since I cannot see atoms, they are not there." Further, it is irrelevant to the status of the first fetus (as a being or a becoming) to say that there may be another human becoming or being created (we know not how) after this one. And once the second has been generated, why should we not give it the same status (being) that the first already has? Becker tries to deny the status of being to the first fetus because two fetuses might be created. But what reason is there for not calling them both beings at whatever time they first exist? To say that we cannot determine how many fetuses the pregnancy will produce is no help, for this is merely an epistemological stumbling block without ontological relevance.

THE MORALIST OBJECTION

One of the more serious charges Becker responds to, in connection with his becoming/being argument, is this: "It might be argued [that] one has abandoned any attempt to make the becoming/being boundary a moral divide" (348). This objection to his biological boundary-setting is raised both by those who see Becker's particular choice of boundary between becoming and being to be devoid of moral significance, and by those who conclude that any defense of boundary-drawing should include substantial moral justification, because this line-drawing is put to uses with burdensome moral implications. The moralists who raise this sort of objection to the biological arguments for the becoming/being and being/has been boundaries are certainly concerned that any line drawn for moral

reasons should at least coincide with the biologically based boundaries we might draw. That is, if we are going to draw lines for any
reason, there must be a biological discontinuity of some sort present.
But the moralists' point is that biological considerations alone cannot dictate the placement of these boundaries. Becker has a fairly
developed and thoughtful response to these critics, but he seems to
be inconsistent on the moral status or usefulness of the biologically
based boundaries he has drawn. Becker expresses his critics' position
thus:

"The end of the metamorphic phase of generative development" does not seem to capture any morally significant
distinction. And the resistance to adopting a morally empty
definition, given our actual use of rough and ready becom-
ing/being boundaries as moral divides is strong. As Tooley and
others have argued, if the legitimacy of moral prohibitions and
permissions [is] going to rest on whether or not the victim had
crossed the becoming/being boundary, then the drawing of
that boundary must be done in terms of characteristics relevant
to the moral justification of those prohibitions and permissions
(348).

Becker sets his becoming/being boundary at the earliest time at
which generative development could be completed—the first week
of month seven of pregnancy. He defends his choice on the grounds
that it is an empirically conservative estimation of this boundary; it is
useful for settling questions of homicide; and its empirical conser-
vativeness favors the fetus's interest in being regarded as a living
human being. If it makes sense to speak of the fetus's interest in being
regarded as a living human being, the burden of proof would surely
fall on Becker to demonstrate that that interest is not present from
conception onwards. But the justifications Becker provides for his
boundary-setting are curious for a further reason as well: these justifications have acquired a thoroughly moral ring. Becker cites a moral
question for which the boundary-drawing is important and defends
the moral interests of the fetus in the process. Why, after all, do we
need to draw boundaries? Because questions of killing, of treating as
alive or dead, of acknowledging or denying the existence of interests
and rights, all weigh upon us. We therefore ask if there are any

morally relevant discontinuities or changes that can be identified in what is clearly a biological process of development and decline. Being told that by the beginning of the seventh month generative differentiation may be complete is not helpful to us. We need an explanation that endows that condition with moral significance, that accounts for the claim that now we have an entity possessing moral value, where we did not even a day or so earlier. At this point, though, Becker's rationale for his boundary choice has developed a moral character and is no longer biological. And he has not achieved the desired result, because he provides no compelling reasons to think that the line he has drawn marks a change in moral status as well. The analogy of the butterfly, even if it applies, generates no conclusion about the moral status of the entity in one phase of metamorphological development rather than in another.

There is a more serious problem with Becker's response to the moralists' objection. He apparently does not intend that his bound-aries coincide with morally significant changes at all, and so we would expect him to provide no moral justification or rationale of the sort just described. Becker sees (perhaps rightly) that the moralists seek boundaries that will settle the moral issues inherent in declaring death, allowing to die, and killing. Becker suggests, however, that such "threshold" questions cannot be settled by a victim-centered analysis. That is, one cannot define what persons are, assume that it is wrong to kill persons, and then come up with an adequate analysis of the conditions under which a homicide occurs. Our conception of homicide, he argues, must be agent-centered as well. His point is that our duty not to kill derives from something about ourselves and our membership in a society of human beings, not just from the rights of victims. Therefore, such threshold questions can never be settled simply by an a priori drawing of lines—which is simply a biological matter anyway. Becker claims that we must settle all such questions on a case by case basis, calculating the relevant features of both victim and agent. He does not consider his biologically drawn boundaries to be of any direct use in settling such threshold cases. "The definition of the becoming/being boundary bears no a priori relevance to this sort of investigation. And if there is a cogent biolog-ical definition of the boundary—as I have argued there is—there is no point in resisting it for the purposes of moral theory" (351–52).

From a biological point of view, Becker feels, there are clearly definable becoming/being and being/has been boundaries. These boundaries will be helpful to us in responding adequately to different moral dilemmas about declaring death, allowing to die, and killing, but they are not necessarily coincident with morally relevant alterations in the human being. It is thus inappropriate to attempt to refute them on moral grounds.

THE BEING/HAS BEEN BOUNDARY

Becker's biologically based arguments are intended to provide a definition of *human being* by specifying a becoming/being boundary (which Becker draws on the basis of his metamorphic argument) and a being/has been boundary. The argument for the latter begins:

> A human being is a biological organism, complete as a living "being" of the species when the metamorphic phase of generative development is complete. Death for such an organism is the same as for any other complex organism. It is a process. The process is, at least in part, a biological one. The completion of the biological part of the process is a necessary condition for its completion per se. This much I take as not needing argument (352).

Some of this is puzzling. If the process is in part biological, what are its other aspects? What is the remainder for which the biological part is a necessary condition? If Becker means the death of the person (that is, the loss of cognitive capacity) is somehow a part of this process, has he not abandoned the biological mode for something different? The death of a complex biological organism like the human is certainly a process, as opposed to a discrete biological occurrence. But I have already argued that regardless of its biological characteristics, there are compelling social and moral reasons for identifying and managing the death of a human being as an event.

Becker's argument for a being/has been boundary continues: "[It is plausible to regard] organic death as the completion of the biological part of the 'exit process.' . . . Death precedes the physical disintegration of (most of) [the] structures [necessary for entry into human-beinghood]" (352). Apparently, the "exit process" of a human being, in its biological part, is completed when organic death occurs. Also, organic death is to be distinguished from the physical disintegration of the organism. But why, if death is a process and we are trying to determine its time of completion, would not the apparent end of the process be physical disintegration? From a biological perspective, some other condition would stand out as the death of the organism only if one is sensitive to the organism's special capacities and if one notes the quantum change—the loss of the capacity for awareness and agency—that follows organic death as Becker defines it. The key lies in Becker's use of the term *exit process* and his qualification of the process of death as partly biological. It must be the remainder, the other aspect of the exit process (however he would describe it) that informs his decision about where to draw the boundary between being and has been. In any event, strictly biological considerations alone will not support any conclusion if one has declared death to be a process.

Next, Becker clarifies what he means by the biological part of the exit process: "The exit process . . . , in its biological aspects, is to be construed as a loss of function, not structure" (353). But why not structure instead of function? What is the biologically relevant difference between them, as far as the line between life and death is concerned? Becker continues, apparently regarding his next point as a consequence of previously presented premises. "The being/has been boundary can . . . not be put any earlier than the biological death of the organism. . . . I shall assume that human beings are mortal in such a way that there is no question but that biological death is a *sufficient* condition for marking the being/has been boundary. I assume, in particular, that consciousness does not persist beyond organic death" (353). Here again is the assertion that biological death is a necessary condition for the death of the human being. Becker then argues that the sort of organic death he has in mind leads predictably to the cessation of any conscious functioning, presumably because such organic death brings about the death of the brain. The cessation of consciousness is probably what Becker thinks of as the other part of the exit process. His definition of organic death is the final piece of the puzzle, however; since organic death completes biological death, the completion of which is a necessary condition for the death of the human being, a definition of organic death is required.

Because organic death entails the loss of the capacity for consciousness and is a necessary condition for the death of the human being, the permanent absence of consciousness, which can coexist with the continuation of organic functioning in Becker's sense, is an insufficient basis for declaring human death. Becker's definition of organic death does not encompass brain death or neocortical death; instead, brain death is seen as a consequence of organic death. Becker continues: "Parts of an organism may die without bringing about the death of the organism as such. Organisms may lose functions necessary to their survival [and remain alive if] these functions are provided mechanically" (353). Following these two seemingly uncontroversial premises, Becker states his definition of organic death: "A human organism is dead when, for whatever reason, the system of those reciprocally dependent processes which assimilate oxygen, metabolize food, eliminate wastes, and keep the organism in relative homeostasis are arrested in a way which the organism . . . cannot reverse" (353). A particular confluence of conditions, then, constitutes organic death. As Becker implied in earlier premises, organic death and the permanent cessation of consciousness are to be distinguished. He now adds, "[In the absence of consciousness], the human organism may continue to function as an organic system. . . . [Therefore], loss of consciousness is not death" (353).

Becker's definition of organic death refers to the integrated functioning of the human body; if such functioning persists, whether spontaneous or mechanically assisted, then the human being is still alive. The iron lung patient is alive for the same reason that the totally brain-dead, respirator-driven body is alive: "the system of . . . reciprocally dependent processes" remains functional. Becker may have generated an inconsistent position at this point. In some cases, when respirators or heart and lung devices have been used to restore integrated functioning in a human body, it is not clear that these processes have not been "arrested in a way which the organism . . . cannot reverse." In fact, it seems clear that they have been arrested beyond the capacity of the organism itself to reverse the process. If Becker commits himself to the view that the totally brain-dead are alive because integrated functioning continues, then he must also commit himself to the view that a human being may undergo death, in the sense that the organism itself cannot reverse the organic breakdown that has occurred, even though that same organism may be returned to life by the timely intrusion of mechanical support systems. Since a persistently unconscious individual is alive, according to Becker's definition, the only concern is the reestablishment of (mechanically supported) integrated organic functioning, not its reestablishment combined with a continued capacity for consciousness. The brain-dead, respirator-dependent patient who was once dead because he could not reverse the dying process himself is now alive, given the presence of the respirator. Consciousness is not a necessary condition for the persistence of organic functioning. Yet organic functioning, spontaneous or mechanically induced, is a sufficient condition for the presence of human life. Becker's argument thus leads to the conclusion that someone dead can come alive. *Death*, the term we use to denote the terminus of life, becomes a reversible process.[2]

Becker clearly holds that consciousness is not a necessary condition for the continued life of the organism. The part of the organism that supports consciousness may die and yet not initiate—or even be deemed a part of—organic death. Loss of consciousness will follow organic death, yet it is not a factor in assessing the life status of the human being. Becker's only argument for this exclusion is this: Since the death of a human organism occurs when the system of reciprocally dependent processes . . . is permanently arrested, and the permanent absence of consciousness is compatible with the continuation of human organic functioning, then loss of consciousness is not death (353). One might agree with Becker that loss of the capacity for consciousness per se does not constitute human death, but argue that the presence or absence of this capacity is relevant to the determination that human death has occurred. Indeed, we might read the Harvard criterion in exactly this way. Becker fails to treat the spontaneity or nonspontaneity of the source of the organic functioning as relevant, since he considers that the presence of such functioning, however effected, is a sign of life. By contrast, David Lamb argues, solely on the basis of what he identifies as biological reasons, that we must determine that brain function is permanently absent at all levels in order to determine whether an individual is dead. The nonspontaneity of lung functioning matters to Lamb, so he concludes that the brain-death criterion is appropriately used to declare death.

One objection to the biological approach bears restating at this point: in the flow of biological events and processes, the conclusion that a given circumstance constitutes death rests on a decision of significance. This claim is borne out by the apparent diversity of views on a biological definition of human death. The fact that Becker and Lamb provide two disparate definitions of human death, even though they claim to base their conclusions on biological reasoning alone, suggests that whatever biological discontinuity is identified as death must be, for some extrabiological reason, endowed with significance.

The second major objection to biological reasoning as the appropriate arena for defining human death is that such an approach gives priority to organic functioning rather than to the capacities of the human organism that distinguish it from other living organisms. While there is considerable argument over what distinguishes the human, there is clearly a distinction to draw. If nothing else, the confluence of certain characteristics (which we abbreviate by using the term *person*) distinguishes human capacity from, say, porpoise capacity. In the biological approach, life and death assessments for humans rest solely on organic functioning—the functioning that unites the human to other life forms. But some argue that the human as person must be the focus in the assessment of life status.

Becker's final point, already made clear in his argument, is the conclusion: "When an organism has failed in such a way that it cannot restart its organic processes [it is dead]" (353–54).

It might be suggested that Becker's definition is useful in that it applies to organic life at all levels. But one could argue as well that this is a moral disservice to persons. Becker tries to avoid the objection that his definition requires too much by reminding us that his definition asks for the conjoint cessation of certain processes, not their simultaneous cessation. Further, he points out that remnant functioning of any of these processes is not an issue; he acknowledges that some "artifacts of vital processes" (354) continue after organic death. But how is it possible, on the basis of biological reasons alone, to draw a line between functioning as a real indicator and as an artifact? Becker claims that residual functioning does not "embarrass the definition of death given here" (354), but he must explain how the biological picture alone allows him to distinguish residual functioning from significant functioning. Do we draw the line between residual and nonresidual function based on our decision about the locus of the being/has been boundary, or vice versa? Our first step would seem to be selecting a being/has been boundary, if it is correct that the biological events do not read themselves.

Becker argues further that his definition of death should be carefully distinguished from the clinical criteria used to establish that an individual has died. His definition has the added characteristics that it "is marked by reasonably unambiguous clinical signs whose 'appearance' . . . takes a relatively short duration" (354) in the absence of mechanical support systems. As long as such systems are in use, the human being has not undergone the sort of organic breakdown required by Becker's definition of organic death, and hence is not yet dead. The clinical tests relevant to Becker's definition are simply the traditional ones—the cessation of heart and lung functions. The unique capabilities of humans (their "higher brain" functions) and the presence of mechanical support systems are beside the point.

A difficulty with Becker's view is best demonstrated with a hypothetical case. Becker's position commits us to the claim that someone who has been decapitated, yet whose body is being maintained so that "those reciprocally dependent processes which assimilate oxygen, metabolize food, eliminate wastes, and keep the organism in relative homeostasis" (353) continue in stride, is alive. Surely we cannot abide this conclusion. A view such as Becker's, overlooking as it does the nature of the maintenance of organic life, commits him to this absurd consequence.

But since we are trying to determine a workable way of defining death—biological, moral, ontological, or other—we must also scrutinize Becker's complaints against the moral approach. His effort to supply a biological definition of death may fail for the sorts of reasons given, yet it may be a worthy effort in that it points out the problems inherent in other major approaches to defining death. We must examine wherein Becker perceives the real strength of his view: what big mistake does it avoid, in his estimation?

BECKER AGAINST THE MORALISTS

Becker's arguments were constructed as a response to the failures and misconceived strategy of the moral approach to defining death. He defends his view on the grounds that it is in accord with common sense, and that it leaves us to address difficult moral issues such as euthanasia directly, resisting the temptation to define away such moral dilemmas by stipulating that some still living patients are dead. Becker sees any redefinition of death as an evasion. Of the brain-death criterion, he says that its proper use is as an indicator of irreversible coma, not of human death. When a patient is determined to be in a state of irreversible coma, it is up to us to decide what ought to be done with him. "To be able to pronounce them dead would be a great convenience" (356), says Becker, but in his estimation it is dishonest:

> Rigging the definition of death to solve this problem, while tempting, is an avoidance of the real issue. The real issue is whether and, if so, when it is moral to give up trying to prolong the patient's life. . . . The typical medical situations—at least the ones in which the temptation to bring in the definition of "human being" arises—are those in which efforts to prolong life are underway, and the question is whether it makes good sense to go on with them. . . . It seems best to face this problem directly—by defining when it is permissible to give up lifesaving efforts—and not evade the problem by introducing an ad hoc definition of death (356–57).

Showing Becker to be incorrect in his claims here will not, of course, vindicate any of the moralists' arguments for redefinition. The moral arguments may fail for reasons peculiar to themselves even if they do not evade the issue as Becker claims. Moralists might argue that the error in Becker's charge stems from his ignoring the distinctive nature of the human being, as well as the need for conceptual revision necessitated by mechanical support systems. That Becker overlooks what is distinctive about human beings can be argued in this way: we cannot meaningfully speak of a patient's life when the subject of that life—a being to some degree aware of himself—no longer exists. According to this view, subjectivity must survive—not mere organic functioning, however integrated—if it is to make sense to say that a human being still lives. Otherwise, Becker is forced to say that a decapitated human body, mechanically sustained, is a living human being. Hence, it is up to Becker to show that his is not an ad hoc definition. In addition, one might argue that the age of machine medicine forces us to draw finer distinctions and to specify more exact meanings than was necessary before. Becker's response seems to overlook this objection entirely. Indeed, Becker may be accused of an intellectual laziness akin to that of which he accuses the redefiners. Now that we can tamper with and interrupt nature as we do, the biological discontinuities that Becker noted no longer exist in the way they did before. They have become possible stages or interludes, not the end of the story; they may now have an aftermath. A new decision-making requirement weighs heavily upon us as a result, if we wish to be sure that we are treating persons and former persons in a morally correct way. But the decisions are no longer simply biological; we can no longer consult nature for answers, because nature is no longer the sole directing force. When nature alone directed events, the biological definition included the conditions under which a person had died. Now the death of the person may precede the occurrence of organic death as Becker has defined it. Now that we direct events through medical intervention, the meaning of a biological approach and definition is largely lost, unless we can use its insights (as Lamb does) to decide that total functional disintegration (a condition masked by a respirator when total brain death has occurred) is death, and therefore that death has occurred when total brain death has occurred.

Although Becker maintains that the being/has been boundary "should not be by itself a moral divide" (357), he stresses in his closing statement the moral usefulness of the boundaries he has drawn: "The definitions proposed here . . . make good sense conceptually, are sufficiently clear for moral purposes, and direct our attention to the moral issues surrounding homicide in a productively direct way" (358). The obvious problem is that Becker has never outlined criteria for conceptual good sense, nor has he shown that his definition fulfills this condition. By his own admission, his divides are not themselves moral divides, so he must provide an argument connecting his biological divides with morally pertinent changes in the human being. He seems to want to have it both ways: his biological divides are not moral divides, but they will be morally useful to us because of their clarity and because they direct us toward the true moral issues in relation to the dying who are brain-dead. Indeed, he assumes that his boundaries may function as moral divides as well, provided we are given the necessary further arguments.

Becker claims that his biological definition of death is to be "rationally preferred" to any morally based line-drawing. His only argument for its rational preference is that it leads us to deal directly with moral issues we should not evade by redefining death. There is some value to Becker's statement, but only as a cautionary assertion. We must not redefine death to suit any other purpose than that of clarifying, as best we can, the real status of the patient. If our redefinition is shaped by other purposes, we have failed to fulfill our primary moral obligation to protect the interests of the most vulnerable human, whose resources for self-protection are permanently absent.

The cautionary force of Becker's claim notwithstanding, there are insurmountable difficulties with his biological argument, which leaves us with the conclusion that the permanent cessation of integrated organic functioning is human death. Even if Becker has succeeded in demonstrating that there are important discontinuities in the biological history of the organism, and has placed the being/has been boundary at the appropriate point, this contribution is helpful only if it responds to the kind of problem we face. Discontinuities do not take on significance, either moral or ontological, without interpretation. If there is good reason to think that our basic problem is moral, ontological, or both, Becker has not taken us far enough. He says that his divides are not moral divides, and so the success of his argument ultimately rests on the nature of the problem to which it is a response.

The central charges against Becker are that his organic definition of death dictates a concept of death at odds with the concept of the human as person, and that his definition avoids the sort of careful thinking that machine medicine requires of us. In assessing what Becker has attempted, we must ask whether it is appropriate to cast a puzzle about the end of personal existence into the language of organic functioning alone. Moral dilemmas about when to declare death arise not because we are unsure about the biological stream of events that takes place during the process of death, but because we do not want mistakenly to consider a person dead before he really is, or to continue regarding him as alive when he is permanently unaware. R. D. Laing points out the nature and implications of alternative foci on the human being:

> Man's *being* . . . can be seen from different points of view and one or another aspect can be made the focus of study. In particular, man can be seen as person or thing. Now, even the same thing, seen from different points of view, gives rise to two entirely different descriptions, and the descriptions give rise to two entirely different theories, and the theories result in two entirely different sets of action. . . . One's *relationship* to an organism is different from one's relation to a person. One's description of the other as organism is as different from one's description of the other as person as the description of side of face is from profile of face; similarly, one's theory of the other as organism is remote from any theory of the other as person. . . . Man as seen as an organism or man as seen as a person discloses different aspects of the human reality to the investigator. . . . Seen as an organism, man cannot be anything else but a complex of things, of *its*, and the processes that ultimately comprise an organism are it-processes.[3]

Can we construct an argument for rejecting Becker's choice of focus on the human being as organism? I address this question in chapter 6. Before turning to the moralists' arguments, there is a second biological view to consider: David Lamb's argument in support of the Harvard criterion as a basis for declaring that a human being has died.

David Lamb's Brain-Death Definition

THE IRREVERSIBLE CESSATION OF FUNCTIONS

Though he agrees with Becker on the adequacy of the biological approach, as well as on the concept of death as the irreversible cessation of organic functioning, David Lamb nonetheless argues for the addition of a neurological criterion of death to our traditional criteria. Lamb's argument is intended both to demonstrate the inadequacies of Becker's position and to justify the use of the brain-death criterion. Lamb prefaces his argument: "A strictly biological definition of death, regarded as a specific event, can be formulated. . . . Such a definition is socially desirable and . . . the brain-stem conception of death, as defined by the Harvard Committee of 1968, is a satisfactory one."[4] Lamb's use of the term *brain-stem death* may be confusing. Many hold that a demonstration of brain-stem death is a sufficient basis upon which to declare death.[5] Since Lamb thinks that the Harvard committee provided a brain-stem-death criterion for declaring death, we may regard his use of the term *brain-stem death* as synonymous with the term *brain death* as it has been used in this book.

As we have seen, Becker's position rests on two central convictions: (1) that the brain-death criterion does not summarize the conditions necessary and sufficient for the irreversible cessation of integrated organic functioning; and (2) that the brain-death definition of death (as Becker characterizes it) is an evasion of our moral responsibility toward those for whom a euthanasia decision is in order rather than a declaration of death. We must appraise Lamb's responses to these two claims.

Lamb addresses the question of whether we should adopt an alternative biological criterion for death. He agrees with what he takes to be the prevalent concept of death, yet sees good reason to change the criterion being used to determine death's occurrence. In particular, he is aware of the implications of mechanical support systems on our "conception of death" (144). He seems to mean that such support systems render the traditional criteria inadequate to their task in some cases. He is not clear about the important distinction between concept and criterion; he presumes that the old notion of death—the irreversible cessation of organic functioning—is adequate to the sorts of cases that arise even in an age of machine medicine. Instead of arguing that both our concept and our criterion need rethinking, he says only that our present mechanical capacities necessitate a new criterion that will tell us exactly what the traditional criteria told us—that irreversible functional breakdown has occurred. Lamb thus provides a version of the view that the traditional and the brain-death criteria presuppose a common heart-centered concept of death. He recognizes that a change is in order but fails to see the dimensions of the change required.

Lamb notes that Becker's definition of death is the irreversible cessation of certain functions, and argues that brain death fulfills the essential requirement of functional irreversibility. He says that Becker's concern about evading euthanasia decisions by defining the brain-dead as dead is not to the point. In fact, he implies that Becker does not understand what brain-stem death is: "What Becker apparently ignores is that the discussion of the diagnosis of brain-stem death is not about giving up, switching off, or withdrawing support from those capable of spontaneous breathing. It concerns the adoption of *alternative* biological criteria which calls into question the orthodox view of the heart as the central vital agency" (146). What Lamb is saying here may well appear confusing. He accepts Becker's concept of death yet argues that the brain-death criterion calls into question the traditional heart-centered concept of death. At first sight, such a statement might suggest that the brain-death criterion entails a change from a cardiac-centered to a consciousness-centered concept of death, rather than that it entails no change in our heart-centered concept of death. But Lamb, by emphasizing that our original concept of death is functional irreversibility (just as Becker holds), is merely stating that the locus of our criteria was previously the heart and is now the brain. Lamb is pointing out that in cases of brain death, the irreversible loss of spontaneous cardiac function has taken place. This feature alone does not distinguish what Lamb calls brain-stem death from the condition of conscious individuals who have undergone the same loss of capacity to respire and will be forever dependent upon a respiratory support system. This distinction is a difficulty for Lamb's view. Apparently agreeing with Schwager, he makes the point that spontaneous cardiac, and consequently respiratory, function is forever lost in cases of brain-stem death. Lamb apparently thinks Becker has failed to grasp this, implying that Becker is guilty of a "superficial reading" of the Harvard committee report, and argues that the committee was discussing irreversible coma accompanied by permanent loss of brain-stem function. (In chapter 2, I argued that cardiac function in the brain-dead patient is spontaneous, and that the Harvard committee recognized this.)

Lamb's assessment of the relationship of the brain-death to the traditional criteria is interesting and important; he indicates that the brain-death criterion is an alternative to the traditional criteria because it does not view spontaneous cardiac functioning as the central vital sign. When there were no respirators and all central organic functions failed pretty much together, our best indicator of total collapse was the cessation of heartbeat, since cardiac tissue will continue to beat for a time even after respiration has ceased. Heart stoppage, then, was a clear sign that all organic functioning was over. Lamb suggests that the brain-death criterion commits us to viewing the brain's functioning as the central vital sign. The heart is no longer necessary or meaningful for diagnosing death in brain-death cases because the respirator's presence will yield a false result. We must look beyond the respirator to determine whether the heart can keep beating when the respirator is turned off.

As I discussed in chapter 2, there is a great dispute in the brain-death literature at this point. I have associated Lamb with the view that the brain-death criterion involves no change in our cardiac-centered concept of death. But what does he mean when he maintains that this criterion "calls into question the orthodox view of the heart as the central vital agency"? This statement may be interpreted in at least two ways, and our choice of interpretation will radically influence the perspective we adopt on the whole redefinition controversy. The two interpretations are these: (1) when brain death has occurred, the respirator-driven body has undergone irreversible loss of spontaneous respiratory activity but retains spontaneous cardiac activity, so that the brain-death criterion is a genuine departure from the traditional criteria; and (2) since brain death necessitates respirator dependency, and cardiac function is maintained as a consequence of the respirator's presence, the heart's function is no longer spontaneous either; hence, to determine that irreversible loss of respiratory and cardiac functions has occurred, we must assess the functional status of the control center for the functions in question, the brain stem. Since the heart is not functioning spontaneously—and this may not be a clear sign of death, as in iron lung cases—we must look not at the heart's functioning (for it is not the true controller), but at the brain's capacity to function. Although the heart functions, its function is an artifact of the respirator.

The second interpretation is compatible with the claim that the brain-death criterion does not entail a change in our cardiac-centered concept of death: our ultimate concern is still with the irreversible loss of integrated functioning. We must look elsewhere in the organism to determine this loss. This interpretation of Lamb's view is consistent with most of his argument; he emphasizes the need for an alternative criterion, not an alternative concept of death. The only statement at odds with this view is his claim that the brain-death criterion represents a paradigm shift. This is strong language if the new criterion is primarily intended to enable us to see when the respirator is masking the irreversible functional loss that Becker is concerned about. In spite of this anomaly, Lamb gives further evidence that he holds the second interpretation: "Since the brain-stem, not the heart, is recognized as the specific area which regulates all vital processes, it follows that after brain-stem death the heart and other organs can never function again naturally" (146–47). Here Lamb assumes that all major organs and organ systems (which he still characterizes as "vital") no longer function "naturally" or spontaneously once brain-stem death has occurred. Since integrated organic functioning persists only because the respirator maintains lung function, Lamb regards all major functions as nonspontaneous in cases of brain-stem death even though they do not all have direct mechanical assistance. To ground this, he appeals to the regulatory role of the brain: the determination of brain death is sufficient to conclude that irreversible loss of organic functioning has taken place, since the regulator (for which we have no mechanical supports or substitutes) is irreversibly destroyed. But why does the nonspontaneity of function matter, such that it is part of the decision that the brain-dead patient is dead? Apparently (and rightly) unsure that this appeal to the brain's role as regulator is sufficient to make his case against Becker, Lamb adds: "At most the heart and lungs can be mechanically operated for two weeks. But during this period one would be merely ventilating a corpse. There are no reversals of brain-stem death. In this respect it differs from cases of severe brain damage where respiratory organs can be artificially maintained almost indefinitely" (147). Lamb thus distinguishes two kinds of respirator dependency: total brain-death cases, in which we can provide mechanical support for organic functioning for two weeks at most; and brain-damage cases, in which such respiratory support can be provided indefinitely. Lamb assigns a puzzling significance to the temporal difference between these two cases; individuals of the first type are really corpses, since mechanical support cannot be maintained indefinitely, but individuals of the second type are alive, since it can. Lamb does not say whether cases of the second type involve a persistent vegetative state or neocortical death, but it is reasonable to suppose that they share this feature with cases of the first type, or we would never consider that the individual might be dead. A troublesome point thus emerges in Lamb's analysis: he determines life status by the length of time we can mechanically ventilate a body—a seemingly irrelevant matter for such a purpose. The imminence of death should never be confused with an argument for its occurrence.

If Lamb's argument for the brain-death criterion is to succeed, he must: (1) demonstrate the inadequacy of the moral approach to the redefinition issue; (2) argue that we must rethink the declaration of death when mechanical support systems are in use; (3) show that applying Becker's criterion to brain-death cases leads to unacceptable results; (4) refute Becker's claim that the brain-dead are candidates for euthanasia rather than a declaration of death; and (5) appeal only to the regulatory relationship between the brain and the functions of the heart and lungs.

LAMB'S CRITIQUE OF THE MORAL APPROACH

Lamb has no convincing argument against the moralists' contention that our concept of death must be justified on moral, not biological grounds. Lamb insists that the criterion is a biological one (which no one would argue), and that the brain-death criterion is also "socially desirable" (144). He must mean by this that the reasons for which society requires a precise time of death are fulfilled by this criterion rather than by the traditional criteria in cases of brain death. If someone were to respond that these socially desirable reasons suggest a need to draw lines that mark a change in moral status, and not merely in biological status, Lamb would say:

> It might be convenient to reply that criteria for death must be socially or legally defined by morally relevant characteristics, not by purely biological ones. Such a course would, however, be dangerous. For example, appeals to social, religious, and moral criteria come both from advocates and adversaries of euthanasia. But the issue of redefining death should not be confused with the quality of residual life or with the decision on when, if ever, lives should be terminated.
>
> According to Lawrence C. Becker a definition of death based on morally relevant characteristics would amount to "passing the buck" to priests, social workers, relatives, and so on. He correctly attacks this view by proposing "decisive biological definitions of the boundaries and giving reasons for thinking that, for moral theory, such biological definitions are preferable to 'morally relevant ones'" (145).

Lamb concludes that it would be dangerous to select a criterion for death on the basis of moral rather than purely biological characteristics. His support for this claim consists of three assertions and is sketchy and inconclusive. He states first that the moral arguments are set forth by those who are for, and by those who are against, euthanasia. But this is hardly a telling point; the fact that individuals hold opposing moral views on an issue does not mean that it would be dangerous to decide that issue based on moral considerations. It may be difficult, or even impossible, but it is not dangerous. Indeed, Becker and Lamb are an example of this very opposition, so this objection, if valid, would undermine the biological approach as well.

Second, Lamb states that the definition issue is separate from, and should not be confused with, decisions about terminating life. Lamb apparently means that we should not define death by raising a question about the value of life for an individual. This claim presumes that the only argument available to the moralists is based on quality of life. But Lamb's is an impoverished view of the moralists' arguments. If his point is intended to connect with his claim about euthanasia, then Lamb must want to avoid a value approach to the definition of death because we will encounter opposing quality-of-life arguments over whether to declare a brain-dead patient dead. Finally, Lamb supports his danger claim by agreeing with Becker that giving the definitional issue to moralists (or anyone else who will reason in a nonbiological mode) is passing the buck. Decisive biological lines can be drawn, Lamb argues, and a biological definition is preferable to a moral definition "for moral theory" (145). Whatever Lamb means by this, it lends no clear support to his claim that it would be dangerous to put forth a moral definition rather than a biological one. We might come to agree that it is wrong-headed to determine when death occurs by raising considerations of value, but Lamb has not demonstrated the danger inherent in doing so.

MECHANICAL SUPPORT SYSTEMS AND THE ADEQUACY
OF BECKER'S CRITERION

Lamb rightly emphasizes a crucial point that Becker intentionally ignores: resuscitative techniques and mechanical means have obscured the occurrence of death. We must look beyond these techniques and means to clarify what constitutes human death in the presence of artificial support systems. Becker saw no need for this: "Where mechanical assistance is provided to maintain organic function, the implications of the definition of the human being/has been boundary are fairly clear. One whose heart no longer functions and who is kept alive by a machine is just that—a human being whose heart does not function."[6] Lamb contends that Becker was ignoring the nature of the cases with which the Harvard committee was concerned.

> According to Becker the Harvard Panel's incorrect conflation of brain-stem death with irreversible coma is an attempt to "rig" the definition of death so that legal problems connected with the removal of still-functioning organs may be avoided. . . . [Becker misses the main point of the report.] Irreversible coma has many causes and not every case of irreversible

coma is associated with the permanent loss of brain-stem function. . . . [The committee's central concern was] "to define the characteristics of a permanently non-functioning brain" (149).

Becker correctly points out an ambiguity in the meaning of the term *irreversible coma* as it is used in the Harvard committee document. At one point in the report, the term is used for persistent vegetative state, a condition of complete unresponsiveness and unreceptivity, which can exist even when the brain stem is functioning. Yet the central point of the document is that the term *irreversible coma* is synonymous with *total brain death*, the death of the brain in all its parts, including the brain stem. Lamb suggests that Becker overlooks this meaning in his rejection of the brain-death criterion. It is difficult to believe that Becker could have made such an elementary error, however. Rather, it seems clear that Becker does not care about the status of the brain stem. He considers the source of persistent integrated organic functioning to be irrelevant in deciding that someone has died. The continuation of this functioning is all that matters for the presence of life.

In addition to the charge that Becker misunderstands the nature of the cases in question and fails to give due attention to brain-stem death, Lamb ingeniously turns one of Becker's criticisms of the brain-death criterion against the criterion that Becker himself offers. If we adopt Becker's criterion, Lamb argues, death becomes a reversible event. Becker's definition of death stresses the arresting of certain integrated functions beyond the capacity of the organism itself to reverse. Lamb comments: "Confusion over the 'reversibility of death' reveals the limits of an exclusive reliance upon traditional criteria. Faced with the possibility of unlimited resuscitation, Becker is committed to talk of death as a reversible event" (151). Lamb is right in this objection to Becker. We would not wish to abandon the core notion of irreversibility in our concept of death; hence, our criterion for death should not commit us to such an abandonment. According to Becker's criterion, however, anyone resuscitated following the sort of functional breakdown Becker labels as death would have been brought back to life. Lamb thus shows that the traditional criteria can lead to unacceptable results in some cases of mechanical dependency, particularly in cases of total brain death.

If it is inappropriate to say that the brain-dead are still alive (given Lamb's refutation of the traditional criteria for such cases), then a discussion of euthanasia in relation to the brain-dead is out of place. Further, Lamb says that public reticence in relation to the brain-death criterion indicates a misunderstanding of the act of turning off a respirator sustaining a brain-dead individual. If the patient has been declared dead, turning off the respirator is not an act of euthanasia. Lamb emphasizes that the reasons for turning off respirators in such cases should never be utilitarian; the machine may be turned off only if it is ventilating a dead person. But Lamb once again compromises the purity of his argument. "What, then, is the dilemma? Provided that the above-mentioned criterion of death has been met, there is little point in maintaining the patient on a respirator; one would only be ventilating a corpse" (152). Lamb's choice of words in this passage is regrettable, for it has the same moral overtones that he himself opposed earlier. The statement above might as well say, "Once brain death has been established, there is no value in maintaining the patient on a respirator." There is no value in such maintenance because the patient is no longer alive. But why is the patient a corpse instead of a living individual? Lamb would respond that its regulatory center has undergone total destruction and that any integrated organic functioning is therefore no longer natural; the functioning heart is no longer to be considered a sign of life in the event of the death of the regulatory center, the brain stem. To say that the functioning is no longer natural is not to answer the central question, however. Lamb must justify calling the patient in this condition a corpse. Why should we consider the brain-dead, respirator-driven body a corpse and not a living, mechanically sustained patient? Lamb must explain why the death of the upper brain matters in this situation, since he considers the brain-dead patient dead but the merely brain-stem-dead patient alive. He does not address the problem of justification any more than the Harvard committee did in its report—unless his argument that the brain is the regulatory or control center of the body can be fleshed out sufficiently to do the job.

THE BRAIN AS THE BODY'S REGULATORY CENTER

Lamb's criterion is based on a point he takes to be noncontroversial: the brain is the body's control center, exercising a regulatory capacity for the body, and since no other organ or organ system relates in the same way to the body as a whole, the ruined brain is an adequate sign of the death of the organism.

Assuming that the lower part of the brain does play this unique regulatory role, why does the permanent absence of the brain's ability to exercise its regulatory function matter in determining life or death? The permanent absence of the regulatory capacity of the brain stem alone would certainly not be taken as a sign of death, but Lamb is willing to take the irreversible loss of regulatory capacity of the whole brain as a sign of death. Brain-stem death alone is not a sign of death because we have developed mechanisms to stand in for the missing regulatory abilities. The permanent absence of the brain stem's regulatory capacity is not the crucial point: what matters is that we can substitute for that loss and retain conscious functioning. Presumably Lamb would agree. Why, then, does he appeal to the absence of the total brain's regulatory capacity per se as a reason to declare death? It cannot be simply because the regulator is lost, for artificial regulators can sometimes mean that life is still present. Lamb's only response is the temporal argument cited earlier: we can maintain the totally brain-dead for two weeks at the most, but we can maintain indefinitely those who are only brain-stem-dead. Such a temporal argument is flatly unacceptable. Imminence and occurrence must not be confused.

Lamb needs to supplement his discussion at two crucial points if his argument is to work. First, he must justify the attention he gives to the brain's regulatory role, for we do not take the death of the brain stem as a sign of death when we can support organic functioning by a mechanical stand-in. Second, he must explain the important difference between the permanent loss of the total brain's regulatory capacity and that of the brain stem alone. This distinction requires him to discuss the relevance of upper-brain functioning to the presence or absence of life.

Michael Green and Daniel Wikler show an initial sympathy with

Lamb's view of the brain as regulator, but then construct an interesting refutation.

> The reader may feel that even if Lamb's appeal to authority fails to establish the centrality of the brain in the body's system of life-functions, that role is intuitively clear. Certainly the brain's work is different from that of any other vital organ. It is the organizer, the integrator; the other organs form the workforce regulated by its commands. And as Becker points out, the body's life is surely a matter of *systemic* functioning: the continued interaction of a hierarchy of biological and chemical subsystems. What we need is a criterion for determining death of the system; and what better candidate than loss of the command center which maintains systemic integration?[7]

There is good reason to attend to the brain, for it bears a different relationship to the body as a whole than do other organs and organ systems. But is its regulatory role (specifically the regulatory role of the brain stem) sufficient to generate Lamb's decision that brain death is human death? Green and Wikler argue that it is not:

> A more careful assessment of the lower brain's role, however, does not support the conclusion that brain death constitutes the cessation of systemic functioning. The fact that the lower brain is the element in the system which keeps other elements acting as a system does not make its continued functioning essential. It is still one among many organs, and, like other organs, could conceivably be replaced by an artificial aid which performed its function. The respirators and other life-supports which maintain body functioning after lower brain death collectively constitute a sort of artificial lower brain, and development of a more perfect mechanical substitute is merely a technological problem. When the lower brain's job is performed by these substitutes, the body's life-system continues to function as a system (113).

Lamb sees the lower brain's role as regulator of respiration and, indirectly, of heartbeat. Green and Wikler point out that what one concludes about the lower brain's role does not license the claim that "brain death constitutes the cessation of systemic functioning" (113). The nature of the lower brain's role does not render its functioning a necessary condition for the continuation of systemic functioning, for it is conceivable that an artificial support system could eventually replace its function. The brain is the body's regulator, but in one important sense its functioning parallels that of other major organs: if we had a mechanical replacement for it, systemic functioning could continue in cases of lower-brain death. Therefore, the loss of the lower brain's regulatory capacity has no obvious bearing on the decision that brain death is the appropriate criterion for death in cases of mechanical dependency. Green and Wikler underscore this point with an analogy:

> The heating system in a home can continue to function even after its thermostat fails, so long as the furnace is turned on and off manually (or by a substitute machine). . . . The source of control is not important; what matters is whether the job is done. The artificial life-supports now in use perform the brain's work rather poorly, as shown by the rapidity with which death of the body usually follows brain death; but not so poorly that the artificially maintained system is no system at all (113).

Brain-stem death leads to the cessation of functions that can, for a brief time, be mechanically maintained. As long as these functions persist and the functional integrity of the organism is preserved, the source of control is irrelevant. If we define death as the irreversible cessation of systemic functioning, as Lamb does, then a brain-death criterion is insufficient for declaring death. If we agree that Green and Wikler succeed in their refutation of Lamb's argument concerning the regulatory role of the brain, then Lamb has failed to justify the brain-death criterion.

The two biological arguments discussed here are unsuccessful. The central reason for their failure has to do with their narrow focus on the human being in its organismic aspect alone; no mention is made of, no relevance attributed to, the function of the upper brain. Hence, Becker must regard a decapitated, artificially maintained human body as alive and must say that in some cases death is a reversible event. The case of decapitation, as well as cases of respiratory dependency in which consciousness persists, argue for the relevance of the permanent absence of conscious functioning in a determination of death. Unfortunately, Lamb's defense of the brain-death criterion appeals only to the brain stem's regulatory capacity, which is not sufficient to generate any conclusion about the implications of the death of the whole brain. Biological definitions appear to fail, then, because they share a common and outmoded concept of death. The irreversible cessation of integrated organismic functioning, measured by the heart-and-lung criteria or by the brain-stem criterion, is a concept that asks too much when measured by the traditional criteria, and too little when measured by a brain-stem-death criterion. If brain death is the death of the human being, as Lamb believes, he must justify this view by appealing to far more than the regulatory capacity of the human brain.

The concept of death that Becker and Lamb hold in common may need significant revision; irreversible loss of systemic functioning is a concept of death compatible with the traditional criteria, but not with the brain-death criterion. Continued use of the traditional criteria in this age of machine medicine yields unacceptable results, as Lamb demonstrates. Our concept of death thus needs rethinking. This task completed, we may find that the brain-death criterion is appropriate in declaring death, or that further refinement in our criteria is in order.

chapter 4

Moral
Arguments

In marked contrast to the views described in the previous chapter, many arguments in the redefinition literature construe the central task as one that requires moral analysis. Such arguments are of many sorts. Although both Becker and Lamb construe the problem as a biological one, they reach different conclusions about the criteria for declaring death. We find the same disagreement among the moralists: some oppose and others welcome the brain-death criterion. Further, some favor the adoption of the neocortical-death criterion. The fundamental reasons for these differences relate both to the concept of human death that the moralists hold and to their understanding of the impact of the brain-death criterion on their favored concept of death. These important lines of disagreement pervade the moral arguments. Before turning to a more specific discussion of several of these arguments, it is important to understand what is meant by saying that the moralists approach the issue as a moral one requiring moral analysis for its resolution.

A moral problem most often reflects an action dilemma, though not every action dilemma is a moral problem. For example, I may wonder what route I ought to take to get to the Canadian border as soon as possible. Clearly, such a dilemma has nothing in common with the one the moralist poses in asking, "When should we declare a person dead?" I shall define a dilemma as moral when its resolution will in some way affect the quality or duration of the lives of sentient beings. The nonspecificity of this definition may be defended by appealing to the differences among sentient individuals. In the moral realm, our decision about what is better or worse is generally determined by reference to universal human needs and desires, but we must also take into account individual beliefs and preferences. For example, when considering whether or not to give a Jehovah's Witness a life-saving blood transfusion, we consider ourselves morally bound to take into account his framework of belief concerning transfusion, and not simply the possibility that we can save his life. Moral analysis and argument are necessary if we are to resolve moral dilemmas rationally. A moral argument provides a moral justification for a moral judgment—a statement in which we resolve our moral dilemma by specifying either that an action is right or wrong, or that an agent should or should not perform a certain action. A complete justification of a moral argument may require us to specify not only the moral rules governing the case, but also the moral principles, of an ascending order of generality, from which those rules are derived. We may even need to defend our most fundamental moral principles. That is, in some cases we must defend our theoretical stance against other possible choices.

For the moralist, then, the redefinition problem is formulated in moral terms: When is it morally justifiable to regard and treat a person as dead? Our action dilemma arises because of the uncertain patient status generated by the use of respirators, and a new arena of human choice is thus created. In order to answer our questions about the brain-dead and the neocortically dead, the moralists suggest that we must consider the quality of life of such individuals, what constitutes their dignified and respectful treatment, and what rights they can meaningfully be said to possess. Because we are posing questions about how we ought to act and about the proper treatment of persons, moralists consider that a moral analysis is the only approach that will enable us to resolve the perplexities of the redefinition controversy. However, it does not follow from the fact that the issue is a moral dilemma, that the reasoning central to its resolution will be moral. That is, just because our interest in redefining death originates in a deep moral concern that human beings be treated as their status and circumstances dictate, this does not mean that moral analysis is sufficient to resolve the dilemma. The primary issues may well be nonmoral, and their resolution may be necessary, though perhaps not sufficient, to provide answers to our action dilemmas concerning the brain-dead and the neocortically dead. Many have simply assumed, however, that brain death is an ethical issue, without really arguing the matter: "Whether irreversible loss of spontaneous brain function is to be equated with death is an ethical question, and one that requires ethical arguments."[1] This assertion appears in a popular introductory bioethics text. The fact that it appears without justification may lead the reader to think that it is commonly assumed that brain death must be an ethical issue. But can the ethical problem of the treatment of the brain-dead be resolved without first settling a nonmoral question about the status of the brain-dead: Are the brain dead still persons? If we decide that they are no longer persons, then should they be declared dead on this account? Surely moral argument is necessary here, though it is not sufficient to resolve all the crucial questions involved in justifying a criterion for declaring a human being dead: in particular, not for the question of whether brain death is the death of the person.

I eventually argue that while the impetus to redefine death is moral, the redefinition requires reflection on the conditions of personal existence—a reflection best carried out by articulating a personal identity theory rather than a moral theory that attempts to connect the absence of rights, or of a minimal quality of life, to death. Since persons have rights, and persons have varying levels of quality of life, we must first decide if the brain-dead and the neocortically dead are persons. We shall then have a basis for placing them among the categories of existing things so that we can determine whether they can possess rights or be a source of obligation for others, and whether a discussion of their quality of life has any bearing on a determination of the conditions constituting their death. Providing this personal identity theory is not sufficient, however; one must justify this concern with the human being as person rather than as organism. This justification will bring us back into the realm of moral analysis in the end.

The moralists appear to be united in the assumption that brain death and other conditions of brain damage pose ethical problems. John C. Hoffman poses the question he takes to be fundamental to the work of the moralists: "What minimal quality of life in a human body possesses sufficient intrinsic value to obligate us to regard it as a living person?"[2] Clearly, this is a moral question. It casts the problem in terms of quality of life, intrinsic value, and obligation. By Hoffman's own admission, some moralists would reject this formulation of the moral dilemma, resisting the implied notion that a human life can, even with drastically reduced functioning, undergo any diminution of value. Instead, they hold that human life, regardless of its condition, has an intrinsic value, and that no change in life status follows a change in the quality of life. This is the view of Hans Jonas, which is discussed below.

Hoffman's question poses a problem of obligation. It presupposes that a functioning human body possesses some quality of life, but it also implies that (1) the quality of an individual's life can dip to such a low level that it no longer has a minimum amount of intrinsic value; (2) intrinsic value is a matter of degree; (3) our obligations toward humans are a function of the degree of intrinsic value of their quality of life; and (4) we are obligated to view humans as alive or dead in accordance with the degree of intrinsic value of their quality of life. Essentially, Hoffman claims that an individual's quality of life may be of such low intrinsic value that we are no longer obligated to regard him as a living human being. It follows that we must regard him as dead. Hoffman is asking about the intrinsic value of one's *quality* of life, not of one's life. Why should we assume that the intrinsic value of the quality of life has anything to do with whether an individual is alive or dead? Hoffman's way of framing the question captures one important assumption of many of the moral arguments: that the matter poses a quality-of-life issue. There is significant objection to this approach by those who argue that the quality of a life has nothing to do with its existence. Green and Wikler pose the problem for the moralists in this way: "The question to be answered . . . is whether the moral proposition that maintenance of the brain dead preserves nothing of value and may be ceased when convenient shows that the brain dead are dead."[3]

I save my consideration of this important objection to the moral approach until the end of this chapter. The moralists I review in the following pages were selected for careful discussion because they best represent divergent moral strategies for resolving the basic question before us: Should the brain-dead (and the neocortically dead) be declared dead? Some of those who maintain that they are pursuing moral strategies appear, upon analysis, to be doing something more complex; their arguments appear to contain nonmoral, specifically ontological elements as well.

The Moralists

HANS JONAS: THE REJECTION OF THE BRAIN-DEATH CRITERION

In an article published in 1970, two years after the Harvard committee report, Hans Jonas argued that the brain-dead ought to be allowed to die, but that they should not be declared dead.[4] By now, of course, this view is out of step with private practice as well as with public policy. Since I argue that the brain-death criterion has not yet received adequate defense, Jonas's argument bears careful scrutiny. He believes both that moral reasoning is relevant, and that he justifies considering the brain-dead to be still living. Green and Wikler contend that the only conclusion that follows from quality-of-life reasoning is that the brain-dead need not be supported—not that they are dead. If this objection is correct, then Jonas is the only moralist who does not go beyond his own quality-of-life argument, for he is the only one who concludes that the worthlessness of the patient's life releases us from the obligation of intruding any longer into his dying, rather than from the obligation of considering and treating him as alive.

Jonas is ultimately arguing for a patient-centered rationale for the management of the brain-dead—a focus the moralists all share. Unlike other moralists, though, Jonas considers declaring death in such cases to be an other-centered response, motivated primarily by transplantation interests and other "practical reasons" having nothing to do with the patient per se. The only valid reason for continuing or discontinuing the support of a brain-dead patient must consider the value of treatment for the patient, Jonas claims. Once such value (or disvalue) has been established, we have reason for continuing or discontinuing treatment, but not for declaring death. Jonas's primary question, then, concerns the value of life for its possessor. But unlike other moralists, he concludes that a life with no value for its possessor should not be prolonged, not that it has already ended. Jonas says that "it is humanly not justified—let alone, demanded—to artificially prolong the life of a brainless body." We have no "duty to prolong life under all circumstances" (136).

Why does Jonas resist declaring death where the body is, as he puts it, brainless? Surely this condition is only a small step removed from Schwager's hypothetical decapitation. While we might agree in general that our duty to prolong life must be assessed in light of the quality of the life involved, is not brain death atypical because it involves an experienceless, as opposed to an experiencing, patient? Are qualitative considerations relevant in cases of brain death?

Jonas has two main lines of resistance to the brain-death criterion. First, he is convinced that declaring death enables us, by defining an individual out of existence, to take whatever liberties we desire with the individual's body; for example, we may take advantage of the respirated condition of the dead body to do research, or to perfect medical and surgical techniques. Jonas believes that the only way to avoid the abominations that can result from placing the brain-dead person in the category of things by declaring him dead is to consider him still alive.

The simple answer is that a declaration of death does not legitimate unconsented use of the deceased. There may have been times when individuals, living and dead, have been used for purposes of research in gross violation of their rights and preferences, but we should not assume that such use is made more legitimate by a revision of our death criteria. We have as much control over such behavior now as we did when we used the traditional criteria exclusively.

Jonas offers a second argument opposing the brain-death criterion. He maintains that the "sacrosanctity [of the patient] decrees that it must not be used as a mere means" (139). The body is an integral aspect of the identity of the person. As long as the body functions, spontaneously or not, it lives, and so the patient is alive. Our duty to the patient is both to promote his dignity and sacrosanctity, and to withdraw treatment on the basis of quality-of-life reasoning, con-

structed from the patient's point of view alone. The sacrosanctity
principle carries with it the duty to treat the patient always as an end
in himself, never as a means to an end. Since the brain-death
definition allows for such morally suspect treatment of the patient,
Jonas maintains, we must resist the option of declaring the brain-
dead patient dead.

Jonas's second argument is a reply to moralists like Paul Ramsey,
who declare death upon demonstration of the permanent cessation
of spontaneous cardiac and respiratory function and hold that the
brain-death criterion is a useful indicator of such loss under certain
circumstances. Jonas replies that the nonspontaneity of a given function must remain a nonissue in assessing the life status of the patient.
To say that the nonspontaneity of the patient's heart and lung function means that he is dead in the circumstance of brain death only, is
to suggest that he is dead because his mental life has ceased. The
elevation of the importance of mental life, in disregard of the continuation of bodily functioning, is a denial of the nature of the
human as both body and mind, and is therefore a retreat into an
inadmissible dualism in Jonas's estimation.

Jonas objects to the brain-death criterion, then, because he con-
siders the source of the lungs' functioning to be of no consequence.
As long as circulation and respiration continue, the patient is alive.
To conclude differently would be to depart from our "definition of
man and of what life is human" (136). Near the end of his article,
Jonas gives us insight into his definition:

> I see lurking behind the proposed definition of death, apart
> from its obvious pragmatic motivation, a curious revenant of
> the old soul-body dualism. Its new apparition is the dualism of
> brain and body. In a certain analogy to the former it holds that
> the true human person rests in (or is represented by) the brain,
> of which the rest of the body is a mere subservient tool. Thus,
> when the brain dies, it is as when the soul departed: what is left
> are "mortal remains." Now nobody will deny that the cerebral
> aspect is decisive for the human quality of the life of the orga-
> nism that is man's. The position I advanced acknowledges just
> this by recommending that with the irrecoverable total loss
> of brain function one should not hold up the naturally ensuing

death of the rest of the organism. But it is no less an exaggeration of the cerebral aspect as it was of the conscious soul,
to deny the extracerebral body its share in the identity of the
person. The body is as uniquely the body of this brain and
no other, as the brain is uniquely the brain of this body and no
other. What is under the brain's central control, the bodily
total, is as individual, as much "myself," as singular to my
identity (fingerprints!), as noninterchangeable, as the controlling (and reciprocally controlled) brain itself. My identity is the
identity of the whole organism, even if the higher functions of
personhood are seated in the brain. . . . Therefore, the body
of the comatose, so long as—even with the help of art—it still
breathes, pulses, and functions otherwise, must still be considered a residual continuance of the subject . . . , and as such is
entitled to some of the sacrosanctity accorded to such a subject
by the laws of God and men. That sacrosanctity decrees that it
must not be used as a mere means (139).

Here we see the conception of human life and personal identity
lying behind Jonas's recommendation that the traditional criteria
remain our only basis for declaring death. The brain-death criterion
entails the assertion that the person is the brain, while the person's
body is merely the medium in and through which the person experiences and is experienced. This, Jonas suggests, is falsification by
exaggeration; each person is a unique combination of brain and
body. The death of a person must be assessed by reference to the
whole; only when the body also ceases its functioning is the person
dead. Jonas's argument stands in interesting contrast to John
Hoffman's (discussed below), which also emphasizes that the
human is both body and mind yet concludes that the conjunction of
mind and body is lost when either brain death or neocortical death
occurs, and therefore that the whole is lost or dead as well.

In defense of his view, Jonas points out that we are identified by
our bodily features and that each of us is therefore a particular body.
Since the nonspontaneity of functioning is a nonissue—Jonas argues that nonspontaneity of brain functioning would not bother us as
long as we could cause the brain to continue functioning by some

artifice—we must say that the person lives as long as his body exhibits the traditional signs of life. But the tie between a particular brain and body, unique and essential as it may appear to us, is a contingency and not a necessity. Simply citing the means by which we are identified by one another (for example, fingerprints) does not establish that we continue to exist as long as our bodies continue to function in certain ways. If a body is not cremated, the fingernails and hair will continue to grow after death. Why not say the person still lives, since the body still functions? What informs our choice of biological functions? Further, that we identify a person's presence by his body's presence does not establish that he is present as long as his body is. We are not our fingerprints, even though we may be identified by them. Jonas, like Becker, has confused epistemic and ontological issues.

Jonas's conclusion about the brain-death criterion is profoundly affected by his concept of human life. He believes that the life of a particular brain/body combination goes on as long as either the brain or the body survives, whether functioning spontaneously or nonspontaneously. To this entity Jonas assigns an intrinsic value that persists even when life no longer has quality for its possessor. We respond to that source of intrinsic value with respect, and Jonas fears that to create an intermediate stage of "machine life" will foster abuses of persons.

Jonas's argument has an ontological and a moral aspect, then: it is ontological in its analysis of the concept of human life, for ontology has to do with the conditions of existence of entities. Jonas argues that persons exist as long as the central bodily functions of circulation and respiration continue, in spite of the occurrence of brain death. Each person is a unique brain/body combination, and only the actual cessation of brain *and* body represents the death of the person. The moral aspect of Jonas's argument is his rejection of the brain-death criterion on the ground that it will foster abuses. The brain-death criterion is, in his eyes, both ontologically and morally unsound.

Jonas's ontological argument deserves careful attention but does not command assent; the moral considerations he cites are not persuasive. In chapter 5, I develop a personal identity theory at odds with Jonas's view, so my full criticism of that view will be postponed until then. The only other objection that bears reiteration here is to his assumption that quality-of-life reasoning is appropriate in relation to nonexperiencing entities like the brain-dead and the neocortically dead. Jonas treats such patients as morally on a par with the sentient dying. Hence, his conclusions for the former cases are consistent with those for the latter: passive euthanasia, rather than a declaration of death, is the response morally required of us.

But there is a significant difference between brain-death cases and the typical euthanasia case: we have an experienceless subject in the former case, but an experiencing subject in the latter. For some, the experienceless subject cannot meaningfully be said to have a quality of life. Such an individual is, according to this objection, off the quality scale, and the question of whether his life has a quality worth preserving or worth labeling life rather than death is a meaningless question.

HOWARD BRODY: A RIGHTS-BASED ANALYSIS

It is clear that Howard Brody construes brain death as a problem that requires moral analysis. He writes: "Whether irreversible loss of spontaneous brain function is to be equated with death is an ethical question, and one that requires ethical arguments."[5] What is not as clear is the actual ethical justification Brody would provide for the brain-death criterion. His only argument in this connection is that discussed in chapter 2—that the traditional and the brain-death criteria are both brain-centered, so the use of the latter does not challenge the prevailing concept of death and requires no special ethical justification. As we saw, this argument is unsuccessful because the notion that the traditional criteria are brain-centered cannot be granted. It is appropriate to add, given Brody's bold claim just quoted, that this argument is not an ethical one at all, and thus fails as the kind of defense Brody requires for equating brain death with death. The only other support he provides for the brain-death criterion is this: "No medical approach to death can be viewed apart from its impact on . . . social and legal considerations; and a new concept such as brain death must be judged for its impact on the entire social structure, not just on narrow medical grounds. All indications are that brain death will meet these tests well, so we are justified in adopting it" (82). Clearly, this is no argument. Brody merely asserts that the brain-death criterion has had favorable impacts legally and socially. But to say that the results of treating the brain-dead as dead have been favorable is not a moral argument showing that the brain-dead are dead. Brody treats the justification of the brain-death criterion as a fait accompli, then, and never constructs a moral argument in its defense.

Brody does present a significant moral argument concerning the management of individuals who, like Karen Quinlan, are not brain-dead but are in a chronic vegetative state, a condition described in chapter 1. Such patients will never return to a "cognitive, sapient state" (82), but they breathe spontaneously. As we saw in chapter 2, some have argued that patients in a chronic vegetative state who are neocortically dead should also be declared dead in accordance with the neocortical-death criterion. That is, proponents of this view recommend a further refinement in our criteria and justify it on the basis of what many consider an additional revision in our concept of human death. (Robert Veatch's defense of this view is discussed later in this chapter.) Brody resists the neocortical-death criterion but provides a moral argument showing that since a patient in a chronic vegetative state is no longer a member of the moral community, he is no longer a person, and any decisions made with respect to him will neither harm nor benefit him. We should examine Brody's moral argument concerning those in a chronic vegetative state before we look at his objections to the neocortical-death criterion. Surely the brain-dead have no higher moral status than the neocortically dead, so Brody's arguments with respect to the latter may suggest moral arguments he is committed to with respect to the former.

First, Brody states an ethical question: "What should have been done with Karen Quinlan?" (82). He then explains how he will work toward an answer to it: "The way we will approach the question . . . is to ask whether Karen Quinlan is still a person, and what personhood means in this context" (83). This is an interesting way to begin, because the question, "Is Karen Quinlan a person?" does not initially seem to be an ethical question at all. Further, to answer this nonmoral question, we must know what a person is, which poses another nonmoral question. But Brody construes these questions as moral and proceeds to construct what he describes as an ethical analysis of the concept of personhood. Building on Joel Feinberg's analysis of "what characteristics a being must have in order to be eligible as a bearer of rights" (83), Brody eventually defines a person as *"a being that could meaningfully be said to be potentially the bearer of rights.* (Or, put another way, a being who could meaningfully be said to be benefitted or harmed for that being's 'own sake')" (86).

Brody jumps, rather abruptly, from Feinberg's conclusion to this conception of personhood. Feinberg's analysis reduces to this line of argument: rights-eligibility requires the capacity to have interests; that capacity requires the possession of wants and purposes, which entail "a minimal level of cognitive awareness existing over time" (83). Hence, an entity permanently lacking this minimal cognitive capacity has no rights. Applying Feinberg's conclusion to patients in a chronic vegetative state, Brody concludes that they no longer have rights, and that all talk of a right to live or a right to die is meaningless in a discussion of what one ought to do with such patients. Brody's next step is the puzzling one. So far, Feinberg's argument has been about bearers of rights; no mention has been made of persons. But Brody attempts to link the moral argument with the concept of person: "If, by a person, we mean a being who is eligible to have rights—to be a member of a moral community—then Karen Quinlan is no longer a person" (84). Brody thus reaches his conclusion about Karen Quinlan's status as person or nonperson, answering the question he considered crucial in deciding what should have been done with Karen Quinlan. But he provides no argument to link the concept of person to that of bearer of rights. Even if he did, the argument linking Feinberg's rights-eligibility argument with Brody's concept of person would not be a moral one, for it would involve inquiry into the nonmoral conditions of existence of persons—a matter for ontological, not moral, reflection. In effect, Brody has adopted a view about the nonmoral conditions of the existence of persons without defending it. He apparently regards being human and possessing "a minimal level of cognitive awareness existing over time" as necessary and jointly sufficient conditions for personhood. But he does not set out to persuade us that this is an acceptable concept—he simply asserts it.

Brody may well recognize the gap between his moral argument

and his definition of personhood, since he presents the matter condi-
tionally: "If, by a person, we mean . . ." (84). Further along in his
discussion, Brody indicates his awareness that the critical linking
occurs between the notions of personhood and cognitive awareness:
"All we require for personhood is the most minimal level of cognitive awareness" (85). He defends this conservative requirement for
personhood on moral grounds, claiming that a more stringent requirement—for example, one that requires the possession of "optimal, rather than minimal, human qualities" (86)—could lead to
abuses of individuals, as well as to the rejection of his argument. He
has failed to provide any reason for thinking that a person continues
to exist as long as a minimal cognitive awareness is present. Further,
the qualification in Feinberg's formulation—"existing over time"—
has disappeared in Brody's final statement. Again, we must reflect
on the conditions necessary for the existence of personal identity if
we are to accept Brody's concept of personhood. This reflection is
reserved for chapter 5.

To what purpose does Brody put the moral argument we have
been considering? Since Karen Quinlan had no rights in her chronic
vegetative state, any decisions regarding her care could, with full
moral justification, have been made on the basis of other-centered
rather than patient-centered considerations. This is not intended to
legitimate unusual uses of patients in a chronic vegetative state.
Instead, it is to emphasize that the comatose have no interests to
foster, protect, or frustrate. They cannot "meaningfully be said to be
benefitted or harmed for [their] 'own sake.'"

One of the ways we can test a moral argument, in addition to
scrutinizing each of its premises, is to consider critically its conclusion. Do we agree with Brody that those who have ceased to be
persons no longer have rights? He writes: "After [Karen Quinlan]
became comatose, . . . it [made] no sense to talk of Karen having
rights or not having rights, because in her chronic vegetative state
she lack[ed] the characteristics that [made] her eligible for right-
bearing at all" (84). If we accept Feinberg's argument about the
conditions necessary for rights-eligibility, then Karen Quinlan was
no longer eligible to have rights. But her case was surely not to be
equated with that of a rock. A rock can never have interests, wants, or
purposes. In this respect, Karen Quinlan was unlike the rock: at one

time she not only had the capacity for, but actually *had* interests, wants, and purposes, thereby exceeding Brody's minimal requirement for personhood. It is for this reason troublesome to assert that she was no longer a bearer of any rights after the onset of her chronic vegetative state. Whether she was aware of it or not, she had a right to respectful treatment and some right to privacy. If one dies, does one thereby lose the moral right to have one's wishes followed (for example, regarding the care of one's children)? This question involves Brody's notion that when personal identity ceases, one can no longer be considered a bearer of rights. It may be correct to say that one cannot be benefited or harmed after one has ceased to be aware, yet incorrect to assert that one is without rights on that account. I return to this issue later in this chapter, in my discussion of Robert Veatch, who holds that moral harm can be done to those who are already dead. Brody must resist this view if he considers that nonpersons cannot be harmed, for the dead are surely nonpersons.

This point leads to a final criticism of Brody's position. Presumably his ethical argument applies equally to the brain-dead, since they are also in irreversible coma. The brain-dead are therefore nonpersons who no longer possess rights. While he has no objection to declaring the brain-dead patient dead, Brody resists the use of a neocortical-death criterion, even though the medical consensus is that patients in a chronic vegetative state who are neocortically dead are irreversibly comatose. While a dead person is a nonperson, not all former persons who are now nonpersons are dead persons. In Brody's analysis, then, one can be a nonperson yet not a dead person. Such a view attributes an essential significance to the continuation of spontaneous organismic functioning. For Brody, that functioning per se is a sufficient condition for human life, though nonspontaneous organismic functioning in cases of brain death is not. Jonas would claim that Brody holds an inconsistent view on the spontaneity issue. As I argued in chapter 2, the irrelevance of spontaneity means that the absence of consciousness must be relevant to Brody's decision about what constitutes human death, since he would regard the conscious, respirator-supported patient as alive yet the brain-dead patient as dead. Since he does not defend the brain-death criterion, we must conclude that he is therefore inconsistent in accepting that criterion while rejecting the neocortical-death criterion.

Brody summarizes several objections to the neocortical-death criterion. Since he takes exception to none of them, he apparently considers them persuasive. He writes:

> A number of objections have been lodged against [the neocortical-death criterion]. For one thing, it stretches our traditional concepts of death much farther than brain death does. A body declared dead by brain criteria, once artificial life support is stopped, becomes dead by traditional criteria in a very few minutes, since it cannot breathe and therefore cannot sustain a heartbeat. A body with a flat EEG but with an intact brain stem may go on breathing indefinitely, however. Many of us would find it hard to imagine declaring such a body dead, holding a funeral and lowering it into the grave, still warm and breathing (87).

This argument, though inadequate, is often encountered in the literature opposing the neocortical-death criterion. Brody's claim that it stretches our concept of death "farther than brain death does" is an interesting assertion, given that he argued that the brain-death and the traditional criteria share a concept of death. His support for this claim, however, comes only from the temporal assertion that the traditional criteria are fulfilled by the brain-dead soon after they are declared dead and the respirator is stopped, but not with corresponding swiftness after the neocortically dead are declared dead. This must be Brody's reason for saying that the neocortical-death criterion stretches our traditional concept of death. We recoil at the idea of burying a body that is still spontaneously breathing, but as an argument, this is merely an appeal to the impact of entrenched human sensibilities. When the neocortically dead patient has been declared dead, we would simply stop the remaining bodily functions by an inexpensive, aesthetically tolerable procedure. Those who administer the means for stopping the remaining functions must understand that the person is already dead, and that their action is therefore not killing. Upon the cessation of functions, death practices may be initiated. It is thus unrealistic to raise the specter of a still-breathing body being suffocated by burial. Brody's appeal to sensibilities is unsuccessful for two reasons: such sensibilities change in new situations and with better understanding; and there is no reason to challenge the sensibilities of those who cannot change their responses, for the spontaneous functioning of the neocortically dead can be discontinued after death has been declared and before funeral services.

Brody's second objection to the neocortical-death criterion is reminiscent of Becker's reason for rejecting the brain-death criterion:

> Instead of trying to answer all ethical questions regarding terminal care by manipulating our definitions of death, we might make clearer and more precise judgments if we recognized a category of human beings that are alive and yet are not persons. Karen Quinlan in a coma fits into this category. An anencephalic infant (one born without any brain apart from the brain stem) would be another example. Depending on your views on abortion . . . , a living fetus might be still another example (87).

Brody's presumption here—that "we might make clearer and more precise judgments" if we treat those in a chronic vegetative state as nonpersons who are alive rather than as nonpersons who are dead—is unsupported. The very prospect that the neocortically dead, the anencephalic infant, and the human fetus might be categorized in the same way suggests that the presumption is dangerous in that it minimizes important differences. The anencephalic infant has never had, nor will it ever have, the sort of personal experiences the neocortically dead individual has had; the fetus has the capacity for such experiences, although it has had none as yet. Surely these differences have ethical ramifications that we should not overlook. There is no obvious support for Brody's assertion then; there is no clear reason to think that "clearer and more precise judgments" will result if we resist the neocortical-death criterion.

Brody has a final objection to that criterion: "We should note that of all individuals in chronic vegetative states, many do not exhibit a flat EEG pattern—Karen Quinlan did not. Thus, even if we adopted a neocortical criterion for death, we would fail to deal with many Quinlan-type cases" (88). This "objection" is only a reminder that the neocortical-death criterion would help us deal with a limited number of patients in a chronic vegetative state. We should adopt new criteria for declaring death only when we have removed any empirical uncertainties connected with their use. If we learn that persons with different patterns of brain destruction remain forever comatose, and if we develop the testing procedures to confirm those patterns of brain destruction, we should feel comfortable in refining our criteria for declaring patients in these chronic vegetative states to be dead. If we have confidence that the individual will never again have life as a person, and if we decide that one dies when one ceases to be a person, there will be no reason to oppose further additions to our criteria, as long as the conditions summarized above obtain.

Brody fails to provide a single telling objection to the neocortical-death criterion. Moreover, his ethical analysis of personhood ends in an unsupported ontological claim, a nonmoral claim about the conditions of existence of persons. That his effort to provide an ethical analysis ends in an ontological assertion raises basic questions about the nature of the concept of person. Is it moral, ontological, or both? I return to this question in chapter 6.

ROBERT M. VEATCH: A MORAL AND ONTOLOGICAL DEFENSE
OF THE NEOCORTICAL-DEATH CRITERION

In chapter 2 we examined the portions of Veatch's argument pertaining to the conceptual changes entailed by the adoption of the brain-death and the neocortical-death criteria. Now we shall trace and critically assess his defense of the latter, delineating the ethical, philosophical, and theological arguments he sees as essential steps in vindicating any criterion for declaring death. Unlike Brody, Veatch admits that his arguments are not exclusively moral ones, for he sees that at least part of his defense of the neocortical-death criterion must consist in metaphysical or ontological reasoning sufficient to clarify our concept of human death. He writes: "The direct link of a word *death* to what is 'essentially significant' means that the task of defining it in this sense is first and foremost a philosophical, theological, ethical task."[6] Veatch recognizes that we must answer several questions in order to construct an adequate defense of any death criterion, and also that these questions pose different kinds of issues for us, some requiring moral, and others metaphysical or ontological, analysis and argumentation. He fails to provide an adequate defense of the neocortical-death criterion because he shortchanges us on these arguments, however.

Why do we choose, and possibly modify, our concept of human death? Veatch responds with a moral assertion: "It is morally wrong to treat a dead man as if he were alive, but it is certainly morally relevant that others may benefit from a clarity of definition. . . . I would argue . . . that even if no one were to benefit . . . it certainly would still be a moral affront to the dignity of man to treat a corpse as if it were a living person" (1976a, 34). This is Veatch's fundamental moral reason throughout his writings for taking the need for redefinition seriously. How are we to understand his claim here? He writes: "There are . . . sound moral reasons for treating the patients as if they were dead. . . . The crucial point is that . . . it is an affront to the dignity of individual persons to treat them as alive if they are dead" (1976a, 35–36).

In an argument to demonstrate that both the traditional and the brain-death criteria are outmoded, Veatch writes:

> In the case of determining whether or not human life exists, . . . it appears that immoral behavior results when either of the two concepts of death is incorrectly chosen. . . . It is a moral infringement to fail to distinguish between a living individual and a former living individual, who should now be appropriately treated as a corpse. To fail to recognize that the essential qualities of humanness have left an individual is a serious assault on the dignity of man. To treat an individual who has lost that which is essential to human life as if he still had it is to say about that individual and about humanity in general that we fail to perceive the essential dignity and humanness of life (1975, 17).

Veatch's primary rationale for reassessing our concept of death is patient-centered. This would overcome the objection of Jonas and others that the adoption of the brain-death criterion was motivated by transplantation interests and had nothing to do with patient-centered considerations. Veatch's statements have the tone of bare assertion, but his argument might be fleshed out thus:

1. Each human life has an "essential dignity and humanness."
2. When one loses what is essentially significant to human life, one dies.
3. It is an affront to the dignity of the human being to treat him as alive if he is dead.
4. If a human being is dead, one should not treat him as alive.
5. Death-assaulting technologies sometimes leave human beings in an inhuman form of existence, since they have lost their essential humanness.
6. Death-assaulting technologies sometimes treat the dead as though they were alive.
7. The use of death-assaulting technologies is sometimes an affront to human dignity.
8. We must eliminate the affronts to human dignity that result from the uses of death-assaulting technologies that treat the dead as though they were alive.
9. We must determine which uses of death-assaulting technologies constitute the treatment of the dead as living.
10. Therefore, we must determine what death is so that we can identify any occurrences of it.

The troublesome claim here is point 3. In what way is it an assault on the dignity of the individual, or a "moral infringement," to treat him as alive if he is dead? If the individual is really dead, then how can we do him any harm, infringe on any of his rights, or assault his dignity? Could we not argue that the false positive declarations are a disservice only to the living, yet one to which the living have no right to object?

Veatch's underlying assumption that posthumous harm is possible is at least consistent with an intuition we all share—that one is harmed if one is murdered, and that the harm is in being murdered as such. To debate this issue would take us too far afield at this point, however.[7] Hence, I resort to the intuitively based remarks above to settle, in a preliminary way, the question of posthumous harm. Since our intuition supports Veatch's assumption that posthumous harm is possible, can we be satisfied with his way of describing the moral harm involved in treating the dead as though they were living? Insofar as we believe that our treatment of human beings should be informed by considerations of their status (for example, age or comprehension), the issue of the individual's life status must be among our most fundamental concerns. If someone is dead, it would be an error to treat him as alive. But would it be an affront to his dignity, or a moral infringement? Brody would maintain that it cannot be, since the brain-dead and the neocortically dead have no rights. Veatch's insight rests on the notion that an entity with the unique and essential features of humanness must be treated in a particular manner. That is, the features that distinguish human from nonhuman entities are such that the human must always be treated with dignity, even in death. To treat someone as something he is not is to ignore what he is—a basic wrong not only to him but to persons generally, since it reflects the quality of one's regard for humanity. Fleshing out Veatch's view in this way gives it the plausibility and strength it initially appeared to lack.

Before we assess Veatch's argument for the neocortical-death criterion, we should consider the language he uses in stating his position. He writes: "It is simply an immoral assault on human dignity to treat a corpse as if it were living" (1975, 17) and, "It is an affront to the dignity of individual persons to treat them as alive if they are dead" (1976a, 36). Veatch's language makes it sound as if the solution to the question of the brain-dead and the neocortically dead is out there for our discovery and not, ultimately, a decision we must make. Death is a quantum change in the status of a living entity, but it is up to us to decide which quantum change we take to be death in the case of humans. Our choice is of such fundamental importance, with such weighty moral and social impacts, that we must defend it to the fullest extent.

As we saw in chapter 2, Veatch contributed substantially to the redefinition debate by clarifying the levels of the debate and by suggesting that different kinds of questions arise at those levels: some are philosophical or ethical, others medical or scientific. Selecting operational tests to determine the death of the brain is not a philosophical problem, nor is it to be settled by philosophical argument; but analyzing the concepts of death lying behind the various criteria, as well as articulating an adequate concept of human death, are the philosopher's concern. Veatch's effort to construct an argument in favor of the neocortical-death criterion centers around these two philosophical projects (see Veatch, 1976b, 3).

If we agree that "death-assaulting technologies" require us to rethink the matter of when a human being should be declared dead, and that a dead human being should not be treated as a living one, then our first task must be to clarify the meanings of death and human death. If these concepts are unclear to us, we will be unable to identify death in all cases, and as a result we may treat some of the dead as still living. As we saw in chapter 2, Veatch begins with the formal concept of death: "In general terms an entity is considered dead when there is a complete change in the status of that entity characterized by the irreversible loss of those characteristics that are essentially significant to it" (1976b, 6).

We cannot apply this definition until we select an entity and decide what characteristics are "essentially significant" to that entity. If we are interested in a precise concept of human death, we must decide what characteristics are essentially significant to the human being, such that their permanent loss constitutes its death. Veatch notes four distinct concepts of human death (based on four different understandings of what characteristics are essentially significant to human life) and argues for the most radical of them: human death occurs when a human being undergoes the irreversible loss of the capacity for consciousness and social interaction. To ground this concept of death, Veatch must show both the inadequacies of the other concepts of human death and the gain in clarity and accuracy of his concept.

He begins his attack on the concepts of death underlying the traditional and the brain-death criteria on the ground that these concepts are "biologically reductionistic" (1976b, 6). Veatch means by this that the use of such concepts reduces the human reality to its identity as a biological organism alone, thus ignoring the refined capacities humans possess in distinction from other living things. To claim that the traditional and brain-centered concepts of death are biologically reductionistic is one thing; to support this claim is another. Using this claim to criticize these concepts requires an argument showing that a biologically reductionistic concept of human death is morally or ontologically unacceptable. Veatch must demonstrate that such biological reductionism is a mistake in the human case, but he never does. He criticizes the traditional concept thus: "The decisive problem with this concept . . . is that it is not only simplistic, but biologically reductionistic. It makes no distinction between the human and the human's body. It is a vitalistic, animalistic notion of the human as essentially a biological species in which the biological functions of respiration and circulation are critical" (1976b, 6).

Respiration and circulation are indeed critical, but it is their *essentially* significant character that is in dispute. To win this point, or at least to be entitled to look further for a better honed concept of human death, Veatch must provide argument, not epithet. What is wrong with the failure to distinguish "between the human and the human's body"? Veatch resorts to an ad hominem argument in response to this crucial question:

> There is no scientific or medical argument against that position. It is fundamentally not a scientific or medical question. If some individuals and some religious and philosophical schools of thought choose to answer the question "What is essential to the human's nature?" by pointing to respiration and circulation, no laboratory evidence will ever refute the stance. It is, however, in conflict with the view of virtually every religious and philosophical group in human history. It could at least be said for the defenders of the idea that death occurs when the soul departs from the body, that they recognized that a human is more than his body and some of its lesser functions (1976b, 6).

Veatch's underlying insight is expressed in the last line of the preceding passage. He must elevate this perspective to the primary role in providing a meaning for our concept of human death. We may agree that a human being is in some sense more than his body, but it is also contingently true that without his body, he is nothing. Further, to say that a human being is more than his body is to make no judgment on what he is; the essentially significant characteristics may be tied to his bodily nature, or to other features or combinations of features.

We must decide, Veatch says, what "functions are the critical ones for deciding that a person should be treated as dead" (1976b, 7). This question puts us in the realm of metaphysics and ethics. The brain-death criterion is an improvement over the traditional criteria because the former tests for functions associated with the brain, which "are more significant than the circulatory or respiratory functions. . . . It seems like this concept of death as the irreversible loss of bodily integrating capacity is philosophically preferable" (1976b, 8). The concept of death underlying the brain-death criterion has now taken "on the character of a reasonably well-established philosophical certainty" (1975, 14). In all of this, the most basic questions never receive a careful answer: What criteria of philosophical preference does Veatch use? What does he mean by a "philosophical certainty"? While Veatch has managed to set out the questions—a task which many engaging in the redefinition discussion have not done carefully or thoroughly—he himself fails to provide a foundational argument for the acceptance of any particular concept of human death.

Veatch is convinced that the essentially significant characteristic of humans is the embodied capacity for social interaction, a necessary condition for which is a capacity for consciousness. Since one can lose these capacities and yet have undergone less-than-total brain destruction, Veatch argues, we must adopt a criterion concerned wih a smaller portion of the brain than is the brain-death criterion. "Is [it] possible that there could be a condition wherein portions of the brain retain their normal functioning and yet for all practical purposes the individual should, according to our philosophical understanding of the nature of man, be pronounced dead?" (1975, 14). Veatch's philosophical understanding of the nature of man, his view about what is essential to human nature, centers on the capacity for social interaction. He indicates that the capacity for experience may be synonymous with this capacity; he can think of no reason why the two would not be synonymous. However, a victim of locked-in syndrome—an experiencing entity lacking any social interactive capacities—may be a case in point. Surely such an individual is to be considered alive because he is aware. Veatch is wrong, then, to consider the capacity for social interaction coterminous with the capacity for consciousness. His concept of human death should fix solely on the latter.

Veatch defends his concept on the ground that it reflects a more "profound understanding" of the nature of the human. He refines this as follows:

> There must be one final comment about that which is essential to the nature of man. Is it simply capacity for experience and social interaction per se, or must there also be some embodiment of the capacity? Consider the bizarre and purely hypothetical case in which all of the information of the human brain were transferred to a piece of magnetic tape together with sufficient sensory inputs and outputs to permit some social functions. Would the erasing of that tape be tantamount to murder? . . . It seems quite possible that our concept of the essential must include some embodiment. . . . Then the essential element is embodied capacity for experience and social interaction (1975, 23).

Veatch's computer-tape thought experiment is challenging because it assists us in sorting out whether we could dispense entirely with a sense of organismic identity and retain the notion that our essentially significant characteristics remain. Veatch apparently cannot do this. Just as he is critical of concepts of human death that are "biologically reductionistic," he is not a mental reductionist either, for he is unhappy with the idea that a self might continue in the disembodied condition he describes in his thought experiment. Veatch thus defines human death as the permanent loss of the embodied capacity for experience and social interaction. We have already seen that his emphasis on social interactive capacity must be disallowed. I return to a discussion based on Veatch's computer-tape example in chapter 5, where it serves as a useful tool in my argument for a theory of personal identity at odds with Veatch's.

While Veatch recognizes the need for argument, he does not always provide it. He is not a clear representative of the moralists, since his moral arguments are meant to show not that the neocortically dead are dead, but that we ought to redefine death so that we do not treat dead persons as though they were living. Veatch recognizes that a part of the argument necessary to defend a death criterion must be ontological, although he fails to defend his own personal identity theory, for he never provides a full-fledged argument for regarding the human being as person rather than as organism. He argues that the essence of the human being is the embodied capacity to experience and to interact with others, and that the permanent loss of this capacity signals death. This view of the human essence emphasizes the personal, not the organismic, aspect of human existence—a choice for which Veatch never argues persuasively. But those involved in the redefinition debate are in his debt, for he demonstrates, as no one has before, the full complexity of justifying a new criterion for declaring death.

JOHN C. HOFFMAN: TWO LEVELS OF MORAL DEBATE

Robert Veatch provided a service when he distinguished these four levels of the debate on redefining death: (1) the formal definition of death; (2) the concept of human death; (3) the locus of death; and (4) the criteria for declaring death. Philosophical analysis is necessary at levels 1 and 2, but Veatch's argumentation at these levels is incomplete. Aware of some of the deficiencies in Veatch's discussion, John C. Hoffman urges a further distinction, one that cuts across Veatch's concept of human death. Hoffman believes that his distinction clarifies our philosophical responsibilities more precisely than Veatch's claim that we must articulate a concept of human death. Hoffman argues that the moralists (he surveys the views of Jonas, Ramsey, Schwager, Veatch, and Schiffer) are divided in their attempt to support various criteria because some of them argue at the primary level, and others at the secondary level, of moral discourse. All, Hoffman contends, should see their task as one at the primary level.

Hoffman is aware that the fundamental choice of a particular criterion concerns whether one regards the human being as person or as organism. He suggests that Veatch's discussion of what is essentially significant to the nature of the human is evaluative, and that Veatch's decision is one resting on what Hoffman terms "primary moral insight."[8] I have argued that Veatch's decision, that the capacity for experience and social interaction is essentially significant to the nature of the human, rests on an unarticulated personal identity theory (a sketch of which can be gleaned from his response to the computer-tape thought experiment). From this I have construed

Veatch's decision as a nonmoral, ontological one. Hoffman considers that all the moralists, including Veatch, respond to the moral question set forth earlier in this chapter: "What minimal quality of life in a human body possesses sufficient intrinsic value to obligate us to regard it as a living person?" (436). Hoffman claims that this question is a primary moral question that must be answered if we are to justify the use of any death criterion.

Hoffman defines the two levels of ethical debate among those engaged in the conceptual arguments as follows:

> Primary moral insight refers to the recognition of discrete occasions of intrinsic value making claims upon us. It is the awareness of specific forms of the good (or of evil) which elicit a sense of moral obligation. Depending upon how we divide up experience, how we conceptualize it, primary moral discourse may talk in terms of qualities or entities of innate worth, goals one properly pursues, experiences or realities one correctly defends and preserves. . . . The participants in the present discussion [Schwager, Ramsey, Jonas, Veatch, and Shiffer] claim this kind of intrinsic value for human life (436).

Applying this description of primary moral insight to the problem of defining human death, Hoffman claims that under some conditions human life possesses sufficient intrinsic value to become the source of certain obligations on our part. He suggests that primary moral discourse may assign intrinsic value to either qualities or entities. Hoffman's question concerns the degree of quality of life that has sufficient intrinsic value to be regarded as a sign of being alive. He says that each of the moralists takes human life to have an intrinsic value but that they differ in their concepts of human life—as we have seen. The problem of justification, then, concerns the concept of human life each holds. By contrast,

> secondary moral insight and discourse are the discernment and articulation of the proper relationship between such values, of the correct priorities among these claims. . . . The basic moral issue . . . would be which claim has the higher priority and under what conditions. This is a different level of moral reflection. Here we seek not specific experiences of moral obliga-

tion, but norms, principles, maxims for ordering our moral
experience (436–37).

Hoffman intends this distinction as a clarification of the two kinds
of moral questions that can arise at the conceptual level. He uses the
distinction to shed light on relationships among the moral views he
surveys in his article, and assumes that all moralists pose the question, "When [should] an individual whom all accept as human . . . be declared dead[?]" (437). The first level, that of primary
moral discourse, is at the heart of the definitional debate: "At this
first level the attempt is to define or characterize human life in order
to be able to determine the occurrence of human death" (437).
Instead of viewing this definitional problem as an ontological one
having to do with the conditions of existence of persons, Hoffman
assumes that it is answered by addressing this question: "What sort of
life, what quality of living is presupposed as the polar opposite in any
definition of death?" (438). This way of phrasing the question implies that death is a qualitative change in status. Hoffman says that
there are, among the views he examines, "competing primary moral
judgments concerning what quality of life is so significant that its
presence provides proof that death has occurred" (438). Ramsey and
Schwager consider that as long as spontaneous respiration and circulation continue, the quality of life is a sufficient sign that death has
not taken place. Jonas, discounting the relevance of nonspontaneity
to any decisions about the life status of the human, maintains that
the continuation of respiration and circulation alone, by whatever
means, indicates the presence of human life. Veatch, Schiffer, and
Hoffman argue that the embodied capacity for consciousness is the
sine qua non of human life. But Hoffman construes this choice as a
moral, not an ontological, one. At the first level of the moral debate,
then, we "clarify our view of human life" (439). But is this a moral or
an ontological task? Some of the moralists might think that they can
solve the definitional problem by raising questions about the quality
of life or about the possession of particular moral characteristics (for
example, rights), but such an approach is bound to fail. Qualitative
considerations do not determine what something is and when it
exists or ceases to exist. These objections to the moral approach are
discussed later in this chapter.

Hoffman's argument has strengths that solve some of the deficiencies of Veatch's argument, though Hoffman is incorrect in placing our central conceptual question in the realm of primary moral discourse. He addresses the issue by recommending a further formulation of the problem: "What is one's responsibility toward the hopelessly unconscious patient?" (442). He then backtracks and says that we must first decide if this patient is dead or alive. We have moved swiftly from a moral question to a question of the life status of an entity. To determine its status, we must first decide what kind of entity it is and then argue for a particular view of the conditions under which such entities may be said to be alive or dead. Hoffman treats the latter project—the delineation of the conditions of existence of the human being—as an issue for moral analysis. Brody, too, treats it as a moral issue yet concludes with a nonmoral assertion about the conditions of personal existence. Veatch argues from an ontological rather than a moral perspective. Hoffman never answers the evaluative question except by implication, and his analysis of human life and death is ontological. He sets out to settle what he sees as the fundamental dispute in the whole debate: "Dispute occurs only in deciding when the quality of whole-life ceases to deserve recognition as human life" (443).

Hoffman pauses to defend Veatch against Schwager's complaint that "the loss of what gives life its value is not identical with the loss of life."[9] He replies that Veatch is trying to define the *esse*, not the *bene esse*, of life. This is a correct assessment of Veatch, but we must ask whether considerations of *esse* or *bene esse* respond to the problem Hoffman has set out, that of "deciding when the quality of whole-life ceases to deserve recognition as human life." Only talk about the *bene esse* of life would seem relevant, yet this is not what Veatch provides. Nor is it what Hoffman provides, as it turns out.

Hoffman indicates that our most fundamental choice—a qualitative one, as he sees it—is between the concept of the human as organism and that of the human as person. He calls them concepts of human whole life because they are taken to embrace the full human reality; all decisions concerning the human depend on this choice, in particular the decision of what constitutes life and death. Hoffman characterizes this disparity between some of the participants in the redefinition dispute as qualitative:

A more significant qualitative difference separates Ramsey and Veatch. Here there is a distinction between those views of whole-life which conceive of the human being as an organism and those which picture the human being as a person. Ramsey, Schwager and Jonas all recognize human life as that which is sufficient to maintain integrated bodily activity even in the absence of the higher mental functions we normally associate with personal existence, e.g., consciousness and social interaction. In contrast, for Veatch and Schiffer, the presence or absence of personal life is the determinative issue in the definition of death. An individual with only organismic whole-life, though possessing life in a human body, is not a living person. The person is dead (443–44).

Is this a qualitative difference? I argue in chapter 6 that the choice of perspective requires a moral rationale. Nevertheless, an ontological problem remains: if we decide to look at the human as person in order to determine the conditions of human death, we must first determine the conditions of existence of persons. Each of the moralists we have examined also has an ontological view, a nonmoral view on the conditions of existence of persons, and Hoffman appears to have moved into the ontologists' territory as well. Is such an excursus into ontology necessary, or can an analysis of the concept of person be provided by moral analysis alone? I address these questions at the end of chapter 5.

Hoffman's "fundamental conception of humanness" is the embodied capacity for consciousness. Persons are a conjunction of mind and body, or "embodied spirit" (444). To stress the necessity of embodiment is to preserve a necessary reference to the body as an aspect, but not as the whole, of the human reality. Hoffman argues "for a holistic image of human life as mind and body, as person and not simply as organism" (446). His argument rests on the fact that "the human mind or spirit we experience in this life is inevitably incarnate" (444). Hence, our experience of a full human existence is one of being alive in mind as well as body. It is the conjunction of a working mind and body that is the living human being. Since brain death and neocortical death destroy one aspect of that conjunction, the conjunction itself is destroyed, and with it the conditions necessary for the existence of the full human reality. Hoffman criticizes the organismic view of Jonas, Ramsey, and Schwager because it ignores a crucial aspect of the human reality: we are not simply body, but embodied mind. This view reduces the human to mere organismic status, while Hoffman's view protects the fundamental union which is the basis for human existence. Hoffman writes:

> The crucial decision concerns the presence or absence of psychic life. To define death as the absence of the capacity for embodied consciousness is simply to see death as the end of full personal existence. Moreover, I would contend that the organismic definitions of whole-life found in Ramsey and Jonas are more properly categorized as dualistic in their neglect of the necessity for mental life, for the spirit, in constituting human existence. The life which is the reference for our definition of death must be the life of the full personal reality, having the two dimensions, psychic and physical (444–45).

Siding with Veatch, and articulating concepts of human life and death that support the brain-death and the neocortical-death criteria, Hoffman equates the loss of the capacity for embodied consciousness with "the end of full personal existence." Support for this equation is implied in an earlier statement: we experience persons as embodied minds ("the human mind or spirit we experience in this life is inevitably incarnate" [444]). The disintegration of that mind-body unity thus marks the end of the human being, even if the body continues to function on its own or by some artifice. Hoffman suggests, as further support for his view, that to consider the human being alive when it is capable of organismic but not higher brain functioning is to hold an unwarranted dualism with respect to the human, because the human is considered alive as long as his mind *or* his body works. Hoffman believes that the human lives as long as his body supports consciousness, the minimal capacity required for the retention of a functioning mind. Ultimately, Hoffman's primary and perhaps only support for his emphasis on "the life of the full personal reality" is his appeal to the way we experience human beings. This justification is not free of difficulties, however. The way we experience the human is a contingent matter. If brain transplants or brain support mechanisms are ever within our capabilities, we shall have to make even finer distinctions in characterizing human life and death, unless we anticipate the need for such distinctions now. If it is hypothetically possible to continue brain life apart from the human frame—or indeed even in a different human body— then we have a case of death, according to Hoffman's view that the human is the conjunction of a particular working body and a particular working mind. We need to think more fully about the relevance of our way of experiencing the human being to a decision about what constitutes human life and death; these matters are given fuller treatment in chapter 5.

Hoffman's argument successfully emphasizes that the full human reality is reflected only through reference to mind, or the higher brain capacities of humans. If our definition of death is to reflect what we are, it must recognize the relevance of conscious functioning in assessing life status. Is this an ontological insight? Hoffman says that persons do not exist when the capacity for consciousness is lost, not that their life is no longer worth living. Since Hoffman defends Veatch against Schwager by saying that Veatch defines the *esse* and not the *bene esse* of human life, Schwager must appreciate the differences between the moral and the ontological questions, as well as the gap between moral and ontological reasoning. Since Hoffman's analysis is an ontological one, I question it more fully in constructing a personal identity theory in the next chapter, against the background of Green and Wikler's ontological defense of the brain-death criterion.

Assessments of the Moral Approach

The assumption that moral arguments can provide a full defense of a criterion for declaring death rests on the conviction that the death of a human being is a moral and social event. On this basis, moralists conclude that a determination of what constitutes human death cannot be supported by appeal to biological considerations; since we choose a moment of death for essentially moral and social reasons, to declare someone dead is to initiate a process of restructuring his rights and our obligations to him. Obviously, such restructuring has significant social impact. This shows, according to the moralists, that we can properly formulate a concept of human death only by asking when such a restructuring ought to occur. The biological deterioration that signals death is chosen on the basis of this prior moral decision. Biological events do not read themselves; we select those that signal death by choosing a particular quantum change in moral status as the death of the human being.

In chapter 3, I argued that nonbiological considerations must be part of our basis for selecting the biological circumstance we think warrants a declaration of death. But does moral analysis per se provide the nonbiological considerations necessary to justify the use of the brain-death and the neocortical-death criteria? Earlier in this chapter, I suggested that our reasons for redefining death may be moral ones—since we want to treat the human being as he ought to be treated, we must determine what his life status is—but that the argument needed to defend a decision of status may not be a moral one at all, or at least not exclusively so.

Before they turned to the task of defending the brain-death criterion on the basis of their theory of personal identity, Michael Green and Daniel Wikler critically analyzed the moral approach to redefining death, showing its inadequacy for the task at hand. The problem, write Green and Wikler, is this: "The question to be answered . . . is whether the moral proposition that maintenance of the brain dead preserves nothing of value and may be ceased when convenient shows that the brain dead are dead."[10] The puzzle, which has been crucial throughout this chapter, concerns the move from a statement of the valuelessness of life to a statement of its status. How is the quality of a life relevant to a determination of a subject's life status? Green and Wikler point out that the worthlessness involved in brain death (to the patient and to others) is the usual reason for regarding brain death as death. Quoting Jonathan Glover, who states that "the only way of choosing (between competing definitions of death) is to decide whether or not we attach any value to the preservation of someone irreversibly comatose,"[11] Green and Wikler claim that such value judgments are not an argument for considering brain-dead patients dead, but only for discontinuing their support. Attacking the evaluative approach to defining death, they argue: "This account of the task of defining death . . . has unacceptable, even absurd, consequences. If our society came to value sports so much that the cripple's sedentary existence was thought to have no value, we would hardly find it congenial to reclassify the lame as dead" (116). This implies that a social consensus on the valuelessness of the supported lives of the brain-dead is no argument for classifying them as dead. The analogy between the brain-dead and the disabled fails, but its very failure supports its conclusion.

While the brain-dead are no longer experiencing entities, the disabled are. Since life is not experienced by the brain-dead, it has neither value nor disvalue for them. It is incorrect to assert, as many moralists do, that the lives of the brain-dead have slipped below a certain threshold of quality. "How much quality of life remains for the brain-dead patient?" is a meaningless question; there is *no* quality to be measured for him. By contrast, we can meaningfully speak of the quality of life for someone who is disabled. The handicapped are in a position to judge the value of life for themselves, and for this reason we are uncomfortable with imposing the disvalue that society attaches to disability upon the handicapped by reclassifying them. To impose socially agreed-upon conceptions of value on persons is to risk violating their most fundamental moral right, since a human being capable of self-determination has an assumed right to be self-determining. One cannot make a similar case for the brain-dead. We are not deciding something for them that they should decide for themselves. Someone trying to defend the quality-of-life strategy in the brain-death case might argue that here society must speak, since the brain-dead cannot. This counterargument shows that there is good reason to resist qualitative reasoning in regard to the disabled, but not in regard to the brain-dead. Hence, Green and Wikler cannot expect their analogy to succeed. Their conclusion can be supported, though, by reiterating the difference between the disabled and the brain-dead. It is meaningless to talk about the quality of life of the brain-dead, but not of the disabled. The brain-dead are off the qualitative scale, not merely at its low end. Hence the value of their life for them cannot be appealed to in deciding their life status. The fact that there is no sensible quality-of-life argument in relation to the brain-dead is a reflection of their "existence" as nonexperiencing entities. That is, because they have no capacity for experience, we cannot meaningfully ask about the quality of life for them. Their incapacity to experience, based on their permanent loss of consciousness, is crucial. We are talking not about quality, but about consciousness; we are asking what conditions must be present for a person to exist. If we are concerned with the full human reality, consciousness would seem to be the sine qua non of human life. Qualitative reasoning is inapplicable to the situation of a nonexperiencing entity.

One final though simpleminded reductio ad absurdum of the quality-of-life approach is available. The moralists are ultimately trying to defend a criterion by arguing that life is valueless for the patient himself—a patient-centered value judgment. If we allow the disabled and the depressed to speak for themselves, they may decide that life has no value for them. But we cannot connect that decision to a change in the way they are classified. A suicidal person does not differ in status from others because he thinks that life lacks sufficient quality to go on. Considerations of quality of life for someone have no bearing on his status, particularly his life status. Green and Wikler emphasize this point by calling our attention to cases in which life has no value yet brain death has not occurred—cases in which few of us would want to go on living yet would not on that account classify ourselves as dead. Any such effort to reclassify persons based on quality of life would lead to "ontological gerrymandering" (116).

Green and Wikler conclude that "the account of defining death which is assumed by the moral arguments is a faulty one" (116). Since several of the moralists accept the brain-death criterion but reject the neocortical-death criterion, and since the nonexperiencing status of the patient is the apparent basis of their claim that the quality of life of the brain-dead is a sufficient indication that they are dead, the moral argument supports equally the brain-death criterion and the neocortical-death criterion. But the moralists using the qualitative approach want to claim that there is a significant difference in moral status between the brain-dead and the neocortically dead. That difference cannot be defended—indeed it is disproved—by the quality-of-life approach.

What can we conclude about the helpfulness of moral arguments in our pursuit of an adequate argument for criteria for declaring death? The situation is complicated, for many share Green and Wikler's view:

> The notion that the brain-dead patient has "ceased to exist as a person" . . . has both a moral and an ontological interpretation. The moral claim is simply that the patient's life now lacks the features that make life more valuable for people than death. Our ontological claim is that the person who entered the hospital, he whose body is now brain dead, no longer exists (though his body or some of its parts may both exist and life) (119n).

If the crucial statement that "the brain-dead patient has 'ceased to exist as a person'" has both a moral and an ontological interpretation, does this mean that either a moral or an ontological argument will achieve a defense of the brain-death, and possibly of the neocortical-death, criterion? Green and Wikler suggest that the argument a moralist might construct in support of this statement (they take Veatch's "intuitive kind-essentialism" [120] as an example) has weaknesses that their individual essentialism does not. While they appeal to intuitions, just as Veatch does, their appeal is "to *conceptual* intuitions, not moral ones, on which there is considerable consensus, and which are used to test a concept (personal identity) which is considerably better defined than Veatch's 'human existence'" (119–20). Their individual essentialism (inquiring into essential features of the individual's existence) is "better methodology if not better metaphysics" (120), they claim. They are not saying that one cannot construct a successful argument for a death criterion on the basis of moral considerations, but their earlier argument from analogy seems to suggest that any moral argument based on quality-of-life assessments is unacceptable. I have shown that all the major moralists eventually construct a personal identity theory or make an unsupported nonmoral assertion about the conditions of existence of persons. Even if an ethical analysis of personhood is possible, no one has yet provided it. The ontological argument then seems to be the primary one; after all, we must know what something is before we can determine how it ought to be treated or regarded. Quality-of-life reasoning leads to inadmissible "ontological gerrymandering," whether reclassifications are based on society's assessment of quality or on hypothetical patient-centered assessments. At best, moral arguments demonstrate only that our obligation to support an individual ceases in the event of brain death. We need a more powerful argument if we are to justify the claim that the brain-dead and the neocortically dead are dead.

What is the role of moral argumentation in redefining death? Veatch argues that redefinition is a moral necessity; moral argument must demonstrate the moral necessity of redefinition to unbelievers like Jonas and Becker, who do not consider the brain-dead patient dead but think instead that such a patient should be allowed to die. Moral argument must also demonstrate that necessity to moralists like Ramsey, Schwager, and Brody, who think that redefinition has gone as far as it ought to. Is there a patient-centered rationale, or just an other-centered rationale, behind our desire to rethink the management of those in chronic vegetative states? Moral argumentation can help us to defend our fundamental perspective on the human being—as organism or as person. However, if the perspective of human being as person is adopted and defended, the next step is a nonmoral analysis of personhood, or the articulation of a personal identity theory. Only by determining what a person is can we decide what quantum change constitutes the death of the person. Although moral analysis can make crucial contributions to the definitional debate, it will not take us the entire route.

chapter 5

Ontological Arguments

The last three chapters bear witness to what Michael B. Green and Daniel Wikler refer to as "the conceptual disarray in the brain death literature."[1] In "Brain Death and Personal Identity," they attempt to clarify the nature of the task of redefining death, and to provide an ontological justification for the claim that the death of a person's brain is that person's death.[2] The use of brain-centered criteria for determining that an individual has died presupposes our acceptance of this claim, which is reflected in the prevailing medical as well as lay opinion concerning human death, and has been further legitimated by its inclusion in the Uniform Declaration of Death Act, our central public policy document on the definition of death. (I evaluate this document in chapter 7.) In contrast to the biologists and the moralists, Green and Wikler define their claim as an ontological one, requiring an ontological defense. An ontological argument addresses itself to the nature of reality and its components. Since persons constitute a central category of existing things, an ontological argument expressing their conditions of existence is necessary, Green and Wikler contend, to ground the claim that brain death is the death of the person. They might seem to be articulating a kind-essentialism—that is, an explication of the essential features of the kind of entity we call a person—but this is not their strategy.

Instead, they construct an ontological argument about the essential features of the individual person, intentionally preempting the issue of the kind of entity the individual is.

From their ontological argument and the conclusion it establishes, Green and Wikler distinguish the reasoning behind the brain-death criterion from an argument to defend its adoption. The defense for the latter must be a moral one, they maintain. Justifying the claim that the brain-dead are dead must be distinguished from justifying the claim that we ought to declare death when brain death has occurred. Likewise, a justification of the claim that the neocortically dead are dead must be distinguished from a justification of the claim that we ought to adopt a public policy based on the neocortical-death criterion. Theoretical arguments do not public policy arguments make.

Green and Wikler provide a wide range of arguments in their article. First, they argue that biological and moral arguments are inadequate to justify the equation of brain death with the death of the person. Second, they argue that ontological considerations are necessary to defend that equation. In this connection, they defend a theory of personal identity from which they conclude that the death of a person's upper brain is that person's death. Sidestepping any discussion of the essence of personhood (a kind-essentialism which they associate with Veatch), Green and Wikler characterize their own theory as an individual essentialism, claiming that the essence of the individual rests on his continued possession of a particular psychological continuity or history. On the basis of this claim about the essence of the individual, they make the following claims: when personal identity is lost, a person has ceased to be; when the person has ceased to be, she has died; brain death (specifically upper-brain death) is the death of the substrate that supports functions essential to the retention of personal identity; and therefore the death of a person's upper brain is that person's death.

Finally, Green and Wikler construct a moral argument defending the brain-death criterion. If they are to vindicate completely that criterion, they must convince us of four points: (1) ontological considerations apply, while biological and moral ones do not;[3] (2) our ontological focus should be on human beings as persons, not as organisms;[4] (3) the continued possession of a particular psychological continuity is necessary for the preservation of personal identity; and (4) the cessation of personal identity (in the sense they intend) constitutes the death of the person.

While a personal identity theory is necessary to defend the claim that brain death (or, more specifically, upper-brain death) constitutes the death of the person, Green and Wikler fail to prove that the essence of an individual is her distinguishing psychological history. This requirement for the preservation of personal identity is too stringent; personal identity is retained as long as some measure of conscious functioning remains, even if psychological continuity has been forever destroyed. [5] Green and Wikler's conditions for personal identity do not exist after brain death, but neither do the narrower set of conditions I will propose. Green and Wikler have provided an argument that justifies the claim that brain death is the death of the person, but no explicit defense of the claim that human death ought to be construed as the death of a person. They thus beg the crucial question in the redefinition dispute.

Green and Wikler's Ontological Argument

Green and Wikler introduce their argument by stating that since each of us has a particular personal identity consisting in a particular set of psychological traits, the assertion, "Patient Jones is still alive" implies both that "the patient is alive" and that "the patient is (remains) Jones." In other words, the patient retains that set of psychological traits we have always associated with Jones. "If we do establish that the patient, even if alive, is not Jones, and if no one else is Jones, then we will have established that Jones does not exist. And this, of course, establishes that Jones is dead."[6]

The circumstance in which the patient is alive, yet Jones is dead, is an uncomfortable one. Green and Wikler apparently use *patient* to refer to the body of Jones (possibly still functioning), and *Jones* to refer to the particular psychological history that has always been associated with that body. Accepting the idea that Jones may be dead yet the patient still alive is to use *alive* and *dead* in two senses with respect to the same entity, a particular human being. Green and Wikler offer this dual approach to the human being because they believe that "Patient Jones is still alive" implies both that the patient is alive and that the patient remains Jones. Many of us lack their ontological sensitivity, however; we use *Jones* to refer to Jones's body as well as to the set of psychological characteristics we associate with him. For several writers, including Jonas and Becker, to say that the patient Jones is still alive need not mean that the patient remains Jones. Green and Wikler define "remaining Jones" as retaining Jones's set of psychological characteristics. It becomes clear in their discussion of the anencephalic infant that they wish to hold one criterion for the aliveness of the human body (namely, heartbeat and respiration) and another for the aliveness of the person (namely, the exhibiting of psychological continuity). On the basis of this distinction, they claim that *"Jones'* death . . . occurs *either* at the time the patient dies, if the patient has remained Jones; *or* at the time the patient ceased to be Jones, whichever comes first" (118). In other words, Jones dies either when Jones ceases to be the patient or when the patient (remaining Jones) dies. But in either case, of course, Jones's death is Jones's ceasing to be.

Green and Wikler's description of the alternate scenarios surrounding Jones's death obscures this, for they imply that Jones's death results either from the patient's death or from Jones's ceasing to be. It would be more straightforward to maintain that Jones's ceasing to be is Jones's death, whatever the causal sequence leading to that ceasing to be. Human death is the ceasing to be of the person (Jones); after that event, talking about the life status of the human body is inappropriate. Viewing the patient's death as a separate event from Jones's death embraces a dualism with respect to the human being. Such a dualistic emphasis promises not only to create confusion, but also to undermine the very view of human death that Green and Wikler favor. One can agree with them that Jones's death is Jones's ceasing to be, yet disagree about the terminology they adopt in relation to the patient. Apparently the case of the anencephalic infant inclines them toward this terminology, for they acknowledge that their personal identity theory also grounds the claim than upperbrain death is the death of the person. They consider the spontaneously breathing anencephalic infant to be alive, but the spontaneously breathing upper-brain-dead patient to be dead—an inconsistent position. If Green and Wikler wish to argue that Jones's ceasing to be is Jones's death, they must apply their argument consistently, construing human death either as the end of a personal existence or as an event in the life of an organism.

There is a more serious difficulty with their argument at this stage. Given the divided nature of the patient Jones in their view, and given their decision to construe Jones's death as Jones's ceasing to be, they begin with an argument about the death of a person, assuming without discussion that human death is to be construed as the death of a person and not of an organism. Since *Jones* refers to a particular personal existence, Green and Wikler's account helps us determine the conditions of existence and nonexistence of persons. But this proof is incomplete without a defense of the claim that the death of a human being is the death of a person. Where *person* refers to a particular psychological history and not to a functioning body, the claim that brain death is the death of the person begs a fundamental question. Green and Wikler seem to admit that they are skirting the issue:

> The approach we take here permits us to remain agnostic on the issue of kind-essentialism and on whether membership in a kind is essential to retention of identity. We offer instead an argument which establishes a claim about the essential properties of a given *individual*. The claim is that the continued possession of certain psychological properties by means of a certain causal process is an essential requirement for any given entity to be identical with the individual who is Jones. Thus, we can afford to remain uncommitted on whether persons are essentially beings with psychological properties and on whether Jones is essentially a person. We demonstrate instead that Jones, whatever kind of entity he is, is essentially an entity with psychological properties. Thus, when brain death strips the patient's body of all its psychological traits, Jones ceases to exist (120–21).

Instead of discussing which features are essentially significant to the nature of persons, Green and Wikler ask a question about Jones himself. Jones "is essentially an entity with psychological properties." His loss of these properties is his ceasing to be. But there is no way to avoid addressing the question concerning the subject of human death. People may disagree on what Jones essentially is.

David Lamb's most recent defense of a biological concept of death, discussed below, is a clear case in point.

Even more troubling is the ease with which we have talked of Jones as "essentially an entity with psychological properties." How can we make such a judgment about him without a discussion of what kind of entity he is? How can one articulate an individual essentialism without reference to essential features of the kind to which that individual belongs? Unless we know that a sufficient set of generic predicates applies to an entity, we cannot determine an essential individual predicate. Green and Wikler do not defend their claim about what Jones essentially is; they slip into this claim as a result of their *patient/Jones* distinction. If we assume that *Jones* refers to a particular psychological history, then it is only in those terms that we can express the conditions of Jones's death.

If we cannot defend a particular concept of human death—one that defines death as the loss of the conditions of existence of persons—then we have established neither the necessity nor the adequacy of a personal identity theory as an ontological defense of the claim that brain death is the death of the person. We must show that we ought to view the death of a human being as the death of a person. That claim defended, we can then determine the conditions under which Jones—a person—ceases to be. The defense of the claim must be a moral one, I believe; we must defend this focus on the human as person on the basis of the moral impacts it will have. I attempt to provide this defense in chapter 6.

There is a possible reply to the charge that Green and Wikler have failed to supply a crucial argument. If they consider the adoption of the brain-death criterion as an indication that we are construing human death as the death of a person rather than as the death of an organism, then the only argument they need provide is one that connects a person's ceasing to be with that person's brain death. A complete defense of any death criterion may require an argument for the concept of human death being presupposed, but Green and Wikler can respond that they are interested only in showing that *if* human death is the loss of personal status, then the brain-death criterion is consistent with an acceptable personal identity theory. In short, they may presuppose what I argue in chapter 2—that the brain-death criterion, unlike the traditional criteria, is consciousness-based. Given that assumption, which implies a focus on the person rather than on the organism, Green and Wikler might maintain that they show by their personal identity theory that the death of a person's brain is that person's death.

Green and Wikler describe the general nature of the argument they are initiating: "If, as we contend, the patient ceased to be Jones at the time of brain death, then Jones' brain death is Jones' death. Thus, if the loss of capacity for mental activity which occurs at brain death constitutes death, it is not for moral reasons, nor for biological reasons, but for *ontological* reasons" (118). This line of argument rests on a particular theory of personal identity. Green and Wikler thus suggest that ceasing to be Jones, in the sense of losing the distinctive psychological traits Jones possessed, is a sufficient condition for Jones's death. While brain death would clearly result in the loss of Jones's distinctive psychological history, ceasing-to-be Jones (in the sense that Green and Wikler intend) is not necessarily a sufficient condition for Jones's death.

For example, the patient could lose Jones's distinctive set of psychological traits as a result of circumstances other than brain death, circumstances in which we would clearly resist the conclusion that Jones is dead. The progressive neural deterioration characteristic of Alzheimer's Syndrome, which results in a severely senile patient with Jones's body but no sense of Jones's life as his life, would be a case in point. Although we might not be able in such a case to identify a moment when the patient ceases to be Jones (in the sense of having lost all Jones's psychological traits), it is certainly possible to say that Jones no longer possesses any of the psychological characteristics he possessed through most of his life and has no memory of his earlier life. We might then say that the patient has ceased to be Jones because Jones's psychological history has been erased, yet be unhappy with the conclusion that Jones is dead, because some mental life remains, supported by Jones's body. Jones's mental life, however impoverished or altered, is still Jones's mental life. Since the process of neural deterioration was gradual, we are unable to specify a time when Jones ceased to be and a second person appeared. If we could determine when the original person ceased to be and the new person came into being, we would have to change proper names to avoid confusion, assign a new social security number, and perhaps assign new rights and obligations to the new person: the new person would not be entitled to the use of the estate of the original person; the children of the original person would have no obvious obligations to the new person; and so on. Such results would be unacceptable. They suggest that there is something important about a continuous link between body and consciousness, however altered that consciousness may be. We must resist the idea that such neural deterioration, by destroying all psychological continuity, is a sufficient condition for the death of the person. Bodily continuity must have a role in personal identity in some circumstances, then, though possibly not in all circumstances.

The patient could also cease to be Jones in the relevant sense as a result of total amnesia, yet we would resist the conclusion that Jones is dead. A memory problem is not an identity problem. We are not tempted to declare an amnesia victim dead and issue a new birth certificate. At least for the time being, given our inability to transplant brains or to preserve them in vitro, personal identity attaches to the brain-body combination, however "undone" brain processes may have become. The loss of psychological history and characteristics is not a sufficient condition for saying that Jones is dead. As long as Jones's body continues to function and his brain supports some set of psychological traits, the person Jones must still be regarded as alive. This supports the more conservative notion of personal identity of Hoffman and Veatch: an individual person is an embodied consciousness. Where ceasing to be Jones results from loss of the capacity for any mental life, it is correct to regard Jones as dead; the person's ceasing to be is a function of the permanent loss of capacity for any mental life—a narrower concept of personal identity than Green and Wikler have proposed. Ceasing to be Jones is a necessary condition for the person's death but not a sufficient one, as they claim. The cases of Alzheimer's Syndrome and amnesia, as well as that of a patient who has undergone a severe personality-effacing stroke, force us to conclude that personal identity is retained as long as some capacity for mental life remains; that identity does not require the maintenance of a particular psychological history, as these counterexamples demonstrate.

Someone might concede that Green and Wikler's requirement for the retention of personal identity is too strong, yet maintain that I have not provided compelling reason for the claim that personal identity is retained as long as even minimal capacity for a mental life remains. I would reply that consciousness provides a capacity for experience; we would be on an exceedingly slippery slope were we to assume that, although we are unable to assess either the level or the meaningfulness of an individual's actual experience, we can nevertheless declare some experiencing humans dead and others not. Experiencing per se, however limited it may be, defines life Entities that are by their very nature unresponsive and unreceptiv —rocks, for example—are the only ones we should categorically not consider alive. There is strong intuitive support for the claim that life carries with it the capacity to receive and respond to stimuli, or to experience. It would be a category mistake to consider nonexperiencing entities as living ones. But we must provide moral reasons for equating the irreversible loss of the capacity for consciousness (and hence for experience) with human death.

Green and Wikler proceed to a statement of their theory of personal identity, supporting it with what they call "familiar cases." They show that their theory attributes a central role to the brain. On this basis, they articulate a corollary of their personal identity theory concerning brain death, from which it follows that personal identity does not survive the death of the upper brain. Hence, when brain death occurs, the person's death occurs. Their argument begins with the passage quoted earlier, in which they offer an individual-essentialism in contrast to Veatch's kind-essentialism. Their theory delineates the essential properties of the individual. They tell us that a given individual is essentially an entity with a particular psychological history. To establish this claim, they defend a version of mentalism, a personal identity theory.

Instead of defining persons, Green and Wikler discuss what is essential to Jones (who happens to be a person) such that its loss would be Jones's ceasing to be, and therefore Jones's death. Though they apparently want to establish that the death of a person's brain is that person's death, they do not seem to recognize that such a claim is about a kind of entity as well as about individuals. This is really their full claim: Jones is essentially an entity with a particular psychological history; the loss of that history is Jones's ceasing to be; Jones's ceasing to be is Jones's death; any entity that is essentially one with a particular psychological history is a person; the loss of a particular personal history is the ceasing to be of that person; her ceasing to be is her death; brain death results in her ceasing to be; therefore, the death of a person's brain is that person's death. An individual-essentialism is the inversion of a kind-essentialism, and vice versa. Green and Wikler may be right in maintaining that their individual-essentialism is better methodology because it is easier for us to recognize and defend our conceptual intuitions with this approach than with kind-essentialism. But kind-essentialism and individual-essentialism are opposite sides of the same coin, and neither can be "better metaphysics" than the other. Further, Green and Wikler's conclusion that brain death is the death of the person requires the argument above, connecting considerations about the essence of an individual to those about the essence of a kind.

> It would be hard to argue for or against [Veatch's kind-essentialism] except by citing one's own intuitions on "man's nature," if any. . . . Though our argument, like Veatch's, appeals in the end to intuitions, it appeals to conceptual intuitions, not moral ones, on which there is considerable consensus, and which are used to test a concept (personal identity) which is considerably better defined than Veatch's "human existence." Our individual-essentialism is relative to Veatch's (and others') kind-essentialism, better methodology if not better metaphysics (119–20*n*).

For Green and Wikler, personal identity consists in "the continued possession of certain psychological properties by means of a certain causal process" (121). They argue for a particular mentalist theory by attempting to correct a deficiency they find in most mentalist arguments. To support the notion that personal identity is a function of the "continuity and connectedness of personality, memory, and other mental phenomena" (121), the mentalist typically appeals to the conceivability of person-body transfers, by which one person may come to inhabit another's body. Green and Wikler agree with the body-continuity theorist that the mentalist must establish more than that we can imagine such body-switching: she must demonstrate how a person could be "serially identical with distinct bodies" (122). Green and Wikler are convinced that a body-switch narrative can be provided to rule out any counterexplanations a body-continuity theorist might produce. One plausible explanation by the mentalist might be this, say Green and Wikler: since all mental events are physical events based in the brain, brain transplantation would bring about the result the mentalist requires to give credence to her personal identity theory. Green and Wikler introduce the term *person-stages* into their discussion: "A person-stage is a person in a given time interval. A person *simpliciter* is a series of person-stages. The problem of personal identity, thus conceived, is to state the criteria determining which person-stages are stages of the same entity" (121).

Transplantation must retain the existing connections among person-stages: "Two 'person-stages' are stages of the same person, just in case the latter is a continuation of the earlier personality and can remember what the earlier one has done" (121). Green and Wikler then explain that the mentalist can provide support for her claim of the conceivability of body-switching along the same lines that we account for the continuity of a person's mental life under ordinary circumstances. They contend that we have an "explanation of the continuity of a person's psychological properties" that accounts for the continuity in ordinary life histories: "Personal identity presupposes a characteristic causal tie between person-stages (what the cause is, exactly, depends on what, empirically, causes psychological continuity). Indeed, this causal tie *is* the criterion of personal identity" (124). Retention of personal identity, then, is the result of the maintenance of "a characteristic causal tie between person-stages." If a person is a particular set of psychological events (person-stages) that are causally connected in a characteristic way, then persons could switch bodies if we had a way of maintaining the causal connections among the psychological events in question. Green and Wikler suggest that since these causes are neural and are located in the brain, a brain transplant would achieve this result. Brain transfer would be person transfer. As long as the brain and its processes remained intact during transplantation, it would retain its characteristic identity; and as long as it retained its characteristic identity, personal identity would be preserved. The retention of personal identity appears to be solely a function of the maintenance of existing causal ties among person-stages. That maintenance requires the preservation of a particular neural organization in the brain. Green and Wikler are convinced that a person could switch bodies by a transfer of her brain to a new body. Personal identity is congruent with brain identity; to preserve the brain in its particular organization is to preserve the person.

But Green and Wikler engage in this elaborate discussion of body-switches to vindicate their assertion that an individual is essentially an entity with a particular psychological history. If we were to agree that Jones's psychological history would survive the move from his former body to a new body, and that Jones would then be alive in a new embodiment, we would be reidentifying Jones on the basis of the whereabouts of his psychological history. Green and Wikler want us to conclude that, since we would reidentify Jones as Jones on just this basis, his individual essentialism consists in his unique psychological history.

But suppose that Jones has an elaborately tattooed left arm, so cluttered with detailed tattoos that no other individual could have an arm precisely like it. Suppose also that Jones has been in an accident that has disfigured his face beyond recognition and has rendered him unconscious. In such a situation, those who knew Jones before the accident would undoubtedly determine his identity by his tattooed arm; they would use Jones's unusual arm as the basis upon which they reidentified him as Jones. But his unique arm obviously does not constitute his individual essence. Hence, our means of reidentifying Jones bears no necessary connection with what the individual Jones essentially is.[7]

There is a further difficulty with Green and Wikler's body-switch scenario. They maintain the conceivability of a body-switch by means of their discussion of brain transfer. If the brain is preserved intact and moved to a new body, the person is preserved and newly embodied. Changing bodies, it is implied, is as inconsequential as changing clothes. But this is to assume that brain-body interactions play no role in the formation and maintenance of personal identity. Can we grant this assumption? If we were to transfer a woman's brain into a man's body, or vice versa, would we have achieved a body-switch? Would we, by a brain transfer alone, achieve a person transfer? The memory criterion would be met, but it seems unlikely that we would achieve person transfer, unless the recipient body were physically and chemically identical with the donor body in all relevant respects. Unless brain transfer also involves the transfer of the endocrine glands, the pituitary and the hypothalamus, we cannot expect person transfer to be achieved simply by moving the brain intact. By contrast, disconnecting a head from the body and maintaining it in some way does involve the transfer of these glands. If brain-body interactions have a bearing on the person each of us is and remains, then we must say that brain 1 inhabiting body 1 is a different person from brain 1 inhabiting body 2. Green and Wikler have failed to dismiss the body-continuity theorist's objection to this line of the mentalist defense.

Nonetheless, they argue that the congruence of personal identity with brain identity "proves to be a happy result in consideration of several of the familiar cases" (124–25). They attempt further to support the transplantation argument by trying to arouse intuitions similar to their own by appeal to "thought experiments." These experiments are not only poor support for Green and Wikler's conclusion, but they raise important questions about the propriety of a mode of argumentation used in many personal identity discussions.

THE DECAPITATION THOUGHT EXPERIMENT

The first "familiar case" Green and Wikler present is that of a "decapitated person whose head and body are each sustained by high technology medicine. . . . If the head can communicate with us, and shows psychological connectedness and continuity with the erstwhile person, there can be little doubt that it *is* that person and the body is not" (125). Their point is expressed hypothetically; if this situation could come about, we would have to agree that the head is (in some sense) the person and the body is not. But maintenance of personal identity in Green and Wikler's sense would seem to require preservation of a complex physical-chemical arrangement. Perhaps this could be achieved without a body, but it would have to be achieved somehow if personal identity were to be maintained.

It is tempting to agree that the person resides in the head, but that is because we would never expect the body to display the requisite continuity without a head. The brain is the body's control center. If we put it in a new body, we are simply providing it with a new "shell" to direct. We want to agree with Green and Wikler, I think, because we would expect the control center, suitably maintained, to be the person, if either the detached head or the headless body could be alone. But we have been forced to choose. It may be that this thought experiment, like many others of the same ilk, appears to succeed because it poses a faulty dilemma. Green and Wikler imply that the person is either where her body is or where her head is. If we must choose, of course we decide that the person is where the head is. But there may be good reason to refuse to make a choice. We would never refer to an entity as a person if we did not experience it as embodied. We identify and reidentify persons by their bodily, not their psychological, characteristics. While we can conceive of the situations Green and Wikler set out, the manner in which we experience persons is not relevant in defining personal identity. To assume that it is would be to confuse an epistemic issue with an ontological one. Our only experience of any individual person is in a particular, unchanging embodiment, but this fact does not support the conclusion that personal identity is a function of a particular kind of embodiment. If Green and Wikler are right in maintaining that the person would survive in a new body following a brain transfer, then the specific body by which we experience someone is irrelevant. Recalling Veatch's computer-tape example, if we are hard pressed to deny that a person continues to exist when the information in her brain has been transferred to a computer tape and she continues to interact with the world through an elaborate input-output arrangement, then the way we now experience and identify persons is clearly irrelevant. We now manage identification and reidentification by relying on a person's bodily appearance. In the future, we may manage these processes differently, depending on the way we then experience persons. The conditions constituting personal identity cannot be made a function of the way in which we now experience persons, as inhabitants of particular human bodies. To this extent, I agree with the mentalist argument of Green and Wikler. However, the continuation of personal identity seems inconceivable apart from some kind of embodiment, be it in another human body, in a chimpanzee's body, or on a computer tape. The central objection to Green and Wikler's use of the decapitation case is that it poses a faulty dilemma, begging the question about the role of embodiment in the retention of personal identity.

THE BRAIN SUBSTRATE/BRAIN PROCESS THOUGHT EXPERIMENT

Green and Wikler argue that personal identity resides in the brain and imply that a brain does not need to be embodied in order to retain personal identity. To avoid a possible confusion about their conclusion that the person is "in" the head (brain), they present a second thought experiment, intended to show that mere brain identity (identity of the substrate) is insufficient for personal identity. What if, in the course of transplantation, the brain is so damaged that it loses its history, its unique series of person-stages? Green and Wikler reply that personal identity is not preserved under such circumstances:

> We feel no urge to regard the individual resulting from placing the unwired brain in a "new" body as the person previously associated with the brain. Brain identity alone is insufficient for personal identity. . . . The ordinary processes which link events in a personal history involve more than spatio-temporal continuity of brain tissue. They also require continuity of certain brain *processes*, carried out . . . in the brain tissue. Two body-stages which fail to be linked by continuity of these processes will fail to be stages of the same person, even if identity of the brain is preserved (125–26).

Green and Wikler wish to establish that the person is not identical with the substrate (the brain material), but with the psychological processes and history supported by the substrate, by a substrate with a particular organization. The undoing of the causal connections among brain events (the "unwiring" of the brain) constitutes the destruction of personal identity, and thus the death of the person.

Like the previous thought experiment, this one does not bear the required weight. The case Green and Wikler describe here is not much different from the victim of a personality-effacing stroke. Green and Wikler speak of the brain becoming "unwired," or losing the personal history formerly associated with it. They attempt to show that such unwiring is the death of the person, even if the brain substrate persists. But their argument requires more than a claim about the conditions under which a personal history is lost; it requires also a claim about destruction of the substrate to the point at which the capacity for any conscious process is permanently lost. The unwiring of the brain must be so complete that the substrate itself is destroyed to such a degree that it can no longer support consciousness. The examples of the amnesiac and the person with Alzheimer's Syndrome show that the loss of a personal history is not a sufficient condition for death, though such loss because of destruction of the substrate (not just its unwiring) is sufficient. Green and Wikler claim that the identity of the substrate is not sufficient for the preservation of personal identity; only the continuation of the brain processes constituting a particular history will allow for the maintenance of personal identity. I would offer this amendment: as long as the substrate supports conscious functioning, it is sufficient for the continuation of personal identity.

At first sight, Green and Wikler appear to have drawn a sensible distinction; it seems reasonable to distinguish between the brain substrate itself and the processes it supports by means of its particular mode of organization. However, this distinction overlooks the intimate connection between the substrate, with its particular mode of organization, and the processes it supports. If the brain's processes were significantly altered, or if the capacity for carrying out such processes were destroyed, the substrate would most likely have undergone significant change as well. The substrate with a particular organization is the basis for certain states and capacities. Were the capacity for a mental life to be erased, the substrate would show marked destruction as well. The distinction Green and Wikler draw between the substrate and its processes is not pertinent in the context of brain death, because alteration of brain processes coincides with alteration in the substrate.

Green and Wikler's terminology has shifted from *person-stages* to *body-stages of the same person.* This seems to be at odds with their earlier conclusion that a brain on its own, that can communicate and demonstrate the continuation of the personal identity hitherto associated with a particular brain-body combination, is the person. Green and Wikler say that we could isolate certain body-stages—for example, body-stage 22 (when the body has no gray hairs) and body-stage 83 (when the body has all gray hairs)—and as long as there is a continuity of brain processes, these body-stages are stages of the same person. The retention of the same brain substrate per se would not be sufficient for this result. The case of Alzheimer's Syndrome is again pertinent, for it shows that destruction of brain-process continuity does not lead us to regard the patient as a different person. The continuation of the substrate, "unwired" yet still linked in appropriate ways to its body, is the basis for concluding that the person still exists. If there were total destruction of the portion of the substrate supporting conscious life, our conclusion would be different.

Whatever the second thought experiment demonstrates, it does not overcome the objection that Green and Wikler fail to give sufficient consideration to brain-body interaction as an aspect of personal identity. In this thought experiment (in which the brain becomes "unwired" during transplantation), the brain-body connection is forever terminated as well. Hence, the difficulties in their analysis of the decapitation case are also present in their discussion of the unwiring example.

BRAIN REMOVAL AND BRAIN DEATH

Green and Wikler claim to demonstrate that brain transplantation involving no alteration or destruction of brain processes would preserve personal identity. I have argued that personal identity is preserved even if the brain becomes severely "unwired," as long as a capacity for some mental life remains. Even if a personal history has been erased, this condition would not be sufficient—unless the substrate could support no mental life at all—to say that the person was dead or that personal identity no longer existed. The point that Green and Wikler require concerns brain destruction: if, in the course of transplantation, the brain is destroyed, and thus can no longer support a personal history at all, then personal identity is erased. In such a case, the person is dead, even if the body continues to function. Such a situation, Green and Wikler say, is like that in which the brain dies in place: the person is dead (personal identity is destroyed) even though the body may still be functioning. Since the brain-body connection has been destroyed, the body has lost the identity once associated with it. Brain death and brain removal have the same consequences for a body: personal identity quits the body in either case. "It is not necessary that the brain actually be removed for personal identity to quit the body. The reason that brain removal cancels personal identity in the donor body, after all, is that the resulting body cannot thereafter have the kind of causal relation to earlier person-body stages which is required for personal identity to hold. Brain death has the same result" (126–27).

Green and Wikler are *not* saying that personal identity requires a particular relation between a body and person-body stages. They are saying only that personal identity leaves a given body either in brain death or in brain removal, not that the body is a necessary condition for the preservation of personal identity. It is a necessary condition only for the preservation of personal identity in that body.

> Brain death and brain removal have much the same result; the dead brain serves only to add bulk to the body if left intact. If, as has been established above, removal of the conscious, functioning brain leaves us with a body not identical to the person formerly associated with it, surely removal of a dead brain leaves just the same thing; and no more remains when the brain dies in place (127).

Green and Wikler conclude that personal identity would survive brain removal, either in the brain (suitably maintained) or in a supporting recipient body. Should the brain die, no matter where, the person dies as well. The preservation of the substrate and its processes is the continuation of the person. The body retains its status as an elaborate biological system, yet it is no more the person than would be a collection of that person's cells in a petri dish.

I have argued that Green and Wikler's criterion for personal identity is unacceptably stringent and must be replaced by a conservative mentalism that ties personal identity to the bare continuation of consciousness. This criterion is compatible with Green and Wikler's claim that personal identity is preserved as long as personal history is preserved. To argue that a person might survive the transfer of her psychological history to a computer tape (Robert Veatch's thought experiment) would strengthen the claim that personal identity is preserved as long as personal history is preserved, and would put to rest any objections that body continuity theorists might raise.

Let us interject ourselves into this situation and consider whether we would choose, if we or someone we love were about to die, to have that person's psychological history transferred to a computer tape with an input-output mechanism that would allow ongoing interaction between the tape and the rest of the world. In order to make the thought experiment fruitful, we must assume that one's psychological history can be put on tape without loss, and that the input-output mechanism will have correlates for all five sense modalities and a means of verbal communication. Assume the transfer has been made, and imagine that in addition to the correlates of all five sense modalities, the tape has a wealth of information acquired throughout a long and rich life. It can tell us that a freshly baked loaf of bread smells and tastes good, and it can react with sorrow to bad news, though not with tears.

While our elaborate input arrangement enables the tape to enjoy a wide range of stimuli, it has no basis upon which to act in the world, except through the instructions it gives to others. It has lost the capacity to be self-determining to the extent that embodied humans are. This lack of self-determination does not, however, indicate a loss of personal identity; we can imagine someone suffering a similar, or even greater, range of deficiencies following total paralysis. Even if we are unable to create a mechanism allowing one-to-one correlates with all the input-output capacities of the normal person, and are thus unable to duplicate for the tape all the kinds of experiences and capacities we have, we cannot therefore conclude that the tape has failed to retain personal identity in the transfer. Its lack of autonomy, though of real concern, is not sufficient reason to conclude that the tape is not the same person.

But suppose the tape's lack of autonomy detracts from its quality of life to such an extent that the tape expresses a desire for termination. It may discover that it is at the mercy of pro-lifers who consider it murder (even though the tape does not) to erase the tape. It becomes an issue of the tape's rights against theirs, and the only people left to defend the tape's claim to be terminated are the ones who think it is the sort of entity that can have no rights in the first place. Hence, they may lack sufficient interest to do their part. While the tape's lack of control over its destiny would not necessarily compromise its status as a person, the lack of self-determination may be a good reason to forgo the opportunity for the tape's sort of embodiment.

If we were to see the tape exhibiting the same knowledge, aptitudes, concerns, likes, and dislikes that the person always exhibited in embodied life, and if we were to see it assimilating and applying new information, we would find it difficult in principle to deny that the tape is the person we knew in a normal embodiment. Veatch concludes that the tape lacks some of the essential characteristics of humanhood. What it lacks is human embodiment. It is therefore unable to be active in the world in its former ways. Is the tape the person continuing under drastically changed or reduced circumstances? Is it just a residual presence of the person, sufficient only to salve our grief? If I give information to the tape that the person could never have known during her normal embodiment, does that person now know something new because the tape knows it?

What if we were to conclude that, whether or not the tape is the person, we have sound reasons to avoid such a transfer? Does this mean that if the tape is a person, it lacks some essentially significant property, a property that does not compromise its status but nevertheless detracts from its quality of life so much that no one could rationally elect such life for herself or for a loved one? Is the tape's life no different, in principle, from that of a quadriplegic? Enshrined on computer tape, it is different. We have total control over whether the tape can communicate with anyone. A flip of the switch and the tape is not a factor in our lives for the moment. Its existence therefore lacks the potential to make continuous claims upon us that the quadriplegic's life has. There is nothing about the tape that is not under our control.

But if we think the tape is a continuing person, we would be no more apt to turn it off at our convenience than we would be to neglect the needs and interests of the quadriplegic. That is, we would consider ourselves under a moral obligation both to respect the tape's right to express its wishes and to make certain that all reasonable wishes were fulfilled. The peculiar nature of the tape's embodiment would not release us from the obligations we normally have to persons in diminished circumstances. This leads us to consider the unsettling social consequences of creating a class of computer persons alongside embodied persons. The world population would be quite different from what it now is. Many of us might elect to make such a transfer when our mental capacities have reached their peak, thus drastically affecting social relationships and institutions. A new industry would have to be developed alongside the health care delivery system, since the limitations on the computer persons' communicative abilities would place an intolerable burden on others, one that could be adequately shouldered only by the creation of a custodial care system for computer persons. Further, barring accidental or intentional destruction, the essential immortality of computer persons would necessitate custodial care in perpetuity. Society would be ill served by such a commitment of its resources, unless of course age and wisdom are positively correlated.[8]

If we cannot conclude that the tape is not a person (indeed a particular person we knew under a different embodiment), and if we are convinced that we must avoid morally disastrous errors by assuming that the tape is a person, then the personal and social consequences of creating computer persons make it an undesirable experiment, even though it provides a way of avoiding the worst aspects of the loss of a loved one. It is difficult in principle to deny that the tape is the same person. Any claim that the tape is not embodied in a human body begs the question. This suggests, contrary to the writings of Veatch, that personal identity is preserved as long as a personal history is preserved, and that embodiment in a human frame is not a necessary condition for the retention of personal identity.

This example does not rule out the claim that some form of embodiment is involved in our ability to reidentify a person as the same person, however. Embodiment of some sort seems necessary for reidentification, but the particular kind of embodiment is not essential to the nature of persons or of an individual person.

Perhaps this conclusion, coupled with the conclusion that an individual person survives as long as bare consciousness (and not a particular personal history) persists, shows that we cannot place too much stock in thought experiments. We seem to have concluded that a particular personal identity is retained as long as a particular personal history is maintained (in whatever embodiment); but also that a particular personal identity is retained as long as bare consciousness persists. What if we decide to embody someone's brain in a new human body, but bungle things so badly that only bare consciousness remains? No one will be able to reidentify the person as the same person. But this scenario does not suggest that something has gone wrong with the personal identity theory I have been sketching throughout this chapter. Our ability to reidentify someone as the same person has no necessary connection with her essence, whatever it is that makes her the same person over time. Personal identity is retained as long as consciousness is retained, whether or not anyone can determine who is there. This might seem to be a counterintuitive claim about personal identity, but it is the least counterintuitive of the options available to us.

Following their argument that brain removal and brain death have the same impact for the preservation of personal identity in a particular body, Green and Wikler tie their ontological argument to brain death. Their argument, which I have cast into premise form to facilitate discussion, is as follows:

[1] A given person ceases to exist with the destruction of what processes there are which normally underlie that person's psychological continuity and connectedness.

[2] We know that [the processes which normally underlie a person's psychological continuity] are essentially neurological.

[3] Irreversible cessation of upper-brain functioning constitutes the death of that person.

[4] Whole-brain death is partly comprised of upper-brain death.

[5] Whole-brain death is also death for persons.

[6] Tests for either [upper-brain death or whole-brain death] will be tests for death (127).

Here Green and Wikler demonstrate the implications of their personal identity theory for cases of brain death. If the theory they have been presenting and defending stands up to critical scrutiny, premise 1 is established. I have provided several arguments that undermine this premise. But to say that the processes supporting psychological continuity are essentially neurological (premise 2) does not license the conclusion that they are simply and solely brain processes, let alone simply and solely upper-brain processes. Yet Green and

Wikler assume the latter in their assertion of premise 3. It is one thing to say that a functioning upper brain is a necessary condition for the maintenance of these functions, and another to establish that the continued functioning of the upper brain alone would preserve them. Yet Green and Wikler try to support their personal identity theory by assuming the latter in their decapitation example. When they speak of the essentially neurological nature of these processes, they mean that they are encoded in the brain, and that the processes will fail if the brain fails.

In premise 3, though, Green and Wikler argue that psychological continuity is destroyed if the individual's upper brain is destroyed. Hence, upper-brain death is the death of the person. Though I agree with their conclusion, they leave a good deal unsaid between premises 2 and 3. The only indication of a filler argument appears in a footnote: "All that we require is that mental life be nomologically dependent on brain-functioning and that the capacity for consciousness should follow the undamaged brain wherever it might go. This we take modern neuroscience to have established beyond controversy" (124*n*). There are indeed many neuroscientists willing to conclude that a functioning neocortex (upper brain) is necessary for consciousness, but this is an empirical issue over which there is some disagreement. Some conservatives claim that we cannot resolve the question of whether the individual is truly experienceless. Even if we disagree with the conservatives on this matter, the fact remains that premise 3 does not follow from premise 2. Premise 4 is a more acceptable consequence of premise 2, since it does not commit us to an exact locus in the brain for the functions in question. Yet Green and Wikler hold, for reasons unstated, that the portion of the brain supporting personal identity functions is the upper brain, a relatively small portion of the total brain mass. The only argument they provide, quoted just above, leads them to depart considerably from their personal identity theory.

They claim in that passage that a mental life—that is, a capacity for consciousness—requires a functioning brain; modern neuroscience has established this claim, they say, and I take no exception. However, a capacity for consciousness is not the same as psychological continuity, which is their condition of personal identity. Consciousness is a necessary condition for such continuity, but it is by no means sufficient to ensure it. Green and Wikler's argument requires that consciousness be nomologically dependent on neocortical functioning, something that modern neuroscience is unambiguously committed to. They further require that consciousness would follow the undamaged brain wherever it might go. This condition is considerably less than their earlier condition, the retention of psychological continuity when the brain is moved. I have argued that mere brain transfer would fail to achieve this result because of the apparent impact of brain-body interactions on personal identity. The chief problem between premises 2 and 3, however, is that no reason is given for thinking that the upper brain is to be singled out as it is in premise 3. As the argument stands, the upper brain's role in the exhibiting of mental continuity must be explained, or additional premises must be included to the effect that psychological continuity is impossible in the event of permanent unconsciousness, and that the possibility of consciousness is forever removed if the upper brain is destroyed. Premises 4, 5, and 6 would be acceptable were the first three premises able to stand.

Implications of the Ontological Argument

Their personal-identity-based definition of death in place, Green and Wikler elaborate three implications of their view. First, if their argument succeeds, we must conclude that the neocortically dead, as well as the totally brain-dead, are dead. But what does this conclusion suggest about the connection between the presence of consciousness and the preservation of personal identity? On this point Green and Wikler discuss the second implication of their view: how do we manage humans born lacking "the substrate of consciousness" (128)—anencephalic infants. Finally, they ask whether their ontological argument and its corollary on brain death allow us to conclude anything about the morally proper care and treatment of the neocortically dead and the totally brain-dead. Their responses to the first two issues in particular muddy the waters considerably.

CONSCIOUSNESS

Green and Wikler write: "Of course, our view does not imply that a person dies with his last moment of consciousness. What matters is the preservation of the substrate, not the psychological states which it produces" (128). Of course, loss of consciousness cannot be a sufficient condition for death, or we would "die" for a time whenever we fell asleep or were temporarily rendered unconscious. But we are worried about the permanent loss of consciousness resulting from the destruction of, or possibly the absence of, the substrate supporting consciousness. Green and Wikler assert that the person has died if the substrate necessary for consciousness is ruined, but not if conscious processes alone cease.

It is worthwhile to distinguish between the substrate and the processes it supports. Clearly, the brain is one thing and its processes are another. Green and Wikler demonstrate this distinction with two examples. The first is the sleeping individual who undergoes brain death while sleeping; the second is a comatose patient with some degree of brain damage: "A person who suffers brain death during sleep dies at the time of brain death, not the time of onset of sleep. Similarly, a person in a persistent coma might be alive if enough of the brain remained structurally and functionally intact" (128). The first example shows only that there is a distinction between being temporarily unconscious and being permanently unconscious. Unconsciousness is not a sufficient condition for death. A person does not die with his last moment of conscious awareness, unless brain death is the cause of the cessation of consciousness. Green and Wikler's observation is useful only as a response to someone who suggests that if consciousness ceases and never resumes, the individual died at the time consciousness originally ceased. Their point is that permanent loss of consciousness as a result of substrate destruction constitutes the death of the person. But there is no reason to belabor this point, for it is difficult to imagine anyone seriously claiming otherwise.

The first example emphasizes that the substrate of consciousness must be destroyed before the lack of consciousness can be considered a sufficient condition for death. Green and Wikler's remarks about the second example—the patient in a persistent coma—are confusing. Earlier they argued that the death of a person's upper brain is that person's death; here they say that such a person "might be alive if enough of the brain remained structurally and functionally intact." These are critical points, yet the authors are vague here. Persistent coma is usually associated with significant upper-brain destruction.

How much brain life is "enough" to ground the claim that the patient is or might be "alive"? Which part or parts of the brain, if remaining structurally and functionally intact, license the use of the term *alive?* Green and Wikler abandon their earlier conclusion that when one ceases to be (in the sense of losing one's psychological history), one is dead. Is it not the ceasing to be, rather than a particular pattern of brain destruction, that is the critical factor here? Should Green and Wikler have added the qualifier *upper* to the word *brain* in the passage quoted? If this was not their intent, they have undermined their initial conclusion that someone whose upper brain is dead is dead. If it was their intent, they should have made the matter clear. They are apparently trying to avoid having to take the view that anyone in a persistent vegetative state is dead, but their argument entails that very view. They themselves emphasized earlier that the critical issue is not the brain substrate per se, but the processes it supports.

In a later article, Daniel Wikler makes explicit the point that personal identity arguments provide the rationale for the claim that cortical death is a sufficient condition for human death. Whole-brain-death definitions of human death, of course, require far more than the occurrence of cortical death. Wikler writes:

> If a "death of the person" argument constitutes the theoretical rationale for a brain-death definition of death, the definition thus supported will involve cortical death rather than whole-brain death. This definition has in fact been urged by Robert Veatch, among others, but it has not received significant medical or legislative support. Fortunately, the practical importance of the difference between definitions involving cortical and whole-brain death is not great. Those who, like Veatch and the present author, support the cortical-death definition due to the acceptance of a "death of the person" argument will also classify whole-brain dead patients as dead, since all of the latter are also cortically dead. The complaint of supporters of the cortical definition against the whole-brain definition will be only that the whole-brain definition does not go as far as can be theoretically justified; it still counts as a step in the right direction and is not to be disputed.[9]

The theoretical argument developed in the course of this chapter provides a direct defense of the claim that brain death is the death of the person, and an indirect defense of the same claim for upper-brain death, since upper-brain death has obviously occurred when whole-brain death has occurred. In the article they author jointly, however, Green and Wikler appear to back away from the implications of their personal identity theory for the eventual use of a neo-cortical-death criterion. The problems are intensified by the fact that their position on anencephaly is inconsistent with that on the implications of upper-brain death.

ANENCEPHALY

Green and Wikler go on to discuss a second implication of the personal identity theory they have presented in their article: "It does not follow from our argument that all humans lacking the substrate of consciousness are dead" (128). This exclusion seems to contradict the most obvious result of their argument. The integrity of the substrate is the point they emphasize repeatedly, yet here the very absence of the substrate is discounted. Green and Wikler have said, after all, that "what matters is the preservation of the substrate, not the psychological state which it produces" (128). They mean by this that just because the brain is not fostering consciousness at a given moment, we should not conclude that the person has died: the brain (substrate) has not, and therefore the person has not. In the argument now before us, the substrate is compromised. If something human lacks the substrate of consciousness (presumably the upper brain), and therefore is never to be conscious, we cannot conclude that that human is dead, they argue. But this statement contradicts their assertion on the previous page, that their ontological argument is connected with upper-brain death. They provide the following example:

> Anencephalic infants are lacking at birth the cortical material necessary for the development of cognitive functioning and arguably, consciousness. Still, due to the presence of a functioning brain stem, they may have spontaneous breathing and heartbeat, and a good suck. Accounts which simply identified life with upper brain function would have to classify these

infants as dead, which they obviously are not. We, on the other hand, need only point out that the identity criteria for the anencephalic, never-to-be conscious infant do not involve causal substrates for higher level psychological continuity. The conditions for life and existence will be those of human bodies rather than those of persons (128).

Whatever their argument has amounted to thus far, Green and Wikler claim here that it has not led to the identification of human life with upper-brain function. They are burdened by the "fact" that the anencephalic infant is "obviously" not dead, but alive. They attempt to sidestep the threat of contradiction this raises for their overall position by providing a separate identity criterion for entities that are genetically human yet lack the substrate of consciousness, the upper brain.

We may view this step, first of all, as an evasion of one of the obvious implications of an upper-brain-death criterion: the anencephalic infant is neither actually nor potentially a living person. Where the condition of personal identity is not fulfilled in a human being's case, that individual is dead; Green and Wikler's assessment of those who have suffered upper-brain death fits this situation as well. The functions present in the anencephalic infant's case are as significant to the decision that she is alive as they are in cases in which the upper brain has died. If this response is incorrect in the infant's case, then the burden of proof lies with Green and Wikler, since they take the radical step of introducing another set of identity criteria for functioning human bodies. This new set of criteria would lead to the conclusion that the upper-brain-dead (who carry on spontaneous breathing and circulation) are alive. It is incumbent upon Green and Wikler to explain why the upper-brain-dead are not in the same category as the anencephalic infant.

A second response to Green and Wikler's argument is that nothing but confusion results from the introduction of a separate identity criterion for the anencephalic. They argued earlier that redefining death in cases of brain death, rather than proposing euthanasia, avoids the moral hazards connected with the latter. Yet their argument here supports a euthanasia argument in relation to anencephalic infants.

A third response is that their argument blurs an important distinction between identity criteria and "conditions for life and existence." Their personal identity theory, when applied to brain death, implies that identity criteria and "conditions for life and existence" are intimately connected; a loss of personal identity is a loss of life. Howard Brody suggests that "the relationship between brain death and personal death, or personal nonexistence, is more troublesome than Green and Wikler assume."[10] Brody thinks that personal existence and personal identity must be distinguished. A personal identity theory will not help us settle questions about the death of a human being, or about the end of a personal existence. I would respond to Brody that the connection is not troublesome. If my counterexamples to Green and Wikler's personal identity theory are valid, then we must accept a more limited mentalist theory according to which the loss of personal identity correlates with the loss of personal existence. We cannot accept a personal identity theory that would allow for the cessation of personal identity but not of personal existence. A consciousness criterion avoids this problem.

Because Brody thinks Green and Wikler fail to justify the claim that brain death is the death of the person on the basis of a personal identity theory, he recommends that we defend the brain-death criterion by the combined use of biological, moral, and ontological arguments. Brody's eclectic approach is convincing only if he can elaborate on the ways in which separate arguments can work in concert for the desired result. He does not accomplish this in his reply to Green and Wikler.

In spite of their methodological disagreement, Green and Wikler and Brody share a common perspective on anencephaly. Brody suggests that the anencephalic infant calls into question the use of a personal identity theory. Green and Wikler compromise their own argument by avoiding the dilemma of anencephaly, suggesting a different identity criterion for the anencephalic infant because it lacks the crucial substrate. It is not clear why they create the new criterion. Is there a danger of trampling sacred rights? Now we have two sets of identity criteria, one for human bodies and one for human bodies that possess or have possessed the capacity for personal status. The latter set of criteria capture as well "the conditions for life and existence." Green and Wikler maintain that the same is true of the first set, but the conditions of life and existence for human bodies are different from identity criteria for human bodies. The body remains, and its identity is a function of the physical characteristics that distinguish it from other human bodies. Criteria for the body's aliveness would be different from those for its identity.

It would be consistent with their earlier argument to say that the anencephalic infant, lacking an upper brain (the substrate of consciousness), is dead. It is not a living person; hence it presents us with the same dilemma Jones (whose upper brain is dead) does, and deserves the same response. I suspect that Green and Wikler are seduced by the fact of the functioning brain stem and the spontaneity of the functions it supports in the anencephalic case. But this is a reversion to the biologically based arguments they dismissed early in their article; their ontological argument is that a human entity lacking certain neurologically based functions (psychological continuity) is dead. Now the presence of a particular set of biological functions (heartbeat and respiration) is the basis for saying that a human entity is alive, despite the absence of the crucial neurological functions associated with the preservation of personal identity.

Perhaps Green and Wikler view the anencephalic infant as an entity with a psychological history, albeit very reduced. Perhaps they mean to avoid criticism by saying that anencephalic infants are not, and never were, persons, and that therefore we need different identity and life criteria for them. If this is their reasoning, it is not clearly expressed in their article. Further, if this were their approach, they would have to demonstrate why we must manage the anencephalic case differently, and why the neocortically or upper-brain-dead patient is not alive as well. If the anencephalic are obviously not dead, then Jones is obviously not dead either. But Green and Wikler tell us that the infant lacks the "causal substrates for higher level psychological continuity," and so its life criteria must be based on the body, not on the person. Their argument might be this: the infant never had the critical substrate; Jones had it and lost it. Therefore Jones, once a person, is now dead; but since the infant was never a person, she is not dead until her body fulfills some other set of criteria. This is the best defense I can construct for Green and Wikler on this matter. It is a defense that treats anencephaly as a unique case and does not contradict the claim that the death of a person's upper brain constitutes that person's death—since the anencephalic infant was never a person.

Still, Green and Wikler should not use such reasoning to introduce a second set of identity criteria for cases of anencephaly. What gains might we expect from such a maneuver, or what harms might we avoid? Their claim runs counter to their reasoning for the ontological adequacy of the brain-death criterion. Green and Wikler argue that such a criterion would eliminate many of the worries and problems involved in making decisions about euthanasia. Not only would that rationale seem relevant in the anencephalic case, but similar considerations of the sort they raise would also seem to apply. There is no good reason to maintain existence, life will end anyway, and the anencephalic infant will never have a conscious life. It is wrongheaded to introduce a second identity criterion for several reasons. In the anencephalic case, identity criteria and conditions of life and existence do not overlap. It is confusing to speak of alive bodies and dead persons, since a similar distinction could be drawn across the board, even in brain-death cases. Finally, the danger of the slippery slope of euthanasia decisions applies here as well.

GREEN AND WIKLER'S MORAL ARGUMENT

Green and Wikler's last commentary on their ontological argument is that they have invoked no moral premises, and their argument yields no moral conclusions. The acceptability of a definition of death is one thing; the morality of elevating it to the status of public policy is another. Green and Wikler believe that their personal identity theory demonstrates that the brain-dead, and more specifically the upper-brain-dead, are dead. What to do with the brain-dead and the upper-brain-dead are separate matters requiring moral deliberation. Green and Wikler specify the conditions under which a person has died and show that brain death and upper-brain death result in the fulfillment of these conditions. When to pronounce death, and how and when to discontinue care, are still open questions. While the death of a person's brain is that person's death, we must decide whether we ought to declare the brain-dead individual dead.

Green and Wikler argue that moral considerations are not helpful in constructing an argument for a particular definition of death. Their analysis is incomplete because it fails to contain a moral argument supporting its presupposed focus on the human being as person. This later portion of their article may be their attempt to provide such an argument, for they defend here the brain-death criterion, given that it rests on an acceptable ontology of persons. Lawrence Becker thinks that an emphasis on redefinition ignores the real issue, and that we must face the necessity of constructing sound ethical arguments to justify the withdrawal of treatment in certain classes of cases, including brain death. He argues that we must face this issue directly and not evade it by an ad hoc definition of death. Green and Wikler say that Becker never shows the definitional approach to be ad hoc. They object to the euthanasia approach to brain-death cases because it puts us on a slippery slope; we can avoid the slopes (the possible unjustified euthanasia) by treating such cases as redefinition possibilities, for there is no tendency to think that the hopelessly senile are dead.

   In addition to the moral security of staying off the slope, Green and Wikler cite a further reason for managing brain-death cases— discussion of upper-brain-death cases is conspicuously absent from the rest of their discussion—as definitional rather than termination-of-care decisions. They appeal to the fact that the public accepts the brain-death criterion, suggesting that the public can live with this approach far more easily than with euthanasia in such cases. But this victory with the public perception of death was not easy; many states have yet to endorse formally the brain-death criterion. Green and Wikler comment:

> Becker feels, as we do, that discontinuation of medical care of brain-dead patients is morally acceptable, even mandatory.
> By Becker's definition of death, such action amounts to giving up life-saving efforts. If this sort of medical action were to be endorsed by statute or other governmental sanction, it might take the form of releasing physicians from the legal obligation to preserve the life of the irreversibly comatose. The standard argument against this sort of policy is that it threatens a slide down a slippery slope: today we endorse the withdrawal of care from the comatose; perhaps tomorrow from the senile, the

moderately retarded, the nonproductive. The likelihood of
such a slide is probably impossible to measure with any confidence, but it surely is not negligible. Some persons now
being retained in institutions for the mentally retarded, after
all, have a cognitive life not much different from Karen
Quinlan's. And the historical precedent (admittedly under
vastly different sociopolitical conditions) has already been set.

Whatever danger exists of a drift toward unjustified euthanasia would be significantly lessened if the statute licensing
termination of care of brain-dead patients were one which
classified them as dead rather than alive; one which, given a
heart-lung definition of death, evaded the euthanasia issue.
For the public, whether justifiably or not, seems willing to
regard brain-dead patients as dead. A brain-death statute thus
has the virtue of leaving official public policy on euthanasia,
presently quite restrictive, apparently unchanged. This legal
step would portend a threat to the senile and retarded only if
the public came to think of them as *dead*, an eventuality
which is most unlikely. The danger of the slippery slope is,
then, blocked by setting a precedent which would be nearly
invulnerable to distortion (128–29).

Here Green and Wikler wish to avoid relaxing the obligations that
physicians have toward the comatose. Far better, they argue, to
define the unambiguous circumstance of brain death as death, and
to retain our present understanding of our obligations to the comatose and the mentally failing and infirm. As I noted above, upper-
brain death has dropped out of Green and Wikler's discussion, probably as a result of their argument concerning consciousness. If my
reasons for extending Green and Wikler's definition of death to cover
all those in persistent vegetative states is compelling, however, the
definitional approach may lead to an equally slippery slope. The
problem is to delineate the parameters of persistent vegetative states
so that we do not declare dead those who are intermittently comatose
or just barely responsive. This does not seem to be an unresolvable
problem, however; nor is it a foregone conclusion that we could keep
our footing on the slope of the euthanasia approach. The argument
Green and Wikler use here can go both ways. Slippery slopes are

dangerous only when people disavow the moral responsibility of drawing precise distinctions. But distinctions must be drawn regardless of the proximity of a slope. In chapter 7, I try to defend a policy that results in a declaration of death, and not the practice of euthanasia, in relation to patients who are known to be in a persistent vegetative state.

The force of Green and Wikler's argument appears to derive from a single fact: the public accepts the idea that the brain-dead are dead. Adopting a brain-death criterion leaves our euthanasia policy intact, is in accord with sound ontology, and avoids the slippery slope problem "by setting a precedent which would be nearly invulnerable to distortion."

David Lamb Revisited

David Lamb agrees that the brain-death criterion has strong theoretical support, but he does not think that it can be provided in the form of a personal identity theory. He attempts to convince us of the strengths of a biological argument as the theoretical basis for the brain-death criterion by arguing that the personal identity approach paves the way for rampant uncertainty and distortion in the declaration of death. In 1978, Lamb made a major contribution to the redefinition debate (which he would surely refer to as the *definition* debate) with the biologically based arguments he presented in the article "Diagnosing Death" (see chapter 3). Lamb has recently elaborated his view, as well as his objections to the "death of the person" approaches taken by Veatch, Hoffman, Green and Wikler, and others. Centered around the opposing approach to defining human death as the death of the organism as a whole, Lamb's freshly articulated position demands attention at this critical juncture in my argument.

Lamb maintains that the novelties of machine medicine have forced us to reconsider the meaning of human death. He concludes that our concept of death is the same as it has always been, a brain-centered concept.[11] Lamb admits that we have come to understand only relatively recently the role and function of the brain in relation to the function of the organism as a whole, but he argues nevertheless that the death of the brain has always been the death of the human being. In fact, he says, the traditional criteria were never adequate for declaring death because they were merely predictive of the imminent loss of whole-brain function, and not directly diagnostic of the occurrence of brain death. In addition, heart and lung function are inadequate signs of death because their cessation is reversible. Lamb views the traditional criteria as brain-centered precisely because they reflect the imminence of brain death:

> It will be maintained here that brain death is a radical reformulation of traditional concepts of death rather than a new concept, since there is no new way of being dead, and that it marks an improvement on cardio-respiratory formulations. [The brain death formulation] is *not so much a new concept as the formulation of a definition of death where previously none existed.*[12]

I refuted this brain-centered view of the traditional criteria in chapter 2. Those criteria were certainly not initially viewed as criteria for the imminence of death, but for its occurrence, and many people will never come to view them in the former light.

The new idea Lamb introduces into the dispute about the concepts and criteria of human death is the suggestion that while our concept of death is brain death, an adequate criterion for declaring death would be brain-stem death, a refinement in brain-related criteria. Lamb appeals to several clinical studies that support the empirical claim that we can draw a conclusion about the status of the whole brain from clinical judgments about the status of the brain stem. Brain-stem death, Lamb argues, is "the physiological kernel of brain death" (4). The brain is the "critical system" of the human body because of its irreplaceability, and brain-stem death is the "point of no return" in the irreversibility of the death of the organism as a whole, relating to the "critical system" as its "vital ingredient" (5). Lamb writes: "Death of the brainstem provides both a necessary and sufficient definition of the death of a human being, in that it provides a physiological substratum for the irreversible loss of function of the organism as a whole" (7).

Lamb's choice of language is crucial in these statements. He embraces the notion of human death as the death of the organism as a whole and holds that brain death is the death of the individual, thus holding that the death of the individual can occur even if integrated, nonspontaneous organismic functioning persists. I would argue that since the nonspontaneity of the respiratory function must be considered irrelevant to any determination of death, a declaration based on the notion of death of the organism as a whole must require the complete cessation of the integrated functioning of the organism, spontaneous or otherwise.

Lamb directly confronts the toughest case for his view: in some cases of maternal brain death (brain death in a pregnant woman), it is possible to maintain integrated systemic functioning long enough to support fetal development to the point of viability. Lamb's view commits him to the claim that the mother has undergone death of the organism as a whole yet exhibits organismic "life" at a level sufficient to support fetal development. This claim seems entirely counterintuitive: in any legitimate sense of organismic death, it is absurd to say that such a mother's body is dead. There must be something amiss either with Lamb's notion that human death is the death of the organism as a whole, or with the idea that a brain-dead individual, simply on account of being brain-dead, fulfills this conception of human death. Lamb comments: "Pregnancy in a vegetative state involves a situation where the mother is capable, with assistance, of sustaining the foetus to term; whereas foetal survival in a ventilated cadaver, following maternal brain death, is simply a situation where physicians are utilizing the uterus of an ex-patient to enhance the probability of a favourable pregnancy outcome" (101).

It is not clear to me that physicians are simply "utilizing the uterus" of the brain-dead mother in such a case. The organism as a whole must be functioning for the uterus to remain a hospitable environment for the developing fetus. At best we have a weak understanding of the physiological and chemical circumstances that sustain pregnancy for all stages of human gestation. Hence, physicians are using the capacity of the mother's body, functioning in an integrated way, to support fetal life. The uterus and its functional contributions to this process are only a part of the total picture. If the mother were conscious instead of comatose, we would have no tendency to think of her body as a "ventilated cadaver," even though it might be equally "manipulated" to support fetal life to the point of viability. Lamb must discuss the relevance of the permanent absence of consciousness—something he never does. Further, we would not think that the mother's uterus alone was being manipulated, were we willing to think along these lines at all.

Brain death and organismic death must be distinguished; the death of the organism as a whole, while an eventual consequence of brain death, has not occurred simply because brain death has occurred. Lamb remarks: "In the case of maternal brain death reported by Dillon *et al.*, the artificial maintenance of certain organs (the womb) to support the foetus was nothing more than another form of mechanical support, equivalent to an incubator. The mother was not supporting the foetus anymore than one who, having bequeathed her organs, can be said to support the recipient after her death" (101). There are errors here. First, the language of this passage is out of place. The mother's body is the source of support—not the mother, and certainly not just the uterus. The support provided by her body may resemble that of an incubator, but the resemblance is slight. Incubators provide a stable, uniformly warm environment, but they provide for neither the transmission of oxygen and nutrients nor the elimination of wastes. They do not bear a close analogy at all to the maternal environment. We involve ourselves in word games if we are unwilling to call the complex function of supporting fetal survival the functioning of an organism as a whole.[13]

Lamb's language relating brain death to the death of the organism as a whole, and brain-stem death to brain death, is also troublesome. In both cases, we are looking at prognostic and not diagnostic relationships. While brain-stem death may be an adequate empirical basis for the claim that brain death will soon occur, it is not diagnostic of the occurrence of brain death. Lamb's discussion of brain-stem death is as follows:

> The brainstem contains (in its upper part) crucial centres responsible for generating the capacity for consciousness. In its lower part it contains the respiratory centre. It is death of the brainstem . . . which produces the crucial signs . . . which doctors detect at the bedside, when they diagnose brain death. . . . The last ten years have seen . . . the gradual realization that death of the brainstem is the necessary and sufficient condition for death of the brain as a whole—and that brainstem death is therefore itself synonymous with the death of the

individual. This latter realization first received implicit recognition in statements issued by the conference of Medical Royal Colleges and Their Faculties in 1976 and 1979. Brainstem death . . . is . . . the stage at which "loss of integration" becomes irreversible (5).

To say that the loss of integration becomes irreversible is not to say that that loss has occurred. Lamb apparently views the brain stem as a sort of mini-brain, responsible for the continuation of the capacities for both consciousness and respiration. This view calls in to question the usual dichotomy between the upper and lower parts of the brain. What does it mean to say that brain-stem death is sufficient for the death of the brain as a whole? Lamb's claim reduces to a temporal one here: while brain-stem death makes the continuation of integrated life impossible, it does not correspond with the cessation of integrated life. Lamb says that "the irreversibility of brain-stem death has been revealed in numerous studies" (63). Irreversibility of a function that leads to brain death, however, cannot be construed as diagnostic of brain death. It must be prognostic of brain death in the same way that the irreversible and irreplaceable functioning of the liver is.

The same error is involved in Lamb's equation of brain death with the death of the organism as a whole: "That structural disintegration follows brain death is not a contingent matter; it is a necessary consequence of the death of the critical system. The death of the brain is the point beyond which other systems cannot survive with or without mechanical support" (37). That other systems cannot survive after brain death occurs is not to say that they are not at this moment still surviving. Lamb must argue that their persisting function in this situation is not significant enough to be called life. But an organismic concept of human death undermines any such argument.

Most important, however, is a recent attack on the notion that brain-stem death provides an adequate biological basis for accurately diagnosing brain death. In an article entitled "Brainstem Death," E. Rodin and others conclude, on the basis of their discussion of a hypothetical case of "a patient who demonstrated the clinical picture of brain death due to discrete brainstem hemorrhage and infarction,"[14] that "brainstem death is not identical with total brain death although it has a fatal prognosis," and that "in presence of life support systems, the clinical examination can only establish a diagnosis of brainstem death but cannot give information about the functional state of the cerebral hemispheres or diencephalon unless spontaneous progressive hypothermia ensues."[15] The authors point out that the brain-stem-death criterion adopted in the United Kingdom presumes the identity of brain-stem death and brain death. They argue that the use of an EEG must accompany the use of the brain-stem-death criterion. Lamb rejects this claim based on clinical discussions from the work of Pallis in particular. Even Pallis acknowledges the possibility of the sort of case Rodin describes, and refers to it as one of the greatest hells one can imagine, "an isolated sentience aware of its precarious existence and with no means of expression."[16] Rodin and others have two crucial responses to Pallis: first, that a patient like the one under consideration may not have a fatal prognosis; and second, that an individual who meets the brain-stem-death criterion may have more than "negligible cortical function." They conclude that without EEG confirmation of cerebral nonfunction, we should neither declare death nor terminate life support. While a quality-of-life approach might be taken here, life can clearly be present concomitant with brain death that is clinically demonstrated on the basis of a brain-stem-death criterion. Hence, an EEG is essential in the determination of whole-brain death; the brain-stem criterion is inadequate for this purpose.

These considerations, perhaps not available to Lamb at the time he wrote his book, suggest that whether we interpret the relationship of brain-stem death to brain death as diagnostic or prognostic, it can result in a false declaration of death in certain cases of partial brain destruction. We must therefore resist Lamb's recommendation for a refinement in our brain-related criteria for declaring death. But what of Lamb's conception of human death, beyond this debate about an adequate set of brain-related criteria for declaring death?

The fundamental perspective that informs Lamb's choice of brain death as a concept of death—one that is at clear odds with the death-of-the-person perspective—is expressed in Lamb's assertions that death is primarily a biological phenomenon (7) and that "life is essentially a matter of organization" (26). Death, then, is the point at which the capacity of the brain to support this organization is irreversibly lost. Since brain-stem death is taken to be the precise point of irreversibility in the process of disorganization, it is an adequate criterion for declaring death. Lamb buttresses his reliance upon irreversibility with his argument that the brain stem is the body's regulator—an argument I refuted in chapter 3.

Lamb needs a clear and compelling rationale for his perspective on human life and death. While it is obvious that being alive requires elaborate biological organization, it does not follow that human life *is* that organization. Lamb's central rationale for his view revolves around his assertion that certainty attaches to the concept of death as that of the organism as a whole, while in Lamb's opinion uncertainty surrounds the concept of human death as that of the person. These assertions about certainty and uncertainty are embedded in a view of what our general concept of death must do.

> If the "loss of that which is essentially significant" is to have any meaning as a concept of death, then it must be framed so that it involves an irreversible state where the organism as a whole cannot function. Only a concept which specifies the irreversible loss of specified functions (due to the destruction of their anatomical substratum) can avoid the anomalous situation where a patient is said to be alive according to one concept but dead according to another. The only wholly satisfactory concept of death is that which trumps other concepts of death in so far as it yields a diagnosis of death which is beyond dispute (13).

Reading this passage as one who espouses the neocortical-death criterion, I offer this reply: human death, understood as the death of a person, is a state in which the function of consciousness has been irreversibly lost as a result of one of several possible combinations of damage to the brain substratum. At this point our understanding of the brain and its functions, as well as our capacity to identify those patterns of damage to the brain substratum that produce irreversible unconsciousness, are limited. However, destruction of the neocortex has been shown to produce permanent unconsciousness and to be an empirically verifiable pattern of brain destruction prior to the failure of the organism as a whole. Since human death is the

death of the person, and the death of the person occurs with permanent loss of consciousness, neocortical death is an adequate criterion
for declaring death. Clearly, Lamb would resist this response, arguing that it rests on a concept that may lead to contested diagnoses of
death. This concept does not "trump" other concepts by yielding
indisputable diagnoses.

We might think that Lamb's use of the word *trumps* is intended to
convey the idea that the death of the organism as a whole is incompatible with the continuation of the life of the person, but he intends
a more limited meaning. This meaning renders his argument unacceptable, however, since some wish to dispute even the status of
the brain-dead. The neocortical criterion may allow someone to
claim that the patient is still alive, but both the brain-death and the
brain-stem death criteria allow the same thing. To think that we can
elaborate a concept of death that is "beyond dispute" is an illusory
goal.

If we cannot expect unanimity in our concept of death, why not
accept a concept that "trumps" all the others in the sense that it
includes them all? That way, whenever death is declared, no one
can complain that the individual remains alive according to some
other concept. The notion of death as that of the organism as a whole
might seem to be the trump card, for it can be viewed as an umbrella
concept: if one is dead in this sense, one is dead according to every
other concept of death as well. But the success of this claim depends
upon what we mean by the death of the organism as a whole. If we
mean the total stoppage of integrated organismic function, then this
concept might trump all the rest. But this is not what Lamb means;
he sees the concept as compatible with the brain-death and brain-
stem-death criteria. Yet we found the links between brain death and
brain-stem death dubious.

There is no compelling reason to assume that one concept might
"trump" all others, so that no diagnosis of death will ever be beyond
dispute. But Lamb favors the organismic concept of death because it
has a certainty that the person-centered concept lacks. This claim
about certainty is an empirical one. To avoid redefinitions of death
that will engender public suspicion and skepticism, Lamb argues
that we need a conception of death that is clear, certain in its meaning and application, and above all not too much of a challenge to

entrenched attitudes about death. The remainder of Lamb's rationale for his focus on the death of the organism as a whole consists in the claim that only this perspective permits a unified view of life and death across the spectrum of living things. "Death is primarily a biological phenomenon. The death of a man is no different from the death of a dog or cat. In all cases the brain is the critical system, and brainstem function its vital ingredient. Essential to the concept of brain death is the belief in the existence of a single vital system whose irreversible loss is synonymous with the death of the organism as a whole" (7).

I would offer a competing set of judgments. Death is indeed a biological phenomenon—that is, it is a process in the life of a biological organism. We have adopted the convention that there is a biologically definable circumstance that constitutes death. We declare an individual dead when that biological condition is determined to have occurred. But we do not choose which biological state constitutes the event of death (which is not just a biological, but also a social, moral, and metaphysical event) on the basis of biological reasoning alone. Death is not simply "a matter of scientific fact," as Lamb would have it. We must make an ethical decision about how best to regard the human for the purpose of declaring death. The death of a person is different from that of a dog or a cat; every death of a person unravels and reconstitutes a complex net of rights and obligations that usually involve many people. Death is not simply an event in the life of the deceased. We must think of human death not in terms of what it has in common with canine death or feline death, but in terms of what it represents for human relationships: abandonment of all roles, the end of all interactions, and the reconstituting of rights and obligations. Permanent unconsciousness, whatever its basis, represents these changes. Any view that would consider someone dead only if her heart and lungs had permanently ceased spontaneous functioning or if she were brain-dead, but not if she were neocortically dead, overlooks the central realities surrounding the death of a human being.

Lamb's objections to the use of a personal identity theory to ground claims about the death of a person, and to construe the death of the person as human death, are twofold. On one hand, he claims that uncertainty plagues the person-oriented concept; on the other, he suggests that this concept attracts us to ethically hazardous slippery slopes. With respect to uncertainty, we must examine where Lamb thinks the uncertainties lie. He writes: "It is by no means clear whether criteria for continuous personal identity reside in either conscious activity or in the structures of the higher brain" (42). Obviously, a disputed theory of personal identity is a source of trouble. But a theory that reduces to the demand that personal identity is retained as long as conscious functioning continues avoids this trouble. Lamb implies that there is a difficulty with the association between the continuation of personal identity and the retention of consciousness. I have argued that this association is not problematic. Lamb's other uncertainty concerns the locus of personal identity. Several commentators on this issue do not share Lamb's concern; what is important, they argue, is that we can say that patterns of brain destruction (for example, neocortical death) entail irreversible unconsciousness. It is also important that we anticipate an ever-expanding ability to correlate patterns of brain destruction with irreversible unconsciousness. Wherever the loci of conscious activity, it is fair to assume that we shall improve our ability to identify them and their irreversible destruction.

Lamb poses a number of other challenges to the person-oriented conception of human death in the fifth chapter of his book. The first is the problem of borderline cases. But a consciousness-based criterion avoids any challenge that a borderline case might raise. Down's Syndrome and severe dementia, for example, do not challenge an adequately stated consciousness-based concept of death. Moreover, the persistence of lower-brain functioning, supporting the functioning of the lungs only, does not and should not challenge a person-centered concept of death. While consciousness might require some functioning in the brain stem (an empirical point), it does not follow that the continuation of the brain-stem functioning supportive only of respiration should challenge our concept of death.

Lamb suggests that neurophysiologists are uncertain as to whether "the cessation of higher brain functions entails a total loss of consciousness and awareness" (43). But Korein is not puzzled about the nonsentient nature of the "life" of such an individual. Lamb is worried about the slippery slope involved in judging that sentience is utterly absent in an individual's case. We must be certain that consciousness is permanently absent; if we are not certain, our moral responsibility is to forgo decision-making, thus erring (if we err) in assuming life rather than death.

Finally, choosing a consciousness-oriented concept of death implies nothing about the extent of our ability to demonstrate that consciousness is irreversibly lost under certain circumstances of brain destruction. This is a medical problem, not a philosophical one. In short, I agree with Veatch that we must "follow safer-course policies of using measures to declare death only in cases in which we are convinced that some necessary physical basis for life is missing, even if that means that some dead patients will be treated as alive."[17]

Lamb's next objection is a familiar one—that the burial of a spontaneously breathing body is morally repugnant. But we need not challenge entrenched sensibilities to such an extent. Lamb seems to think that if we do not bury the spontaneously breathing neocortically dead, our only options are "benign neglect" on one end of the spectrum, and "active euthanasia" on the other (44). Surely our options are more varied and less morally troublesome than these. If we replied that the remaining spontaneous functions of the neocortically dead ought to be stopped in a quick and tolerable manner, Lamb would no doubt respond that this policy mandates the creation of a class of medical executioners in our society. It is odd that an objection would be lodged against the creation of "medical executioners" (a misleading term, given that the neocortically dead are already dead) while the same objection does not occur to a class of legal executioners in our society.

The chief objection to upper-brain formulations of human death is in the form of slippery slope arguments: "If a diagnosis of death is based on permanent loss of the content of consciousness, then this category can be extended to include a wide range of disorders that should not be considered as death, or even close to death" (45). Slippery slope arguments rest on the empirical assumption that one specific step must lead to another, less morally desirable step, and on to another until we have lost our footing completely and find ourselves in moral quicksand. Such arguments are compelling only if the empirical connections they presuppose are reasonable. The difficulty is to determine whether personal-identity-based arguments carry us too near the slopes—in this case, whether the adoption of a consciousness-based criterion for declaring death can be expected to drag us down into the moral quicksand. The usual argument, that such a criterion will undercut our broadest moral principles, suggests that such a decision about the neocortically dead will seriously compromise our regard and treatment of the retarded, defective newborns, the chronically or terminally ill, and others. Such an argument presumes that no clear line can be drawn between these cases and that of neocortical death. But the permanent cessation of consciousness due to demonstrable destruction of relevant portions of the brain is immune to the sorts of distortions feared by those who argue that this criterion leads to a slippery slope. As Lamb himself points out in his defense of the whole-brain formulation of death, it is not the acceptance of criteria per se that leads to the slide down the slope. Rather, such an outcome can result only from general attitudinal changes toward human beings in the categories mentioned above. Such attitudinal changes are the issue: there is no reason to think that a shift from an organismic understanding to a person-centered concept of human death would erode our respect for human life and our treatment of human beings in diminished circumstances.

Lamb's argument for the certainty of his own position fails, and his objections to the death-of-the-person approach are ultimately unpersuasive. His work in *Death, Brain Death and Ethics* is of inestimable value in the redefinition debate, because it elaborates and defends a position about death based on the assumptions that human death is ultimately a biological phenomenon, and that the central conclusions necessary to defend a particular criterion for declaring death can be generated on the basis of biological considerations alone. My fundamental disagreement with Lamb concerns the status of human death. Our concept of death is not a fact awaiting our discovery; rather, it must be chosen on the basis of ethical reflection.

In the final section of their article, Green and Wikler emphasize their points of divergence from other arguments that the death of a person's brain is that person's death. The biological arguments, they claim, mistakenly emphasize the brain stem and its functions in the determination of the death of the person. This is a mistake, they say, because the loss of upper-brain function alone constitutes the person's death. As we have seen, however, their discussion of the anencephalic infant is inconsistent with their rejection of the biological arguments. Moreover, reference to upper-brain death drops from their discussion of the implications of their position. If Green and Wikler want to argue that separate criteria for personal identity should be used for those who have never had upper-brain functioning and for those who have had such functioning and lost it, they must provide good reasons for drawing such a distinction. Otherwise, they commit themselves to a dualism with respect to the human being. In order to hold a consistent view, one must choose either the organismic or the personal concept of death. David Lamb makes a clear choice but does not defend it persuasively.

Green and Wikler argue that the death of the brain stem is no more the death of the person than is the death of the kidneys—apparently because we have mechanical stand-ins in either case. But if we developed a mechanical replacement for the upper brain—for example, a qualitatively identical computer correlate of Jones's upper brain which we could link up to Jones's body—would the person Jones still be alive? Our discussion of Veatch's computer-tape experiment demonstrated how difficult it is to conclude that Jones is not in some important sense still alive. I would agree with Green and Wikler that the biological arguments are inadequate, that there must ultimately be some decision of significance on which declarations of human death rest. But Green and Wikler do not give sufficient reason for rejecting these arguments. In the past, the brain failed when the heart and lungs failed, and so the biological "facts" were self-evident. A decision of significance lay behind the use of the traditional criteria, but it has not been necessary until now to make that decision more precise. Forced to articulate and justify such decisions, we now see that the decisions of significance underlying the traditional and the brain-death criteria are radically different.

Green and Wikler assume throughout that the loss of personal existence is at issue. They therefore assume that a theory of personal identity is the proper ontological route for concluding that a person has died when her brain has died. But are we concerned about persons, about their coming to be and their passing away, or about the cessation of function of human organisms? If our concern is about persons, then the persistance of organismic functioning is irrelevant to the determination of death. If there is no capacity to support the consciousness necessary for a personal existence, then the entity exhibiting integrated organismic functioning is dead. Moral principle will dictate how we restructure rights and duties, since we are no longer discussing a living person. But the moral argument of Green and Wikler is inadequate to defend the initial choice of focus on the human as person. "Should we consider the human as person for the purpose of determining what constitutes death?" is a different question from "What reasons support the brain-death criterion, given that it presumes that the death of a person's brain is that person's death?" We need moral argument at two levels of the redefinition debate: first, to justify our approach to the human being, and second, to defend a particular policy with respect to declaring death. If we accept that death is to be declared when the conditions necessary for a personal as opposed to a vegetative existence are removed, then articulating an adequate theory of personal identity is our essential philosophical task.

Green and Wikler make an important effort to argue, from ontological premises, that the death of a person's upper brain is that person's death. Their personal identity theory is not adequate, but a more modest mentalist theory may be. Consciousness, a necessary condition for psychological continuity, is the sine qua non of personal existence. Since upper-brain death results in the permanent absence of consciousness, it is the death of the person. Green and Wikler correctly argue that the body without a brain is not the person. But this conclusion is compatible with a number of other theories that they do not rule out: the person may be identical with a particular set of upper-brain processes; the person may be a particular set of such processes connected with a particular body; the person may be a particular set of such processes connected with any body having a particular physicochemical structure; or the person may be identical with a computer correlate of a particular set of upper-brain processes. These are just a few options. Green and Wikler's conclusion is appealing because upper-brain death generates at best a vegetative, not a personal, existence; a person in such a situation is dead. But the justification for an upper-brain-death criterion would be better enunciated thus: the individual's essence consists in the possession of a conscious, yet not necessarily continuous, mental life; if all mental life ceases, the person ceases to exist; when the person ceases to exist, the person has died. Upper-brain death destroys all capacity for a conscious mental life, and it is therefore the death of the person.

chapter 6

Redefining Death

In chapter 2, I argued that we depart from an organismic concept of human death when we adopt the brain-death criterion, for the concept of death underlying that criterion emphasizes the permanent loss of the capacity for consciousness. In chapter 5, I claimed that one who retains the capacity for consciousness, even in the most minimal form, must be considered the same living person she was when her mental life was richer. Such a claim does not imply that the individual retains the same moral status; she may have undergone such loss or change of mental functioning that her rights and responsibilities must be recast. I have also argued that the concept of human death underlying the brain-death and the neocortical-death criteria is the same. The redefined concept presupposed by these criteria is that human death is the irreversible loss of the capacity for consciousness. In response to the objection that the circumstances of brain death and neocortical death differ dramatically, since organismic functioning is nonspontaneous in the former case and spontaneous in the latter, I would invoke Jonas's argument to demonstrate the irrelevance of nonspontaneity in determinations of death. We would surely rank a conscious individual among the living, even if all her functioning (heart, lungs, and brain) were nonspontaneous. The source of the functioning is immaterial; the kind of functioning is not. In chapter 5, I argued also that a conservative, mentalist, personal identity theory was compatible not only with the brain-death criterion, but with the neocortical-death criterion as well.

Throughout this book, one question has recurred: in determining what constitutes the death of a human being, should we focus on the human being's status as organism or as person? The two choices yield different and incompatible results. We must defend our choice if we are to justify completely a particular criterion for declaring death. I have waited until now to present my own justification, hoping by this means to ensure a fair critical analysis of the many analytical approaches and arguments that have figured in the re-definition debate. It seems accurate to say that no one whose view we have surveyed has taken this matter sufficiently to heart, except perhaps John Hoffman. But some others engaged in the debate have been sensitive to the need for argument on this crucial matter. For example, Youngner and Bartlett write: "We further believe one must specify the type of living entity in question—a human. Other-wise, one runs the risk of identifying the life or the death of the wrong kind of entity."[1] We need to defend the choice of the person-cen-tered concept of human death before any argument for the brain-death and the neocortical-death criteria will be complete.

In addition to this central argument, there are other matters to discuss in this chapter. In chapter 4, I examined Veatch's argument that death ought to be redefined. I restructured and recast portions of that argument to render it more compelling, and it became clear that a moral argument is necessary. Veatch urges redefinition by suggest-ing that it is an affront to the dignity of a dead human being to treat her as though she were alive. I will elaborate on this claim, arguing that redefinition is morally mandated. Further, the argument con-cerning the focus we take (on the human being as organism or as person) is also a moral argument crucial to whether we accept the necessity of redefining death. That is, if we undertake a redefinition to ensure the moral treatment of former persons, then we must recognize that the organismic formulation of our concept of human death may fail to achieve that result.

Chapters 3 and 4 cast doubt on the adequacy of the biological and moral approaches to defining human death and justifying a criterion for declaring death. At the deepest level, the disagreement between some representatives of these approaches and proponents of the ontological approach is a disagreement about the essential features of human existence. Some conceive of the essential in organismic terms, others in personal terms. If we adopt the personal focus, the claim naturally follows that a justification of the brain-death criterion requires an analysis of the concept of person (which Green and Wikler direct into an analysis of the conditions necessary for the preservation of personal identity). Since an individual-essentialism (a personal identity theory) and a kind-essentialism (a theory of personhood) are opposite sides of the same coin, the choice between the two approaches is not a major dilemma. It is, however, more manageable philosophically to think in the former rather than in the latter terms, and I have therefore constructed my own argument on the basis of personal identity.

Both approaches commit us to the adequacy of ontological analysis to the task at hand. But since some moralists contend that moral analysis gives us a better handle on the necessary and sufficient conditions of personhood or personal existence, I must vindicate the adequacy of ontological analysis. Although Brody's moral analysis of the concept of person is deficient, we should not therefore conclude that moral analysis per se is not as well suited to our task as ontological analysis is. To clarify this matter more thoroughly than I did in chapter 5, I examine Daniel Dennett's and Michael Tooley's views on analyzing the concept of person. While Dennett holds that concept to be a normative one, Tooley suggests that its primary analysis must be in its descriptive or ontological use. If there is a significant disagreement between them, deciding the issue in favor of the ontologists will vindicate the use of an ontological instead of a moral theory. Since the personal identity theory I presented in chapter 5 defends both the neocortical-death and the brain-death criteria—a point on which Green and Wikler were vague at the end of their article—I must now supply a moral argument for or against a public policy statement incorporating conditions governing the use of both criteria. To show that human death ought to be considered the death of the person, and that both criteria rest on a sound and common ontology, is not to argue that we ought to use either criterion in declaring death, nor to argue for a particular public policy.

There are thus four claims I must support in order to complete my argument: (1) we ought to reconsider the meaning of human death; (2) we ought to analyze the concept of human death as the death of a person; (3) an ontological approach is better than a normative approach for determining the essential characteristics of persons in the context of an analysis of the concept of human death; and (4) we ought to adopt a public policy statement allowing the use of both the brain-death and the neocortical-death criteria, and remain open to further refinements in our criteria for declaring death. In the final chapter, I assess the prevailing public policy on declaring death, the Uniform Declaration of Death Act, and defend my own public policy recommendation.

Reconsidering the Meaning of Human Death

Throughout this book, I have discussed the implications of the elaborate "death-assaulting" technologies of our era. Without these technologies, total brain death would always lead immediately to organismic death, given the relation of lower-brain functioning to the functioning of the lungs; conversely, cessation of heart or lung functioning would lead immediately to brain death. For most of us the only anomaly—a morally troublesome one—is neocortical death, which does not necessarily lead to organismic failure. Nor, for that matter, do persistent vegetative states which result from other patterns of brain destruction. Patients in persistent vegetative states are, as a rule, not dying; hence, they pose a real dilemma. Since passive euthanasia is essentially a policy for allowing the terminally ill to die, we may consider euthanasia for patients in persistent vegetative states only because the rationale typically appealed to in such cases seems appropriate: remaining alive is no longer of value to the patient. But that rationale addresses the unacceptable quality of the terminally ill patient's experiences—not the fact that a patient no longer experiences at all. Even the usual rationale therefore has only marginal relevance in cases of persistent vegetative states. We must therefore inquire about the status and management of such patients. Is there reason, particularly since we now associate death with the absence of brain function, for considering these patients dead because they lack the capacity for consciousness, and thus lack any brain functions that are essentially significant to human existence? Do these patients fail to fit into existing policy, thus requiring us to fashion a policy specific to them? In what follows, I focus on neocortical death because of the relative clarity of this situation compared to other persistent vegetative states. Our understanding of the many circumstances of brain damage that result in truly *persistent* vegetative states, and our ability to confirm that a patient is in such a state, are limited. But our medical or scientific inabilities have no impact on the adequacy of our concept of human death.

Why is neocortical death a morally troublesome case, causing us to conclude that a redefinition of human death is morally required? In the case of the brain-dead, it can be argued that death-assaulting technologies interfere with nature's dictate that the integrated functioning of the organism should cease. In the case of the neocortically dead, we cannot appeal to the dictates of nature, for nature dictates nothing—unless we leave the neocortically dead alone and let nature take its course, a decision many find morally objectionable. Since the situation of neocortical death is detrimental to the well-being of the living and fruitless for the patient, some believe that the life status of the neocortically dead ought to be carefully considered. We must show that the spontaneity of heart and lung functioning is no longer to be regarded as a sign of life. The point of Jonas's argument is that nonspontaneity is not an issue. That spontaneity should not be an issue in some cases must be decided on the basis of the common conceptual commitment underlying the brain-death and neocortical-death criteria. In the case of brain death, if nonspontaneity is not an issue, then permanent unconsciousness determines that the brain-dead are dead. Since the neocortically dead are also permanently unconscious, we must likewise rethink the meaning of consciousness in relation to them.

Do these reasons concern only the worthlessness of the patient's situation to herself and to others? The quick reply is that the brain-dead and the neocortically dead are not persons any more, and that this change in status ought to be regarded as the death of the human being. But this reply works only if we can defend an analysis of the concept of human death as the death of the person. The claims that we ought to reconsider the meaning of human death and that we ought to analyze the concept of human death as the death of the person are closely connected. In order to complete my defense of the first, I must defend the second, which is central to a full justification of both the brain-death and the neocortical-death criteria.

Human Death as the Death of the Person

If I can show that we ought to analyze the concept of human death as the death of the person, then I will have completed my argument that we ought to redefine human death. The full claim to be defended is this: for the purpose of determining what constitutes the death of a human being, we must consider the conditions of existence and nonexistence of persons. Becker and Jonas were unwilling to consider a permanently unconscious individual dead because of the presence of integrated organic functioning, even if mechanically sustained. Michael Tooley shares the view that the death of a human being is the death of an organism. He maintains that we may, with complete moral assurance, kill the brain-dead and the neocortically dead (because one is killing merely the human organism), but that we may not regard persons in either category as dead beforehand.[2] By contrast, I claim that any integrated organismic functioning concomitant with the permanent absence of consciousness is irrelevant to the decision that the human being is alive or dead. The death of a human being should be construed as the death of the person.

If such acts as turning off a respirator supporting a brain-dead patient or killing a neocortically dead patient are morally inconsequential, as Tooley claims, how can the bare continuation of organismic function provide any moral reason for retaining the concept of human death as the death of the human organism? Tooley views the human being as the unity of personal and organismic life with a disjunctive capacity for life. Hoffman views the human being as the same unity, yet argues that it has a conjunctive capacity for life. Tooley supports his position along lines that echo the policy statement issued by the President's Commission:

> The concept of being a *living* thing is a *general* biological concept, applicable to all species, both plant and animal. The concept of death, however, is simply the concept of the cessation

of life. So just as the concept of being a living thing is a general concept that applies to individuals belonging to all species, the same must be true of the concept of death. But this means that if those processes, such as growth, and repair and reproduction of parts, which characterize living things in general, are still going on in a human organism, then that organism cannot properly be characterized as dead, *unless* it can be argued that it is not enough that such processes go on: they must also be sustained by the organism without artificial assistance. But it seems clear that this cannot be plausibly maintained, since it would imply, for example that humans who are otherwise normal, but who cannot survive without artificial help, are not alive.[3]

Tooley accuses his opposition of the confused view that brain death "is an acceptable criterion for the death of a human organism" (65). As we saw in chapter 2, some of the participants in the redefinition debate maintain that both the traditional and the brain-death criteria are heart-centered—a view that cannot be upheld. As I will show in chapter 7, the President's Commission articulates two versions of the whole-brain formulation of human death. Each assumes that the criteria we would use to determine death of the human organism as a whole will reflect the occurrence of the death of the whole brain. In this assumption, each formulation errs. Tooley is right if he is saying that the criteria for determining the death of a human organism are not also criteria for diagnosing whole-brain death. He is equally right if he is arguing the converse—that brain death does not entail organismic death in the sense of the permanent cessation of spontaneous heart function. The more important view—one that Tooley rejects in favor of what I call "the unity of living things" view—is that since the death of the person can occur before organismic failure, the death of the person should be considered the death of the human being.

Since Tooley sets out to show that we are dealing with a living human organism, he must be using the terms *human being* and *human organism* interchangeably. (In my own analysis, I use *human being* to refer to the kind of entity in question, and *person* and *organism* to reflect the two central aspects of its functioning—namely, consciousness and the integrated bodily functioning promoted by the heart and lungs.) Our difference in terminology is of no real consequence. Tooley's argument merely gives compelling reason for concluding that organismic death has not occurred in the case of either the neocortically dead or the respirator-supported brain-dead. His argument holds up only if his perspective on the unity of living things can be upheld. I assume here that demonstrating the necessity of a person-centered conception of human death will undermine the focus on the unity of living things.

A CONTRACTARIAN METHODOLOGY

In determining how we ought to regard the human being for the purpose of defining human death, we must be responsive to the nature of the problem we are addressing. This determination must be viewed as a public policy choice—indeed, as the most basic public policy choice we face in the redefinition debate. Since our end is the articulation of a public policy about the criteria for declaring persons dead, and since any such decision requires a conceptual framework to support those criteria, our public policy choices have many levels and include fundamental philosophical decisions. At the deepest level of the debate, we must choose one conceptual framework—personal or organismic—over the other. If it is acceptable to view this as a public policy choice, it is a choice that will have strong moral overtones: our highest concern must be to provide for the most appropriate and respectful treatment of human beings of different ontological status. We need a rational methodology to assist us in selecting among alternative public policies that present difficult ethical decisions. I shall attempt a practical justification of my policy choice in the form of a hypothetical contractarian argument.

It is useful to begin by determining what we expect of our chosen methodology. Certainly it must foster rational choice. That is, it must promote the fullest possible appreciation of the diverse aspects of the problem (social, legal, economic, philosophical, religious, and ethical); it must lead us to generate several policy options; and it must enable us to weigh the impacts of these diverse options. Any methodology that did not meet all three requirements would fail to foster rational choice. In addition, our methodology must be accessible to persons of various backgrounds. As I argue in chapter 7, there is a public education problem connected with the redefinition issue. An ethical methodology enabling as many people as possible to think constructively about the central moral dilemmas associated with redefinition must be favored over one that is abstruse or highly technical. The methodology I employ has long been developed and refined, and has received a highly technical and sometimes abstruse discussion in contemporary philosophical literature, but it can nonetheless be conveyed straightforwardly to persons with no extensive schooling in ethical theory. The defense of this methodology as an adequate ethical theory leads us into a philosophical thicket, and I leave this discussion to such writers as David Gauthier, Jan Narveson, Richmond Campbell, and others.

The method, simply conveyed, is this: what two people would contract to do in relation to one another, as long as their contract is made under circumstances of perfect mutuality, would be morally acceptable to each of them. A morally justified rule or policy choice must be one they would agree to in a fair bargain in which they were pursuing mutual advantage. This is a necessary but not a sufficient condition of a morally justified rule or policy. The words "perfect mutuality" and "fair bargain" obviously bear a very heavy burden here. What conditions guarantee perfect mutuality and a fair bargain? Perfect mutuality need not mean that each person seeks or obtains the same end. Rather, it concerns the relationship between their individual objectives and the result they work out between them; one's interests are as much a force in that result as the other's, and the result probably will not serve either set of interests perfectly.

The purpose of the contract is to arrive at a solution to a joint problem, a solution that will satisfy each person because it succeeds in harmonizing their interests—the sort of outcome that each person realizes in advance is optimal for both, given the nature of the problem. That is, each realizes in advance that the best she can hope for is not the full serving of her own interests, because both sets of interests cannot be served fully. Given their common concern to agree on a rule or policy governing their interactions, mutuality constrains them to strike a bargain that harmonizes their interests, rather than to pursue the domination of one another's interests. To say that the contract is the result of a fair bargain presupposes certain features of the contractors: each must be equally and adequately informed, competent to enter into the bargaining situation, and capable of engaging rationally in the bargaining process. Everyone may not always exhibit these features, but if two persons were so situated, any contract they would strike would be morally acceptable to both. Their willingness to enter into the contract means that each views it as sufficiently protective of her interests, and that each accepts the obligations it places upon her in relation to others. While each has sought maximally to serve her own interests, she has done so under the constraint that the other is seeking to do the same. Such a mutual constraint forces them to a higher, or at least a different, ground despite differing and to some degree incompatible interests. On that ground, a harmonious balancing of interests occurs.

Our question concerns a public policy choice, not the formation of a contract between two individuals, but if we can demonstrate that it would be in everyone's interest to contract in a particular way—namely, to adopt the personal rather than the organismic concept of human death—then the social policy in question would have strong moral justification. Actual contracts are not at issue here, only hypothetical ones. To suggest that it would be in everyone's interest to contract in a particular way does not mean that they would do so if they had the chance. We are assuming an idealized contractual situation in which all parties to the contract are fully informed, competent, and rational. Since the conditions governing the choices people actually make vary widely from our ideal, I speak not about the contract people would form, only about the one they ought to form.

We must determine which of the two policy choices it would be in everyone's interest to follow. Our argument must address two questions: first, we must ask of each policy whether it would be in everyone's interest to follow it; second, recognizing that we cannot all agree on a concept of human death, we must ask whether a harmonizing of interests is possible with either concept of human death. We must first determine what those central interests are. The decision we make will have the morally important consequence of drawing the boundary between life and death. The point at which that line is drawn will have powerful impact on our rights and obligations in relation to one another. To make a decision, we must entertain as thoroughly as possible the two scenarios in question: continuing to regard the human being as alive as long as its orga- nismic functions persist, even if consciousness is forever absent; and regarding the human being as alive only as long as a capacity for consciousness is retained.[4]

We can agree that consciousness per se (the most conservative criterion for the preservation of personal identity, and the only one that is defensible) is a sufficient sign of the continuation of a personal existence. Such an agreement allows us to avoid the necessity of making any qualitative and quantitative determinations about the presence or absence of life. We may on this conservative basis classi- fy as persons those individuals whose lives we would regard as less than worth living, but since we do not want to make such judgments on another's behalf, we agree that no one will make them about anyone. We are agreed, then, that as long as consciousness persists, the person survives; and as long as the person survives, the human being is alive. We must now decide whether we should adopt this person-oriented concept of human death, knowing that some human beings will thus be considered dead even though they would not according to the organismic concept we have held exclusively until now. The policy we choose will be a statement that brings into a morally acceptable balance what we want for ourselves and what we are willing to provide for others; on that basis we can make a decision about the entitlements and obligations each of us is to have. These are the simplest terms—although they are not simple—in which to think about the issue.

THE APPLICATION

The most straightforward approach to determining a contrac- tually based agreement is to consider what contract would be in everyone's interest for the management of Jones, a hypothetical, permanently insentient individual in a persistent vegetative state. What rights should Jones have? What obligations should others have to her? If the organismic perspective on human life is adopted, then Jones must not be declared dead, since her heart and lungs continue to function spontaneously. Recent developments in medical tech- nology, in particular the perfecting of elaborate support systems, generate increasing numbers of patients who do not fulfill the traditional criteria for death, yet who are irreversibly comatose. These patients are either brain-dead or in persistent vegetative states. In either case, they are permanently insentient.

Those in persistent vegetative states pose special concerns. While our society has come to consider brain death an appropriate basis upon which to declare the death of a human being, most of us cannot dominate our feelings about the spontaneous functioning of the heart and lungs. Such functioning has always been central to our concept of life, and it is difficult to alter our perception of their importance. But we must consider that Jones represents a burden to a health care facility and health care professionals. Useless ministrations to Jones detract from the medical staff's ability to give maximal care to others, and the involved yet fruitless care they must provide her compromises their emotional well-being. Most important, Jones's maintenance is clearly of no value to Jones, who is indifferent to the care she receives.

How should we respond to Jones's situation? We might decide that rather than being considered dead already, she ought to be allowed to die. But this choice is difficult, for Jones is not dying. From the broader perspective of public policy, we do not have an alternative policy to handle the situation Jones presents. If we were to allow her to die, it would not be in the usual way of withdrawing extraordinary treatments or support systems, but in the unusual way of failing to provide fluids and nourishment. So it would not be properly described as allowing Jones to die, but as causing Jones's death. Since Jones is not dying, we must develop a rationale for ceasing ordinary treatment in such nonterminal cases, making certain to avoid any slippery slopes in the policy we recommend. Genuine dilemmas will occur whatever policy we adopt. A passive euthanasia approach would have to be greatly redesigned and be specified to handle persistent vegetative state cases. Since most of us find the killing of a human being problematic under any circumstances, an active euthanasia approach would require an argument for justified killing in such cases (contrary to Tooley, who finds killing unproblematic under these circumstances). A declaration-of-death approach will at least initially cause considerable discomfort and repugnance for many. No policy solution obviously recommends itself.

Before we settle on one of these policy alternatives for patients like Jones, we must consider other factors as well. The worthless and costly medical ministrations that Jones requires are a potentially crushing financial burden for her family. Society at large pays for Jones's care, either indirectly, through increased insurance rates, or directly, through subsidies for her care. Since her lifespan is indeterminate, it is conceivable that her care may drain her family of all financial resources. The economic realities of Jones's situation cannot be ignored. Nor can another social reality: if Jones has declared herself an organ donor, organ removal and transplantation would have a far greater chance of success if the remaining organismic functions were not considered signs of life. Thus, if she were declared dead prior to the cessation of integrated organismic functioning, others might be enabled to live full lives—an option Jones no longer has.

Further, a concept of death that sees Jones as still alive exacerbates the emotional drain on her loved ones. A person-centered concept of death would alleviate their extended false hopes, the diffusion of their ability to redirect their lives in Jones's absence because she is not yet dead, and the feelings of guilt that would attend a euthanasia decision. Such cases are agonizingly difficult to decide not only for loved ones but for medical professionals. To declare someone dead, rather than to decide that she ought to be allowed to die, clarifies the situation and avoids the wrenching dilemmas for the family and care-givers that the euthanasia option would create. While avoiding ethical dilemmas is no justification for redefining death in this way, avoiding *unnecessary* ethical dilemmas is.

Adding an important legal consideration, let us suppose that Jones's situation resulted from an assault on her life. She has clearly suffered a harm equivalent to that sustained by someone rendered brain-dead under the same circumstances; Jones's loved ones have suffered both an equivalent loss and at least an equal harm—a harm we would expect to increase proportionately to the length of her "survival" in a persistent vegetative state. Not to consider these harms and losses morally equivalent would require elaborate moral gymnastics. For the law to declare Jones dead if she is brain-dead as the result of an assault, but not if she is neocortically dead from the same cause, is a serious inconsistency. Justice cannot be served unless the two cases are acknowledged to be equivalent crimes against victims and their survivors, and therefore subject to the same legal penalty.

The legal and social functions following upon a death are postponed unless we regard Jones as dead. This has no implication for Jones herself, but it has dramatic implications for her survivors. If she is not declared dead, her will cannot be executed, and her estate is not accessible to those who might need it. If she is not dead, the appropriate redirection of the lives of the survivors cannot begin. Their lives are in a limbo that parallels that of Jones's suspended life.

Such reorganizing behaviors are appropriate for the survivors, given Jones's circumstances. She is in an important sense gone, but unless she is regarded as dead, she still exerts the same moral and legal hold on loved ones, as well as on society. Her rights, and the obligations of others to her, have not yet undergone the dramatic alteration we associate with someone's death. Nonetheless, the obligations of survivors and the rights still accorded to Jones bear no connection to any discernible interests on her part. It is difficult to make the case that someone has an obligation to do something for someone who has no discernible interest in the act.

It would not be in anyone's interest to contract in such a manner that Jones would still be considered living. Whether she is considered alive is of no direct consequence to her. She would suffer no loss were we to shift to a personal conception of death. In a broader sense, however, the matter is of consequence to Jones because she would probably wish to spare her family undue economic and emotional distress, and to have them reorganize their lives as soon as possible. Jones would thus favor a person-centered concept of death on these grounds. The only reason Jones might want to be regarded and treated as a living being is that she may have held a philosophical or religious conviction that requires this definition. But this difficulty can be managed by an appropriately worded public policy statement, as I show in chapter 7. Beyond this, there is no reason for us to think that we ought to retain the organismic focus on the human in determining death.

The interests of others would be best served if they were to hold only productive obligations to Jones. One way to determine the extent of those obligations is to decide exactly what Jones's rights are under the circumstances. But this is not an easy matter. In the formula Joel Feinberg recommends, rights and interests have an important link. Not all interests constitute a basis for rights. Clearly, everyone has an interest in being happy, but not necessarily a right to be happy. We have an interest in having shelter, and it is at least arguable that we have a right to that shelter even if we cannot secure it on our own. We have an interest in being helped in times of physical or emotional trouble, and a right to such help from those individuals who have an obligation to provide it to us. Some interests ground rights claims; and some rights claims ground obligation claims. If we can determine Jones's rights, we will have a basis for deciding whether someone has certain obligations to her, since she cannot secure her rights on her own. Clearly, no one would have an interest in contracting for virtually unlimited obligations to Jones. However, if we are legally, socially, and economically committed to her—commitments the organismic concept of death seems to encourage—then our obligations to her are virtually unbounded. But Jones's rights, being a function of her interests, are limited. As I suggested above, Jones has an interest in the well-being of those who survive her; by an argument in chapter 4, Jones also has an interest in being treated respectfully. But the obligations that these rights yield have nothing in common with those we have to Jones if we assume that the death of the human being is the death of an organism.

The contractual approach reminds us that our choice of focus results in an arrangement of rights and obligations, and that we must ask which arrangement better harmonizes the many interests involved. It would not be in anyone's interest to regard Jones as still living. Our choice, then, is to view the human being as a person for the purpose of declaring death; this policy deprives the patient of nothing, while the opposite policy gains nothing for the patient. The former policy also furthers the interests of those who are called upon to support the patient. The contractual approach thus enables us to decide how to manage a class of cases which would otherwise be handled on a case by case basis, probably inconsistently, thereby increasing the ethical agonizing that inevitably attends such situations. Our methodology enables us to arrive at a morally acceptable clarification and balancing of interests and needs, apart from the trauma and turmoil that actual situations unavoidably create.

It might be objected that my focus on Jones's case has led me to overlook important larger questions. How can we move from discussing one case to a conclusion that we should, as a general policy, construe human death as the death of a person, committing ourselves to the claim that all patients in persistent vegetative states are dead? In particular, how can we maintain that this policy choice would harmonize interests better than would a euthanasia policy? And how would the management of such cases be conducted?

Euthanasia policies entail euthanasia choices in particular cases. Traditionally, euthanasia has been viewed as an option for a terminally ill patient whose quality of life has reached such an abysmally low ebb that pain can no longer be managed. In short, an individual's life has become only a source of agony for her, and considerations of mercy compel us to allow her to die. I refer here to passive euthanasia. It cannot be argued either that life has become a source of agony for the patient in a persistent vegetative state, or that our allowing life to end in such a case is merciful. Hence, the standard defenses of passive euthanasia decisions are not helpful. We must defend allowing the patient to die solely on the grounds that her life has become worthless to her. While such arguments are part of passive euthanasia discussions, the matter is complicated by the fact that the typical patient in a persistent vegetative state is not dying. There is no naturally occurring disease process that we shall no longer oppose. Instead, we must withdraw normal supports, thereby promoting dehydration, malnourishment, and starvation.

While such a course of action does not cause the nonsentient patient any discomfort, it is not aesthetically tolerable for most of us. More important, it fails to treat the patient with dignity and dishonors the sensibilities of the survivors, who must stand by and wait for the end to occur. During this time, the patient is still a drain on medical resources and a source of stress for medical care-givers. If we are to pursue a euthanasia policy here, it would seem preferable to pursue one of active rather than passive euthanasia. In either case, a serious difficulty arises for public policy. If the argument for terminating the lives of patients in persistent vegetative states rests on claims about the worthlessness of life for the patient—as it must—the slippery slope objection is much stronger than it would be to a policy permitting the declaration of death.

Consider the March 1986 ruling of the AMA's Council on Ethical and Judicial Affairs, that all supports, including feeding and hydration tubes, may be withdrawn from patients with persistent vegetative status. The intent of this ruling is to honor the wishes of the patient or family, and to allow the patient to die with dignity, on the apparent ground that continuing to live is not worthwhile for her even though her death is not imminent. This radical departure from present practice openly creates a new category of patients: those who can be caused to die because their life is no longer worth living. While the import of living wills and death-with-dignity legislation has been to disallow extraordinary life-prolonging interventions that retard a dying process already underway, the AMA ruling allows for the causing—and therefore the hastening—of death. Since the justification for causing death is the worthlessness of continued existence, the ruling positions us alarmingly close to hazardous slopes. The AMA ruling is not an extension of a euthanasia policy, then, but something entirely new.

By contrast, the policy that treats permanent nonsentience as the ground for declaring death, and allows only the demonstrable permanent absence of the capacity for consciousness to qualify as permanent nonsentience, disallows slippery slope objections. Only those for whom there is no experienced quality of life—and not those for whom life has become worthless—would be candidates for a declaration of death. Further, the adoption of a euthanasia policy legitimates the claim that one does a lesser harm, or inflicts a lesser loss, by rendering a person neocortically dead rather than brain-dead—a point that cannot be sustained. A policy of redefinition steers clear of such an outcome.

If my argument here is compelling, our public policy regarding human death ought to involve a change in our orientation to the human being. Human death should be regarded as a person-centered occurrence. Since permanent unconsciousness is the sign of personal death, the brain-death and the neocortical-death criteria are consistent with this concept. Treating such individuals as living human beings must be disallowed on the grounds that there is no moral cost to them in our considering them dead, and high moral cost to others in our considering them alive.

How shall we manage patients who are demonstrably in persistent vegetative states, once we have declared them dead? The status we assign them, coupled with their retention of spontaneous organismic functioning, present us with the anomaly of the breathing corpse. From an emotional perspective, the situation is pure paradox. Between the declaration of death and preparation for cremation or burial, what should the sequence of actions be? While the removal of feeding tubes will eventually result in organismic cessation, the corpse will meanwhile continue to strain medical resources and care-givers needlessly, and to challenge the sensibilities and well-being of both care-givers and loved ones as long as the organismic shut-down is occurring. From a contractual perspective, some active means of promoting organismic cessation is preferable to the removal of feeding tubes. This active means, to be aesthetically tolerable, must be a simple act with an immediate result—for example, an injection of potassium chloride. Of course, only one who is entirely comfortable with this act should be asked to perform it.

When a patient in a persistent vegetative state is to be an organ donor, the sequence of actions must be different, just as it is now when a brain-dead donor is maintained on a respirator until the organ is removed. Neither the passive withdrawal of feeding tubes nor the active injection of potassium chloride would promote the patient's declared interest in being an organ donor or the recipient's interest in receiving a viable organ. Organ removal itself will be the proximate cause of organismic cessation. Again, the sensitivities of the medical personnel asked to participate in organ removal must be accommodated.

A contractarian approach provides telling moral reasons for regarding human death as the death of the person, and guides us in the central decisions concerning the management of patients in persistent vegetative states after death has been declared. The moral argument supporting the decision that the death of the person constitutes human death supports the whole project of redefinition. If human death is the death of the person, and if heart and lung criteria are inadequate indicators of whether personal status is retained in many cases, we must determine what functions are essential to existence as a person, locate these functions in the human organism, and devise tests to determine if the capacity for these functions persists.

But what is the better approach to determining which functions are essential to existence as a person? That is, what sort of analysis is more useful for analyzing the concept of person? There is a basic division between those who take the concept to be a descriptive one and those who consider it a normative one, to be sorted out by moral and not by ontological analysis. In the context of a concern with human death, understood as the death of the person, we must decide whether moral or ontological analysis is more defensible.

The Ontological Approach to the Conditions of Personal Existence

Daniel Dennett claims that even though the concept of person consists of a metaphysical notion and a moral notion, it is an "inescapably normative" concept. Dennett's central argument defines six necessary conditions of moral personhood which he says are not also sufficient for moral personhood because "the concept of person is . . . inescapably normative."[5] He concludes with this view:

> Now finally, why are we not in a position to claim that these necessary conditions of moral personhood are also sufficient? Simply because the concept of person is, I have tried to show, inescapably normative. Human beings or other entities can only aspire to being approximations of the ideal, and there can be no way to set a "passing grade" that is not arbitrary. Were the six conditions (strictly interpreted) considered sufficient they would not ensure that any actual entity was a person, for nothing would ever fulfill them. The moral notion of a person and the metaphysical notion of a person are not separate and distinct concepts but just two different and unstable resting points on the same continuum. This relativity infects the satisfaction of conditions of personhood at every level (285).

Contrary to Dennett's claim that the moral and metaphysical notions of person are different and shifting points on a common continuum, I shall argue that our concept of person functions descriptively and normatively, and that the moral uses of the term must be justified by descriptive analysis. The considerations underlying the choice of a particular concept of human death must take into account our metaphysical or descriptive notion of person. This conclusion is lent support by the fact that each of the moral approaches to defending a particular concept of human death surveyed in chapter 4 engages in nonmoral or descriptive analysis of the concept of person. Brody's argument consists of moral and ontological claims ineffectively combined. While Hoffman's central question is a normative one, his analysis of the concepts of person and of human death is an exercise in descriptive metaphysics. Veatch's argument is an elaborate combination of the ontological and the moral, in which he derives ontological conclusions from normative premises.

Dennett begins by observing that "we recognize conditions that exempt human beings from personhood, or at least some very important elements of personhood. For instance, infant human beings, mentally defective human beings, and human beings declared insane by licensed psychiatrists are denied personhood, or at any rate crucial elements of personhood" (267). Certainly we do not take the class of human beings and the class of persons to be coextensive; some humans are not persons because they lack "important elements of personhood." The human beings Dennett has in mind are those whom we cannot (for a variety of reasons) consider responsible for their behavior. They are thus not persons in the complete moral sense in which we commonly use the term. Since we apply the concept of person to some and withhold it from others, Dennett says, "one might well hope that such an important concept . . . would have clearly formulatable necessary and sufficient conditions for ascription" (267).

It is difficult to articulate any such set of necessary and sufficient conditions, however, because the concept of person has a double aspect: "Roughly, there seem to be two notions intertwined here, which we may call the moral notion and the metaphysical notion" (268). Here Dennett states his central puzzle:

> Does the metaphysical notion—roughly, the notion of an intelligent, conscious, feeling agent—coincide with the moral notion—roughly, the notion of an agent who is accountable, or who has both rights and responsibilities? Or is it merely that

being a person in the metaphysical sense is a necessary but not sufficient condition of being a person in the moral sense? Is being an entity to which states of consciousness or self-conscious-ness are ascribed *the same* as being an end-in-oneself, or is it merely one precondition? (268).

Dennett is asking what the relation is between being a person in the metaphysical sense and being a person in the moral sense. He defends this distinction on the basis of this example: "When we declare a man insane we cease treating him as accountable, and we deny him most rights, but still our interactions with him are virtually indistinguishable from normal personal interactions unless he is very far gone in madness indeed. In one sense of 'person,' it seems, we continue to treat and view him as a person" (269).

This example shows, for Dennett, that within the concept of person are the two distinct notions of person he has delineated. Metaphysical personhood, he adds, is "a necessary condition of moral personhood" (269). Granting Dennett's distinction on the basis of his example, to say that the metaphysical sense of being a person is a necessary condition of the moral sense means that the conditions of the former must be met if an entity is to fulfill the latter. However, the fulfillment of the metaphysical conditions will not guarantee that one is a person in the moral sense. Dennett next discusses six descriptors of persons, each of which he takes to be a necessary condition of moral personhood. He is providing six conditions of metaphysical personhood, each of which is necessary for moral personhood and no combination of which is sufficient for moral personhood. We need not review Dennett's discussion of the six conditions of metaphysical personhood, but we must consider his view that an entity never fulfills any of these conditions to perfection. Whenever one ascribes the concept of person to an entity, one assumes that the entity fulfills one or more of these conditions to some extent. This is Dennett's reason for talking of the "inescapably normative" character of the concept of person. If this is all he means, then he is not arguing that the concept of person requires a moral rather than a nonmoral analysis. Indeed, one can agree with Dennett so far and yet conclude that ontological analysis is the most promising means of clarifying our concept of person. That is, one can agree that the concept is "inescapably normative" and that metaphysical personhood is a necessary condition for moral person-hood. But we must resist this point of Dennett's analysis: "The moral notion of a person and the metaphysical notion of a person are not separate and distinct concepts but just two different and unstable resting points on the same continuum" (285).

If consciousness is the sine qua non of metaphysical personhood, then one may have such personhood without having moral person-hood, because one is no longer considered a possessor of rights or responsibilities; an example would be a hardened criminal about to be executed. We clearly have two very different concepts of person in such a case. While there is usually a correspondence between meta-physical and moral personhood, the correlation is not a necessary one.

A concern about analyzing the meaning of the concept of human death as the death of a person, however, is a concern with a termi-nus. It is not a question about the degree to which a human is still a person, but rather one about the conditions that must obtain for her to have ceased being a person. Our problem is to determine the terminus of the continuum, not some point along it. It is in-comprehensible to suppose, as Dennett does, that there is only one continuum along which both metaphysical and moral changes are charted. The concept of the continuum is acceptable, because per-sons do expand and diminish in both metaphysical and moral status throughout their lives. Our judgments about changes in moral status are commonly justified, however, by describing how the individual has changed in the conditions of metaphysical personhood. Hence, the easier picture to adopt is of two continua—one along which we might chart an individual's metaphysical personhood, the other along which we might represent her moral personhood. As I sug-gested earlier, changes in one aspect will usually correspond with changes in the other, but this need not be the case. A further reason for maintaining that the metaphysical and moral are two distinct though importantly related concepts of person is that the latter has an aspect of conferral that the former does not. We may, for example, deny that the hardened criminal has moral personhood, but not that he has metaphysical personhood. Hence, Dennett's picture of a single continuum along which the two concepts of person range must be rejected.

The notion of two continua leads us to appreciate the heuristic role of moral considerations in the analysis of our concept of person. Michael Tooley writes:

> It seems advisable to treat the term "person" as a purely descriptive term, rather than as one whose definition involves moral concepts. For this appears to be the way the term "person" is ordinarily construed. Second, however, it seems desirable that the descriptive content assigned to the term "person" be guided by moral considerations, in order to have a term that can play a certain, very important role in the discussion of moral issues.[6]

Since moral appeals to rights and quality of life are notoriously open to objection, we should use moral considerations not as the basis for our analysis but as a guide in framing that analysis so that it will be maximally useful in resolving the conceptual problem at hand. Dennett's argument is flawed in that it analyzes the concept of person as a single normative concept. It thereby obscures this concept in its most usual descriptive use, and fails to reflect that we commonly and most easily defend conclusions about moral personhood by appeal to features of metaphysical personhood.

Redefining Death

I have tried to lay the philosophical footings for declaring brain-dead and neocortically dead individuals dead. By means of a contractarian argument, I have defended the change in our concept of human death that each of these practices requires. Ontological analysis is the most suitable philosophical tool for examining our notion of the death of a person. My analysis helps us specify the conditions under which a person ceases to exist, and as a result we can see that the onset of permanent unconsciousness is a person's death.

In chapter 5, I surveyed Green and Wikler's moral argument supporting the use of the brain-death criterion. Their ontological argument shows that the death of a person's brain is that person's death. Their moral argument defends the use of the brain-death criterion. Not only are brain-dead persons dead, but we ought to declare them dead.

At this stage in the discussion, I must provide my own moral argument for supplementing the traditional and brain-death criteria with the neocortical-death criterion. Such an argument must take into account the wide range of issues any public policy decision must address. What sorts of social, moral, legal, religious, political, and economic consequences might this criterion generate? Certainly its use will be confusing, and possibly damaging, to those who are unable to shed their attachment to the residual spontaneous functioning of the heart and lungs as signs of life. Is our debt to them greater than it was to those who opposed the brain-death criterion? Reluctantly, I must say that I think our debt *is* greater here. Our immediate goal mut be to improve public comprehension of all that is at issue, to improve people's ability to confront rationally situations of death and dying. Although I have concluded that the brain-death and the neocortical-death criteria share a solid ontological footing, I cannot conclude simply on that account that the latter ought to be put into use immediately. Without public education, we risk substantial personal trauma to some of the living. From a contractual point of view, it might initially appear that the use of the neocortical-death criterion should not be mandated, but I will argue that eventually it should. It might be objected that a public policy mandating the use of any particular criterion will inevitably force some in our society to live with what they consider the rationally indefensible views of others, and that any mandate is prejudicial to those who desire the use of a specific criterion in their own case.

Is there a better way to serve justice in this matter than simply gearing up for public education and hoping for change in the future? A reasonable interim policy might be the best long-range policy as well—to allow for personal choice in the matter through an appropriate legal mechanism. I develop such a policy recommendation in the next chapter. Since persistent vegetative states arise from a variety of conditions of brain destruction, another implication of my argument is that we must remain open to further refinements in our criteria for declaring death. The issues surrounding the use of new criteria will be empirical ones; we will have to demonstrate that other patterns of brain destruction entail permanent unconsciousness, and that we have adequate operational tests to detect those patterns. Only then will we be in a position to refine further our criteria for declaring death. But these are problems for the medically minded, not the philosophically minded. I hope that the necessary philosophical work has been completed.

chapter 7

Public Policy
Considerations

In July of 1981, the President's Commission for the Study of Ethical Problems in Medicine and Biomedical and Behavioral Research published *Defining Death: A Report on the Medical, Legal, and Ethical Issues in the Determination of Death*. In this chapter, I examine its theoretical arguments and evaluate its central policy statement, the Uniform Declaration of Death Act, with reference to the conceptual framework I have defended in the previous six chapters. In the final section, I recommend an alternative policy statement. In analyzing the commission's report, we must assess both the supporting theoretical argument and the central policy statement itself.

The Theoretical Argument

WHOLE-BRAIN FORMULATIONS OF DEATH

In its third chapter, the commission reviews three kinds of formulations of the meaning of death—two whole-brain, two higher-brain, and two nonbrain formulations—and considers the policy consequences of each. The commission prefaces this discussion with the following claim: "The Commission has not found it necessary to resolve all of the differences among the leading concepts of death because these views all yield interpretations consistent with the recommended statute."[1] As I have argued, the difference in the concepts of human death supporting the traditional and the brain-death criteria is so substantial that our conceptual choice legitimates the use of quite different criteria. There is no way to reconcile the brain-death criterion with the concept of death underlying the traditional criteria, though the reverse is not true: someone who is dead according to the traditional criteria will, within ten or fifteen minutes, also be dead in terms of the brain-death criterion. Even if we adopt the death-of-the-person concept, we can still use the traditional criteria in certain clearly definable cases. Further, I have argued that the death-of-the-person view provides an adequate theoretical basis for both the brain-death and the neocortical-death criteria. Since the commission considers that an upper-brain criterion like the neocortical-death criterion would involve a dramatic shift in our concept of death (7), it cannot argue that an upper-brain-death-oriented conception of death is consistent with an organismic concept, or with the concept that the commission assumes the traditional and the brain-death criteria share. The passage just quoted is therefore puzzling.

The commission notes that there are two whole-brain formulations, which are "mirror images" of each other; they are complementary and hence "enrich [our] understanding" (32) of the whole-brain formulation. The first whole-brain formulation claims that death is the irreversible breakdown of "the integrated functioning of the body's major organ systems" (32). Those systems are of course the lungs, the heart, and the brain. The latter is considered central "since it is neither revivable nor replaceable" (32). On this view, the traditional criteria "detected an irreversible cessation of integrated functioning" (33) among the three interdependent systems. The proponents of this formulation further maintain that the brain-death criterion can be used to detect precisely the same breakdown when a respirator is in use.

This formulation generates a host of imponderables. What precisely is meant by "integrated functioning" of the lungs, heart, and brain? What constitutes the "irreversible cessation" of such an integrated system? How is the death of the upper brain related, if at all, to the irreversible cessation of integrated functioning? What is the basis for ruling that nonspontaneity of a particular system's functioning means that there has been an irreversible loss of integrated functioning? And why is the irreversible loss of integrated functioning so essential as to constitute human death?

While the interdependence of the heart, lungs, and brain is clear, the exact relationships among them must be considered. In the situation of brain death, the heart beats spontaneously. The brain stem, now dead, is not responsible for the functioning of the lungs. The lungs still supply oxygenated blood to the heart, but their function is nonspontaneous. In the absence of brain death, the triangle of functions is different only in that the lungs' function is neurologically produced. According to the first whole-brain formulation, the "break" in the integrated system in cases of brain death is an adequate basis for concluding that the integrated functioning of the three major organ systems has been irreversibly lost. The mere continuation of circulation and breathing is not life, then. "When an individual's breathing and circulation lack neurologic integration, he or she is dead" (33). Overlooking for the moment the faulty implication that the heart needs a neural locus of support, we must remember that the neural locus of the lungs' functioning is not in the whole brain but in the brain stem. In a fully functioning human body, the upper brain receives oxygenated blood, of course, but the only part of the brain that contributes to the integrated functioning of the major systems is the brain stem.

There is no reference in the first whole-brain formulation to the significance of the permanent absence of consciousness. The triangle of integrated functioning defined as life by this formulation includes the heart, the lungs, and the brain stem. If a patient is brain-dead and on a respirator, then the neurological piece of the tripartite system (the brain stem) is absent, the integration is broken, and death has occurred. But it must be the permanent absence of consciousness that makes this sort of breakdown of integrated functioning sufficient to be considered death. If someone is considered dead because the loss of integrated functioning of the major organ systems has occurred, then an artificial replacement for one of the system's relevant functions will not change the patient's status. If the heart were replaced by an artificial pump, for example, the patient would still be considered dead, because the functional triangle has been broken and one of its functions must be replaced by a mechanical device. This is a fatal flaw in the first whole-brain formulation. Either the view must be amended such that the irreversible cessation of integrated functioning is not considered death unless consciousness is permanently absent as well, or it must be admitted that this conception of death fails as an adequate *whole*-brain formulation.

The second whole-brain formulation "identifies the functioning of the whole brain as the hallmark of life because the brain is the *regulator* of the body's integration" (32). The first formulation appears to be the view that both the traditional and the brain-death criteria focus on integrated organismic functioning, while the second formulation subsumes both criteria under a neurological, brain-centered concept of death. The commission refers to the second formulation as the "primary organ" (37) version of the whole-brain formulation: the brain is the irreplaceable center of consciousness as well as the body's control center. Hence, its irreversible loss of function is the death of the human being.

Both formulations purport to focus on the integrating and regulatory capacities of the whole brain. As we have seen, however, only the brain stem is involved in the continued integrated functioning of the major organ systems, and only the brain stem is the body's regulator. Brain death involves permanent unconsciousness, a factor that does not figure in either the loss of integrated functioning (the criterion of the first formulation) or the loss of the primary regulatory organ (the criterion of the second). Hence neither formulation should be called a whole-brain formulation.

The commission is marginally critical of both formulations on two grounds. First, it asks whether either the integrating or the regulatory capacity of the brain "is as distinctive as [these formulations] would suggest" (34). Other organ systems are as essential to life as the brain. Admitting that the view of the whole brain in both formulations is an arbitrary choice, the commission defends each on the ground "that this choice overwhelmingly reflects the views of experts and the lay public alike" (35). The commission assumes that the brain is generally viewed as central because of its integrative and regulatory role, and because of the immediate impact of brain death on the status of the organism as a whole. Reliance on consensus or prevailing opinion is a poor justification for any formulation, yet the commission seems to use that very method when the theoretical arguments become confused and apparently faulty.

A second criticism of both formulations is that integrated functioning ceases only when the relevant functions, however supported, have ceased. If the respirator effectively replaces the brain stem, the individual will live as long as the heart and lungs continue to function. The commission chooses to reject this criticism. It maintains that the respirator replaces only the functioning of the intercostal muscles and the diaphragm, not the brain stem itself. If the neural control of these structures is lost through destruction of the brain stem, their functioning must be produced in some other way. The intercostal muscles and the diaphragm must move in certain ways for oxygen to be drawn into the body. Normally, a neural mechanism generates the relevant movements, but if the brain stem is destroyed, a machine must make the movements occur. The muscles and the diaphragm must be manipulated to get the desired result—intake of oxygen, expulsion of carbon dioxide. The respirator works the muscles and the diaphragm just as the brain stem used to, but the commission says we are not replacing a part of the brain stem, only substituting for a muscular function.

A respirator-driven body, the commission says, is not an integrated organism but "a group of artificially maintained subsystems" (35–36). But if we admit that the introduction of some artificial supports can restore integrated functioning, how do we decide which ones accomplish this end and which do not? We need some principled basis for this decision; I would suggest the condition of the capacity for consciousness. The commission apparently shares this insight, for it appeals to the case of the decapitated, artificially maintained body, which it says lacks the "requisites of human life" (36). Such a body exhibits integrated functioning, though without the usual neural locus of respiratory functioning. It does not exhibit the tripartite integrated functioning we associate with most human beings, however. Does the absence of brain life per se ground the claim that this entity lacks the requisites of human life? I have already argued that the absence of brain-stem life per se cannot deprive someone of the crucial requisite for human life; if it did, an artificial heart would have the same consequence. It must be the absence of consciousness that is the crucial requisite of human life, though the commission never says this. Death is the loss of a cluster of attributes, we are told. (There is safety in clusters). The commission writes: "While it is valuable to test public policies against basic conceptions of death, philosophical refinement beyond a certain point may not be necessary" (36).

Obviously, the commission feels no obligation either to refine further and defend the concept of whole-brain death as an adequate formulation of death, or to address the incompatibility of two ways of viewing the traditional and the brain-death criteria in relation to a particular concept of human death. The commission ultimately accepts a whole-brain formulation of death on the basis of a consensual rather than a theoretical argument. But surely the commission must defend its claim that the need for "philosophical refinement" extends no further than the articulation of the two whole-brain formulations—neither of which accounts for the element of permanent unconsciousness in the decision that the individual is dead. As the two formulations read, the loss of the integrative and regulatory capacities could occur in the presence of consciousness; these are thus whole-brain formulations in name only, and brain-stem formulations in deed.

The commission sees no problem with combining the two formulations into a unified conception of death: "Further effort to search for a conceptual 'definition' of death is not required for the purpose of public policy because, separately or together, the 'whole brain' formulations provide a theory that is sufficiently precise, concise and widely acceptable" (36). At the time the Uniform Declaration of Death Act was written, the commission had the luxury of knowing that medical and lay opinion was overwhelmingly in favor of the whole-brain conception of death. While this consensus may have required a long and difficult acceptance process for the public, the time of controversy had clearly passed, and the commission could afford to overlook the genuine differences between the two whole-brain formulations. While both ultimately refer only to the functioning of the brain stem and not of the whole brain, the first construes death as a breakdown among systems, the second as the breakdown of a single regulatory system. To conflate the two, one would have to reject my argument that the recipient of an artificial heart would have to be regarded as dead for the same reason a brain-dead, respirator-supported body would be. The first formulation is concerned with the maintenance of the functional triangle of heart, lungs, and brain stem. The burden of proof lies with proponents of this formulation to show why the nonspontaneity of respiratory function matters to a decision that death has occurred.

By contrast, the second formulation construes death as the death of the body's regulator, the brain stem. Instead of the participatory role it was assigned in the first formulation, the brain stem is now seen as the unique regulator of bodily function, whose death is the death of the human being. One primary organ is the focus of the second formulation, not the interactions among three major organ systems. Although both formulations are presented as "whole-brain" formulations, each reduces to a different claim about the brain stem alone. The two formulations yield two very different concerns, as the commission goes on to admit: "For patients who are not artificially maintained, breathing and heartbeat were, and are, reliable signs either of systemic integration and/or continued brain functioning (depending on which approach one takes to the 'whole brain' concept)" (37).

The commission also addresses the public policy implications of its discussion of the two whole-brain formulations. When brain death occurs, there is no "comprehensive integrated functioning" (37). The commission recognizes that the two formulations could lead to different public policy statements. This fact alone should call into question the claim that any significant reconciliation between the two can be worked out at the theoretical level.

The most likely policy statement corresponding to the second, or primary organ, formulation would be that death is the irreversible loss of total brain function. The commission thinks that one could hold the second formulation and issue a second definition of death as the irreversible stoppage of respiration and circulation. The commission refers to these as two "standards," and defends the second as a "surrogate" for the first.

The policy statement corresponding to the first whole-brain formulation would be that death is the irreversible loss of the integrated functioning of the organism as a whole. The traditional or the brain-death criterion could be used to determine death's occurrence depending upon the situation, the commission suggests. This is the view of David Lamb. But this view is incomplete without an argument to the effect either that the permanent absence of consciousness is crucial to the decision that someone has died, or that the nonspontaneity of lung function is a sufficient ground for concluding that someone is dead under some circumstances.

The central reason that the commission sees no big difference between the two whole-brain formulations is a pragmatic one: no matter which formulation one adopts, it suggests, both the traditional and brain-death criteria will be acceptable bases for declaring death under the appropriate conditions. The commission concludes that two "standards" should be part of our public policy—a cardiopulmonary and a brain-based standard—even though we conclude that death is the irreversible loss of total brain function. However, this dual standard diffuses any commitment we have made to a whole-brain formulation of death, no matter how flimsy the theoretical basis of that commitment. To suggest that a statute containing alternative standards of death is acceptable "as a practical matter" undermines the claim that "the loss of spontaneous breathing and heartbeat are *surrogates for* the loss of brain functions" (38; italics mine). At some point the commission must defend its obvious policy choice of deference to the dictates of what it perceives as practical necessity rather than to those of sound theoretical justification.

HIGHER-BRAIN FORMULATIONS OF DEATH

The commission distinguishes two versions of the higher-brain formulation: the first defines death as "the loss of what is essential to a person" (38); the second defines death as the loss of personal identity or the ceasing to exist of the individual person. The commission sees the whole-brain and the higher-brain formulations as different views of what is "essential to being a person" (39). The two higher-brain formulations fall victim to a common defect, claims the commission: there is no consensus on personhood or on a theory of personal identity, and hence neither formulation would be suitable as a basis for public policy. The only significance of a higher-brain formulation is confirmatory; the loss of the capacity for consciousness and for the person-related functions we associate with the higher brain are elements of our conception of death. Since a whole-brain formulation includes the loss of these capacities, a higher-brain formulation just lends it further credibility.

The commission gives several reasons for opposing higher-brain formulations of death. First, no one agrees on the underlying perspective on person or individual person, so it would be impossible to come up with an unassailable higher-brain formulation of either kind. This objection is suspect; it does not follow from the fact that there are different theories of personhood and personal identity that we would be unable to agree on a higher-brain formulation of death as part of our public policy statement. It is conceivable that a harmonizing of interests on this issue could be achieved among those who favor higher-brain formulations. Since all such proponents agree that higher-brain death constitutes the death of the individual, even though they might rationalize their position on different grounds, they share a belief that higher-brain death (for example, neocortical death) must have occurred for death to have occurred. If all agree, say, that the neocortical-death criterion is necessary for their formulation of death, there is no dilemma. A dilemma would occur only if the higher-brain formulation incorporated in the public policy did not require the occurrence of neocortical death—which a memory-based theory of personal identity would not. We can acknowledge the conceptual disagreements among proponents of higher-brain formulations, but this does not necessarily undermine the possibility that a single such formulation might harmonize interests and block the extension of the higher-brain formulation to cases in which it has no bearing (for example, the victim of permanent amnesia).

There is another objection to the commission's refusal to work around the problem of multiple and competing concepts of personhood and personal identity. As we saw in its discussion of the whole-brain formulations, the commission tacitly invokes criteria for acceptable theoretical arguments as well as for successful combinations of theoretical arguments. It should apply these criteria consistently in relation to whole-brain as well as higher-brain formulations. Why should we not combine all higher-brain arguments into some unitary view, as the commission claims to do with the whole-brain formulations? If higher-brain functioning is destroyed, proponents of higher-brain formulations agree that the patient has died. If those proponents wish to argue that she is dead for a reason specific to their personal identity theory, yet not dead according to a higher-brain formulation of death, they are suggesting a further formulation of death that we would have little difficulty dismissing.

The commission has another reason for opposing higher-brain formulations: discussions of personhood and personal identity are technical and abstract, and hence an unstable basis for the elaboration of a public policy. In short, the commission suggests that even if we were persuaded that a particular personal identity theory was rationally acceptable in comparison with its alternatives, and that it concluded that the death of a person's upper brain is that person's death, we would have to reject it because of its "abstract technicality" (40).

We should certainly be concerned about the abstract technicality of a particular conception of human death. In particular, we should make sure to develop ways of educating the public so that it can think about alternative views of death, since the discussion is of necessity abstract and technical. But the abstract technicality of some of the arguments should never be the ground for leaving the lay conception of death unchallenged or for allowing that conception to determine public policy. To do so would set a dangerous precedent indeed.

The commission also raises the expected slippery slope objection to any higher-brain formulation of death. If we decide that a grossly retarded individual is not a person, the commission argues, then a higher-brain formulation would enable us to declare her dead. We never would wish to support a conception of death that promotes such slippage in its application. Any formulation that enabled such errors or abuses would be inadmissible. But not every higher-brain formulation has this flaw. My own recommendation centers on the irreversible cessation of consciousness, a criterion that keeps the door to error and abuse decisively closed and locked.

What about the spontaneous continuation of respiration and circulation in cases of upper-brain death? "The implication of the personhood and personal identity arguments is that Karen Quinlan, who retains brainstem function and breathes spontaneously, is just as dead as a corpse in the traditional sense. The Commission rejects this conclusion and the further implication that such patients could be buried or otherwise treated as dead persons" (40). The claim of an advocate of a higher-brain formulation would be that Karen Quinlan was indeed dead, but not according to the concept of death we associate with the traditional criteria. She was dead for the same reason that someone who is brain-dead is dead: consciousness is permanently absent, and remaining organismic functioning is of no consequence save as a possible source of confusion, misunderstanding, and discomfort to the living. In deference to entrenched human sensibilities, the remaining spontaneous functions should be stopped prior to burial or cremation. In the meantime, the patient is to be treated as a dead person, difficult though this might be for some to comprehend. It was no doubt an equal challenge for people to convince themselves in the early 1970s that death had already occurred in brain-dead, respirator-driven bodies. We ought to defer to entrenched human sensibilities to an extent, but they should not be honored to the point of disallowing the theoretical adequacy of higher-brain formulations of human death.

Youngner and Bartlett refer to this suspect move as "the psychological fallacy":

Emotional forces are also influential, partly because they are not rational. Normal human contact does not involve the analysis of which life functions are so essential that a person could not survive without them. When we hold someone we love, we feel their warmth, heartbeat, and breath. We see their facial expressions change in response to our words or touch, we hear them sigh and see them move in their sleep. When confronted with a person maintained at the edge of life, the situation compels us to think differently; but it is not easy to feel differently. We have been conditioned to associate even the most mundane physiologic functions with life. The importance of certain vital functions, like breathing and heartbeat, is not easily dismissed on the grounds that the brain's integrative function determines whether they are essential to life. [The commission claims that the discomfort some feel about regarding the brain-dead as dead is not an adequate ethical argument against the brain-death criterion.] Yet they, as well as other advocates of the whole-brain criterion, sometimes use these same considerations to reject a criterion based only on higher brain functions.[2]

With respect to the actual formulation of a public policy statement, the commission maintains that there is no way clearly to articulate a higher-brain formulation of death. The commission's basic contentions are that we are fairly ignorant about the relationships between consciousness and brain function, and that we lack the medical and scientific expertise to identify the pattern of brain destruction present in most cases. Hence the commission argues that even if we knew what aspects of brain functioning are nomologically tied to consciousness, we would lack the medical and scientific know-how to be certain in our assessments of these conditions. But the fact that we labor under both these limitations does not preclude the possibility of formulating a public policy statement that speaks meaningfully to the questions of patient status posed by persistent vegetative states. In my own policy statement I avoid any impact that these two objections might be thought to have.

The final reason for the commission's rejection of any higher-brain formulation is the notion that such a concept of death represents a radical departure from "the traditional standards" (40). The framework of criteria and concepts I defended in chapter 2 is entirely different from that presupposed by the commission, which suggests that a higher-brain formulation of death implies "that the existing cardiopulmonary definition had been in error all along, even before the advent of respirators and other life-sustaining technology" (40–41). There is no reason to believe this statement, however. Before respirators were used, the cessation of the heart and lungs was the only adequate basis for any judgment about the future of the organism as a whole. Since there was no understanding of the roles of the brain, the only possible referent in a declaration of death had to be the organism as a whole. The traditional criteria were the only measurements at our disposal and were adequate under the circumstances to determine death's occurrence. According to the higher-brain formulations, the use of the traditional criteria is now overkill, which is probably the point the commission is trying to make. But in the original context of their use, the traditional criteria were our best way of determining that death had occurred. There was no error connected with their use when no resuscitative machinery was available. That their early users had an incorrect conception of death is only a function of the state of their biological knowledge. While we might now say that they defined human death erroneously, their criteria were certainly adequate for declaring death. Their error, if we really want to call it that, was a function of limitations in their knowledge—certainly not an error in the usual sense of an avoidable mistake to which we would attach blame.

NONBRAIN FORMULATIONS OF DEATH

The commission considers two nonbrain formulations of death. The first is the strict application of the traditional concept of life and death, in which continued circulation and respiration, regardless of their source, indicate that life is still present. I have rejected this approach because it eschews the moral obligation we now have to resolve the dilemmas modern medicine has generated. The commission says that to retain this early conception of death will lead us to overlook the significance of the fact that the patient is "totally unresponsive to its environment," and so just a "perfused corpse" (42). This is the commission's first reference to total unresponsiveness, the first reason the commission gives for thinking that a brain-dead patient is nothing more than a "perfused corpse."

The other nonbrain formulation is the soul's departure from the body. I forgo discussing this formulation because it lacks an empirical referent.

THE RESULT

The commission consciously adopts a conservative posture that allows new ways of diagnosing whole-brain death, but does not, in its own estimation, commit us to a radical change in our concept of death. "On a matter so fundamental to a society's sense of itself— touching deeply held personal and religious beliefs—and so final for the individuals involved, one would desire much greater consensus than now exists before taking the major step of radically revising the concept of death" (41). I shall call this appeal to consensus, which is integral to the commission's overall position, the *consensual strategy*. The commission uses this strategy at the theoretical level as well as at the level of policy selection. The consensual strategy consists in the claim that some policy questions by nature require us to incorporate a consensually held view into public policy. Stated another way, it is the claim that for some policy questions, a public policy that does not reflect consensus should not be adopted. The commission is strongly committed to the latter form of the consensual strategy, which entails the first form.

But such an appeal to consensus is a poor defense where redefining death is at issue. The only consensus that existed when the brain-death criterion was introduced was a medical consensus, one that apparently arose despite the fact that there was no deeper medical consensus on a theoretical justification for the use of that criterion. It is certainly correct to say that there is no current consensus, medical or otherwise, in favor of a higher-brain formulation or a neocortical-death criterion. But at least we are proceeding in the proper order, first defending a particular concept of death, then choosing criteria for declaring death that reflect this concept.

In addition, we must question the commission's reasons for thinking that determining a societal definition of death is such that our policy ought to reflect consensus. The commission suggests that since "deeply held personal and religious beliefs" are involved, and since our discussion will be "so final for the individuals involved," both our concept of death and our public policy ought to be based on consensus.

The commission relies heavily on a consensual strategy, not to be confused with a contractual strategy. An appeal to consensus is only as strong as the reasons supporting the individual decisions that lead to consensus. A position that has the force of consensus behind it cannot be assumed to reflect a common, let alone a rationally based, decision on the part of individuals. People often have many and conflicting reasons for the conclusions they share with others, so consensus per se is not necessarily a rational basis for policy choice. The underlying policy problem in a democracy is to determine which decisions ought to be based on consensus. It seems clear that some societal decisions should not be based on the prevailing consensus position—our policy of defining death is included.

We want to have a uniform standard for declaring death so that the treatment of individuals reflects their status, and so that we have a firm basis for treating like cases alike. The "deeply held personal and religious beliefs" of individuals must sometimes give way to overwhelming societal concerns. Were this not the case, we would still be living in a far more racially and sexually prejudiced society than we are. Some issues require a broader perspective than most of us can achieve; personal convictions may prevent us from thinking in terms of broader societal needs and goals. Our public policy defining death is one such issue and thus should not be based on consensus. In my policy statement, I temper a necessary disregard of consensus with a mechanism of toleration in the form of a conscience clause—a mechanism that enables individuals to opt out of the effects of the policy in their own cases on conscientious grounds. Since I have shown that the commission is mistaken in its claim that a higher-brain formulation of death represents a radical alteration in the understanding of death underlying the brain-death criterion, the first order of business is to demonstrate this mistake to medical professionals, lawyers, policy makers, and the public. In this way, the slow and difficult process of conceptual clarification and change (which has not yet occurred adequately even with regard to the brain-death criterion) can begin.

Even though the higher-brain formulation does not involve the radical conceptual change that the commission thinks, a public policy based primarily on a higher-brain rather than a whole-brain formulation will be perceived as a radical policy change. Therefore, some would argue that the latter formulation should remain central to our policy statement, as it is in the Canadian statute discussed in the next section, because it will be perceived as an incremental rather than a radical policy change. The distinction between the incremental change represented by a whole-brain-death policy and the radical change represented by a higher-brain-death policy is obfuscation, given the theoretical argument of this book. But we must always be concerned about the way a policy of defining death will be perceived by the majority of citizens, and about the way in which it will challenge the beliefs about life and death that some of them hold. Simply because some will regard the incorporation of a higher-brain formulation into public policy as a huge departure from the status quo, should we adopt what will appear to be an incremental departure only? The various formulations of death that might be made central to our public policy statement *do* alter the status quo by altering our default standard on death. That is, the circumstance under which death is normally declared will be different depending on whether the whole-brain or the higher-brain formulation of death is embodied in our policy statement. Hence, if we adopt a public policy based on the higher-brain formulation, the resulting change in our default standard must be defended.

The Uniform Declaration of Death Act

The Uniform Declaration of Death Act proposed by the President's Commission reads as follows:

> 1. [*Determination of Death.*] An individual who has sustained either (1) irreversible cessation of circulatory and respiratory functions, or (2) irreversible cessation of all functions of the entire brain, including the brain stem, is dead. A determination of death must be made in accordance with accepted medical standards.
> 2. [*Uniformity of Construction and Application.*] This act shall be applied and construed to effectuate its general purpose to make uniform the law with respect to the subject of this Act among states enacting it (73).

Some crucial explanatory statements immediately follow the proposal:

> The proposed statute addresses the matter of "defining" death at *the level of general physiological standards* rather than at the level of more abstract concepts or the level of more precise criteria and tests. The proposed statute articulates *alternative standards*, since in the vast majority of cases irreversible circulatory and respiratory cessation will be the obvious and sufficient basis for diagnosing death. . . . The Commission prefers to employ language which would reflect the continuity of the traditional standard and the newer, brain-based standard (73–74; italics mine).

The commission makes it clear that it is setting forth alternative "general physiological standards." Hence, its definition of death is presented as two standards which relate equivalently to the formulation it favors in its chapter on alternative formulations of death. The commission does not explicitly state the whole-brain formulation in the act itself. According to paragraph 1, death can be determined on either of two bases. The "Determination of Death" clause tells us that someone is dead if she has undergone either of two conditions, but the statement says nothing about the relationship of those conditions. There are two ways of being dead, then, and we have lost the sense of death as a "unitary phenomenon." The concept of death elaborated in the commission's supporting arguments was that of the "permanent cessation of integrated functioning of the organism as a whole" (33). Thus, the two general physiological standards it provides are on equal footing in diagnosing the occurrence of death in the sense just given.

The crucial question is whether the two conditions specified in paragraph 1 relate in the same way to this conception of death. Other commentators on the act have also pointed out the importance of this question.[3] It is fairly easy to show that the two conditions do not relate in the same way to the whole-brain formulation of death. The requirement of irreversible cessation of circulatory and respiratory functions is ambiguous in a way that the requirement of irreversible cessation of all functions of the entire brain is not. Circulatory and respiratory functions may occur spontaneously or nonspontaneously. Brain functions, if they occur, do so spontaneously, since we have no mechanical support systems for the functions of the entire brain. But if we interpret the first condition as a statement about spontaneous functioning, it would appear that the iron-lung patient is dead. If we interpret it as a statement about nonspontaneous functioning, then the artificially maintained decapitated human body is alive. Neither conclusion is tolerable. Moreover, if it is a statement about nonspontaneous functioning, the decapitated patient is alive according to the first condition and dead according to the second. Obviously, then, the two conditions do not relate in the same way to death.

It is thus clear that both conditions cannot be considered general physiological standards for death. A choice must be made, and the role of the condition not chosen will require clarification. As we saw in the last section, the commission opts for a whole-brain formulation, but on the basis of arguments that have no reference to the functioning of the brain as a whole. Focusing as it does on the lower-brain vegetative functions to the exclusion of the higher-brain cognitive ones, the commission's concept of death reduces to an organismic one. Since the commission claims to be articulating two general physiological standards equally compatible with a whole-brain formulation, though, I shall assess the adequacy of its policy statement in these terms.

The commission clearly aims to elevate the entire brain and its functions to the level of a general physiological standard of death. But it has either failed to realize that it cannot do this without rethinking the role of the traditional criteria, or simply tried to finesse the matter. Since the two conditions do not relate in the same way to death, and since death is the irreversible cessation of all functions of the entire brain, including the brainstem (the commission is convinced of this because of the medical consensus that this condition is death), then the second condition must be our general physiological standard of death, and tests for both conditions will be separate ways of testing for its occurrence.[4] This is how the matter should have been presented in the act, consistent with a whole-brain concept of death. This emphasis would convey the necessary message that death is a unitary phenomenon.

Several unresolvable difficulties surround the first section of the proposed act. The commission felt itself under an obligation to respond to two serious matters: the presence of a clear medical consensus that brain death is death, and the obvious lay inclination to regard death as an organismic breakdown centered in the heart and lungs. Bernat, Culver, and Gert report that the problem, as the commission saw it, was to incorporate "the theoretically correct standard of death—irreversible cessation of all brain functioning—but also allow, for practical purposes, irreversible cessation of cardiopulmonary functions to be used as a test of death in the overwhelming majority of cases."[5] Recognizing a society divided on the issue of the central vital agency, the commission fashioned a proposal that would be least troublesome for representatives of both groups. Indeed, that proposal has received favorable responses from the American Bar Association, the American Medical Association, representative lay groups, and others. Each group reads the act as compatible with its own underlying conception of death, not recognizing the inconsistencies the proposal harbors. Trying to be all things to most people at the expense of theoretical precision and consistency is a dangerous strategy.

The basic difficulty lies in elevating the public's conception of the functioning of the heart and lungs as the central vital agency to a primary level of concern in policy formulation. Substantial portions of the public have, by degree, come to see the centrally important and irreplaceable role of the brain in the life of the human being. To jerry-rig a public policy statement to appease those who either have not been confronted by the situation of brain death or have not been intellectually concerned enough to sort out the role of the brain as opposed to that of the heart and lungs is a gross abuse of the policy-maker's role. Policy-makers cannot view themselves as instruments of democracy per se. In this case, they must articulate a new understanding of death if developments in modern medicine suggest that our older understanding is inadequate. In line with the new concept of death they recommend, they must demonstrate which general physiological standard should be used to determine death's occurrence. If they choose the second condition, then the first is ruled out as a general physiological standard, and vice versa. Since the commission clearly wishes to choose the second condition, it must rearticulate the relationship of the conditions, for they no longer have equal standing.

I am not suggesting that the public's thinking about death is irrelevant to our policy choice. The formulation of public policy has a theoretical and a practical dimension, and the two must at least be consistent with one another. While pragmatic considerations may dictate, for example, that we do not draft a policy statement relying exclusively on a higher-brain formulation of death even if we have a theoretical defense of this conception, we should not draft a policy that undermines the theoretical formulation of death we have previously defended. The commission's policy has this unfortunate effect upon its own theory. The formulation of policy must be a function of both sound theory and sensitivity to public response, but it should not be guided by public relations concerns. We should worry about public response as a factor in statutory formulation only if that response is linked to deeply held (and in our system, protected) moral or religious beliefs. If, however, the public holds the view it does either because of outmoded or incomplete physiological information, or because of a simple reluctance to change, we should not feel obliged to try, within the statute itself, to minimize problems the public might initially have with the statute.

The apparently formidible worry that the commission felt about public response is far surpassed by the worry it should have felt about those who might want language incorporated into the statute that would support the use of both a brain-death and a neocortical-death criterion. Admittedly, the commission's conceptual framework was too narrow to license the use of the latter, but it could have added a conscience clause for those whose concept of death centers on the loss of higher-brain functions, and still have held to the whole-brain formulation overall. If the commission had added a higher-brain option to their statute—a step they flatly rejected—I could understand the importance of trying to reconcile the new concept with the old, for such an addition would appear to be a deep challenge to either of the standards of death the commission suggested. Such an apparent departure from standard practice would require careful management were it to be written into the statute, even if only as an elective for those who might want to be declared dead in such a circumstance.

There are fundamental errors in the conceptual framework the act presupposes, as well as in the policy statement it issues. Given the theoretical footing favored by the commission, only one general physiologic standard of death can be allowed. Since the second is the only one consistent with the commission's formulation of death, the first must be relegated the role of a test for the second under circumstances not involving the use of artificial support systems.

The specific difficulties that have emerged in our analysis of the Uniform Declaration of Death Act are avoided in the finely crafted model statute of the Law Reform Commission of Canada. In particular, the Canadian statute corrects the central deficiencies of the act on the connection between the two conditions. The Law Reform

Commission of Canada issued the "Criteria for the Determination of Death," of which this model statute was a part:

> A person is dead when an irreversible cessation of all that person's brain functions has occurred. The cessation of brain functions can be determined by the prolonged absence of spontaneous cardiac and respiratory functions. When the determination of the absence of cardiac and respiratory functions is made impossible by the use of artificial means of support, the cessation of the brain functions may be determined by any means recognized by the ordinary standards of current medical practice. . . . To remain faithful to the popular concept, the proposed legislation must recognize that death is the death of an individual person, not of an organ or cells.[6]

The Canadian statute manages the relationship of the two conditions appropriately. Death is now a unitary phenomenon: it consists in the cessation of all brain functions. Depending upon the patient's circumstances, death is determined on the basis of either the traditional criteria if no artificial support systems are in use or the brain-death criterion if they are in use. The Canadian statute is a great improvement, then. Its meaning and use are abundantly clear; there is no confusion between the general physiological standard of death and the criteria for declaring death. Given the similar intent of both the Uniform Declaration of Death and the Canadian statute—that individuals can be declared dead in accordance with either the traditional criteria or the brain-death criterion, whichever is appropriate—the Canadian statute is clearly preferable.

Given the commission's understanding of this straightforward and adequate statement, it is puzzling that the Uniform Declaration of Death Act does not have more in common with the Canadian statute. The commission explains why it rejected the Canadian formulation:

> Although conceptually acceptable (and vastly superior to the adoption of brain cessation as a primary standard conjoined with a nonspecific reference to other, apparently unrelated

"usual and customary procedures"), the Canadian proposal breaks with tradition in a manner that appears to be unnecessary. For most lay people—and in all probability for most physicians as well—the permanent loss of heart and lung function (for example, in an elderly person who has died in his or her sleep) clearly manifests death. As previous chapters in this Report recount, biomedical scientists can explain the brain's particularly important—and vulnerable—role in the organism as a whole and show how temporary loss of blood flow (ischemia) becomes a permanent cessation because of the damage it inflicts on the brain. Nonetheless, most of the time people do not, and need not, go through this two-step process. Irreversible loss of circulation is recognized as death because—setting aside any mythical connotations of the heart—a person without blood flow simply cannot live. Thus the Commission prefers to employ language which would reflect the continuity of the traditional standard and the newer, brain-based standard (74).

The commission begins by admitting the "conceptual acceptability" of the Canadian statute. Apparently, the commission must interpret the alternative statute's insistence that "death is the death of an individual person" to be compatible with its own statutory definition of death. Despite its conceptual acceptability, though, the commission rejects the Canadian statute primarily because it represents an unnecessary disruption of tradition. Here again is the argument that for the public (and for many physicians) heart and lung failure is the signal that death has occurred. The commission now uses the consensual strategy to argue for the opposite of a point made earlier: in the first instance it invoked the consensual strategy to defend the acceptability of the whole-brain formulation of death. Now it suggests that brain death is not the sole general physiologic standard in the policy statement because most of us, including physicians, associate heart and lung failure with death. This position undermines the whole-brain formulation for more reasons than one. On the face of it, it seems simply to rule out declarations of death as long as support systems continue to function. It radically undermines the recommendation of the Harvard committee, whose approach is to declare death when the brain is determined to be dead, and at some later time to turn off the respirator. According to the commission's consensual argument here, the patient should be considered alive until integrated functioning ceases, which requires that the respirator be turned off prior to a declaration of death.

The commission also notes that the claim that the brain is the central vital agency results from our scientific understanding of the brain's role in the organism, as well as from the brain's dependence on a continuous supply of oxygenated blood. The commission disagrees with the elevation of the brain over the heart and the lungs because most of us do not go through the following reasoning process:

X's heart and lungs have permanently ceased to function.

Therefore, X's brain is dead.

Therefore, X is dead.

Instead, the commission says, most of us reason:

X's heart and lungs have permanently ceased to function.

Therefore, X is dead.

But our way of reasoning to a conclusion that X has died has no necessary connection with what death is. We have already seen that X is not dead simply because her heart and lungs do not function, if all we mean by that is spontaneous function. The commission is worried about placing heart and lung functioning in a subordinate role to brain functioning, insisting that there is a continuity between the two that can be preserved only by implying that they bear the same relationship to death, whatever death is. This continuity simply does not exist, and hence no policy statement designed to express such continuity can possibly be acceptable.

Recommendations for Policy Change

Public policies that depart substantially from a justified conceptual or theoretical position are suspect. While there is ample room for argument about what the connection between theory and practice ought to be, let me preempt this argument with a minimalist criterion. It would be odd, to take an example from another area, to consider that we had articulated a cogent and defensible concept of distributive justice, yet to adopt a welfare policy that either ignored or contradicted the basic provisions of that concept. The same is true in the redefinition of death. Policies that undercut their explicit or implied conceptual foundations must be rejected in favor of those that do not. Given the argument of this book, we are under two conceptual constraints: to convey that the death of the person constitutes human death; and to allow for a declaration of death in cases of persistent vegetative state. In addition, social, ethical, religious, political, and legal factors constrain us as well. While it is inappropriate to allow the latter constraints to affect our articulation of a conceptually sound formulation of human death, they must be accommodated in a reasonable public policy.

It is thus possible that a public policy statement may be a good one, yet not one that perfectly mirrors the results of a well-grounded conceptual position. I have shown that the Uniform Declaration of Death Act does not mirror its conceptual arguments well, though this fact alone does not automatically count against it. In this case, however, there are reasons for rejecting it on this ground; the act engenders conceptual confusion far more than it fosters conceptual clarity and rigor, and it undermines its own notion of an adequate formulation of death, the whole-brain formulation. Further, I have shown that the conceptual arguments to which the commission appeals are grossly unacceptable as support for the whole-brain formulation of death. I turn now to formulating a public policy that has an acceptable fit with the conceptual framework I have defended, and is responsive to the social, ethical, religious, political, and legal factors at issue when a society adopts a policy for defining death.

In what follows, I take for granted the argument that has developed throughout this book. I am assuming that any human being in a persistent vegetative state is dead, even if respiration and circulation continue unassisted. Some readers may be unwilling to acknowledge my entitlement to this central claim. From a policy-making perspective, though, they must admit that there is a growing number of persons in our society who hold this conception of human death. I assume that those who object are committed to a principle of toleration roughly like our society's principle of religious freedom. Whatever one's principle of religious toleration, it need not commit one to tolerating the religious vision and activities of a Tom Jones, and so it is not a principle of absolute toleration. As a society, we are committed to a principle of toleration that dictates that our public policies enable maximum freedom, consistent with an equal degree of freedom for all. How responsive should our policy regarding the declaration of death be to the diversity of conceptions of death among us, given the link between deeply held personal and religious convictions and conceptions of death? How responsive should it be to a conception that has the strength of consensus behind it?

Three policy choices strike me as reasonable ones to consider. First, we could commit ourselves conceptually to the higher-brain formulation of death and frame a policy that defines death as the permanent absence of a capacity for consciousness, but otherwise parallels the Canadian statute. Second, we could make a commitment to a whole-brain formulation of death in our policy, yet include a conscience clause for those among us who hold a higher-brain formulation. Finally, we could adopt a policy based on the higher-brain formulation of death, yet which allows conscientious objection for those holding the whole-brain formulation. Intuitively, the third option would seem to be the weakest. It is certainly the oddest of the three, for it ignores the necessity of observing some sort of consensual strategy in the formation of public policy, and it alters the status quo by changing our default standard for declaring death. Like the first two policies, it unambiguously commits itself to the higher-brain formulation of death, and it incorporates a conscience clause in order to enable maximum freedom where matters of personal conviction may have been seriously challenged. Defending the third policy is a difficult task, but I think it is the best of the three policies before us.

The first policy alternative is the friendliest to the conceptual argument of this book. The emphasis on the death of the person is the appropriate frame of reference for the first policy, but by contrast with the Canadian statute, it rests on the view that the same person continues to exist only as long as consciousness remains. P. D. G. Skegg constructs a slippery slope objection to a consciousness-based criterion:

> The problem would be shifted, rather than avoided, if patients in an irreversibly non-cognitive condition were regarded as dead. It would then be possible to point to those patients whose brains were damaged to such an extent that they could never have more than a minimal degree of cognition. Why, it could be asked, should the possibility of such an extremely limited function be considered so significant as to warrant making such a fundamental distinction between this patient and one in whom this very limited capacity was absent?[7]

Skegg's point is that the irreversible loss of consciousness is the lowest common denominator in all conceptions of human death that focus on the loss of either personhood or personal identity, but that there is no reason why we would be likely to preserve that concept of death in practice. I would reply that there are two very good reasons for thinking that a consciousness-centered concept provides solid, and not slippery, footing. First, the line between consciousness and permanent unconsciousness is indeed a line, and reasoning about individuals on either side of that line must proceed in quite different terms. Judgments about the status and care of an intermittently conscious or semiconscious individual are quality-of-life judgments and are therefore of an entirely different kind from the judgments that lead us to say that a permanently unconscious individual is dead. In this latter case there is no sensible question to raise about the quality of life, for there is no longer any capacity for experiencing life, and thus no quality of life to be evaluated. Second, as I argued in chapter 6, we should avoid social policies that require us to make quality-of-life decisions on behalf of others. A definition-of-death policy that directs us to think in qualitative terms should be a source of great worry to us. For this reason, we eschew qualitative approaches and thereby block any relaxation in the consciousness-based criterion of human death. Immune to slippery slope objections, then, the first policy is a clear departure from the Canadian statute, for it focuses explicitly and solely on a higher-brain formulation of death:

Human death is the death of an individual person.

A person is dead when an irreversible cessation of brain functions necessary for consciousness has occurred.

Such cessation can be determined by the prolonged absence of spontaneous cardiac and respiratory functions.

When this determination is made impossible by the use of artificial means of support, the cessation of these brain functions may be determined by any means recognized by the ordinary standards of current medical practice.

When cardiac and respiratory functions continue spontaneously, the cessation of these brain functions may be determined by any means recognized by the ordinary standards of current medical practice.

This policy is the model statute I would recommend on the basis of the full argument I have developed in this book. It does not commit us to a higher-brain locus of death, but instead focuses on the permanent absence of consciousness, the sort of functioning we associate with the higher brain. Since it changes our default standard for death and contradicts consensus, this policy statement is radical indeed. It can be expected to have few strong supporters. As I have already admitted, there are limits to what one can expect the public (and perhaps many medical professionals as well) to accept as a public policy. The President's Commission was right in recognizing that policy-makers must take the pulse of the public. However, the commission bent its policy statement into a distorted and confused directive in its concern to appease as many groups as possible.

There is no denying that the first policy may be criticized as an unrealistic public policy for our time, because the psychological leap from considering the brain-dead patient dead to considering the permanently unconscious patient dead is too great for most of us. This concern is, of course, a version of what Youngner and Bartlett called the psychological fallacy. But even though psychological concerns were not foremost in anyone's mind when the brain-death criterion was adopted, we are still obligated to arrive at a policy statement that does not challenge lay sensibilities beyond necessity. If those sensibilities must be challenged, we must allow individuals some mode of adjustment or adaptation. Hence, I cannot be content with the policy statement that follows strictly from the conceptual arguments I have developed. The philosopher who would remain in such an ivory tower in the present context is indefensibly aloof. I must provide a policy statement that speaks more justly, more humanely, to the individual and societal needs at stake. The second policy recommendation returns to the whole-brain formulation and hence leaves our default position on death intact:

A person is dead when an irreversible cessation of all his or her brain functions has occurred.

This cessation can be determined by the prolonged absence of spontaneous cardiac and respiratory functions.

When artificial support systems are in use, the cessation of brain functions may be determined by any means recognized by the ordinary standards of current medical practice.

Conscience clause: An individual who believes that a person is dead when an irreversible cessation of brain functions necessary for consciousness has occurred may give advance legal effect to the desire to be declared dead under such circumstances. The cessation of these brain functions may be determined by any means recognized by the ordinary standards of current medical practice.

This policy departs from the Canadian model statute only in its inclusion of a conscience clause. A defensible principle of toleration would support this policy alternative, I believe. However, the President's Commission opposed a "conscience clause," maintaining that "such a provision has no place in a statute on the determination of death. Were a non-uniform standard permitted, unfortunate and mischievous results are easily imaginable" (80). In defense of the second policy, I would argue that the inclusion of the conscience clause does not compromise it to the point of setting up a nonuniform standard. To allow persons to choose among the traditional, the brain-death, and the neocortical-death criteria would result in a nonuniform standard, but to allow those who desire it to elect this single further option on grounds of conscience, for themselves only and by means of an advance legal declaration, would be as unlikely to result in a nonuniform standard as is our allowance of conscientious objection to war. Further, what "unfortunate and mischievious results" are foreseeable given the restrictions I have recommended? No one can make this choice for another, and no one electing the narrower brain-death criterion would do so lightly or in ignorance, for the full initiative remains with the individual.

It is reasonable to amend the Uniform Declaration of Death Act so that it reflects a person-centered conception of death, construes brain death as the death of the person, leaves our default standard intact by allowing the use of either the traditional criteria or the brain-death criterion, and contains a conscience clause for those holding a consciousness-based concept of death. The conscience clause represents an improvement over the Canadian model statute, for it implements our societal commitment to toleration, which is necessary when deep personal convictions are challenged and their expression represents no threat to others. The central place accorded the whole-brain formulation in this policy honors our societal commitment to consensually based public policies.

In spite of these solid gains, the second policy is seriously deficient, as is clear when we consider the impact it will have on our ability to resolve certain legal dilemmas. Since the point of a uniform statute like the Uniform Declaration of Death Act is to provide a legal framework within which questions of status, rights, and obligations may be settled, any policy choice must be evaluated in terms of the central legal conceptions it yields—in this case its definition of legally equivalent harms and losses. I raised this issue in my defense of a person-centered concept of human death. To provide an adequate system of protection and redress for individuals, the law must supply a basis for the decision that someone has visited an equivalent harm and loss in X's case when she has caused X to become either brain-dead or simply permanently unconscious. Likewise, the law must recognize that an equivalent harm and loss have been visited upon X's survivors in either case. Since the centrality of the whole-brain formulation in the second policy suggests that death is something more than the permanent cessation of consciousness, it undermines the legal recognition of the equivalence of these harms and losses. As such, this policy will promote a multitude of injustices. The law must speak for us here, determining a default standard that will acknowledge the underlying moral insight that equivalent harms and losses have been inflicted in such cases. To do this, our default standard must be based on a higher-brain rather than on a whole-brain formulation of death. If some individuals wish to have their status determined by the latter formulation, they must indicate their preference in advance.

The second policy permits self-determination (and self-determination only) through its conscience clause. It is desirable to let this decision rest with the individual alone; if family members are permitted to make this choice, we run the risks of conflict of interest, guilt, and serious emotional trauma. But the mechanism of a conscience clause is not without its difficulties. There are adults who will not entertain the question in time, and so we will not know their genuine wishes. Likewise, some will never be capable of such a decision. A conscience clause does not take us far enough, it might be argued; in the case of those who either have not or cannot fulfill its requirements (competent but uninformed adults, children, and the mentally infirm, for example), we might fail to fulfill an individual's genuine wishes or to make a decision that successfully realizes her best interests.

These are problems we face whenever we must make decisions on behalf of others, not problems that arise specifically because a conscience clause has been included in our policy statement. However, because of both the presumed difficulties of a conscience clause and the difficulty of designing a policy that will result in the like treatment of like cases, we need a policy centered on a higher-brain formulation of death that includes a conscience clause rather than on a whole-brain formulation that includes a conscience clause. To promote the principle of justice that equals must be treated equally, it would be preferable to select the policy with the strongest conceptual rationale, along with a proper conception of the relationship between conceptual and criteriological decisions. To center our policy on a formulation of death that is a partial truth rather than the whole truth will promote inconsistent legal judgments. Only a consciousness-based formulation of death provides a basis for treating relevantly like cases alike; that is, only in this formulation do we recognize that brain death and a persistent vegetative condition represent equivalent harms to victims and equivalent losses to survivors. A conscience clause would promote toleration and would place the decision to treat a relevantly like case differently with individuals speaking for themselves alone. Only in this way would our public policy foster adequate protection without overdetermination. A third policy thus results from the unlikely marriage of the first two:

Human death is the death of an individual person.

An individual person is dead when an irreversible cessation of brain functions necessary for consciousness has occurred.

The cessation of these brain functions can be determined by the prolonged absence of spontaneous cardiac and respiratory functions.

When artificial support systems are in use, the cessation of these brain functions may be determined by any means recognized by the ordinary standards of current medical practice.

When cardiac and respiratory functions continue spontaneously, the cessation of these brain functions may be determined by any means recognized by the ordinary standards of current medical practice.

Conscience clause: An individual who believes that a person is dead only when the functions of the entire brain have ceased may give advance legal effect to the desire to be declared dead only under such circumstances. The cessation of the relevant functions may be determined by any means recognized by the ordinary standards of current medical practice. For the purposes of criminal justice, however, the death of an individual is considered to have been caused when an irreversible cessation of the brain function necessary for consciousness has been caused.

There are many good reasons for favoring this policy over the alternatives; these reasons can be spelled out in relation to the challenges the policy will probably elicit. First, it may be objected that public policies should change incrementally, and that this policy's change in our default standard is an unacceptably radical move. From a practical perspective, the change appears radical; from a theoretical perspective, the radical change was made years ago. If the moral argument in chapter 6 stands, advances in medical technology have ruled out incremental policy change. Further, this policy rests on a solid conceptual edifice: our theory and our practice coincide in it. It is critical that theory and practice do coincide, as the discussion of the legal implications of alternative policies has clearly demonstrated. Second, it might be claimed that the policy's departure from the consensus position is indefensible, since our policy defining death touches convictions of a deeply personal and religious nature. I would reply that a conscience clause is a reasonable way to compensate for the decision not to translate the consensus position into public policy. Assuming that the consensus position would favor a policy based on the whole-brain formulation of death, a consensus-based policy would promote legal injustices by promoting the treatment of relevantly like cases in an unlike manner. This would be a more serious social consequence than that of allowing individuals to opt out of the policy on conscientious grounds.

The third policy does not commit us to a nonuniform standard of death any more than the second does. Since it is a more radical departure from the status quo than the second policy, it necessitates public education and thinking about death by pressing individuals to make a decision either for or against a particular definition of death. Any policy that remains centered on the whole-brain formulation of death cannot be expected to prompt individual decision-making to the extent that the third policy would, even if it includes a conscience clause. For the most part, the second policy will only prompt those already interested in being declared dead by appeal to a consciousness-based criterion to execute an advance legal directive to this effect. The third policy will generate much more thought and discussion about death, and will result in more individuals making conscientious choices than will the second. This is not to say that more people will avail themselves of the conscience clause in the third policy than would under the second. I mean simply that individuals will be more likely to see the matter as one for thought and decision, that the choices they make will be carefully considered, and that public discussion will provide an arena for their decision-making. This policy is highly conducive to public education and deliberation, then, precisely because it *is* a departure from the status quo.

Of course, some persons either will not make or will be unable to make the decision to exercise the option represented by the conscience clause in the third policy. This is a common problem, and we already have in place some mechanisms, albeit imperfect ones, for managing it. If I were not an organ donor, my next of kin could make this choice for me. As a parent, I must make some choices for my children, unless it can be shown that I am failing to do so in light of reasonable and informed assessments of their interests. For the incompetent, we make an effort to determine what the individuals' wishes would be were they competent. There are unsettling and unsettled questions here, to be sure, but they do not refute a particular conception of death or the consistency of certain criteria with it, nor should they be allowed to defeat a particular policy choice. We must address these questions in their own right and refine our surrogate decision mechanisms in light of careful ethical discussions, but we must not allow them to undermine the progress we have made in removing the vast range of dilemmas surrounding the declaration of death.

The third policy remains true to the conceptual framework I have defended in this book. It does not threaten to undermine a well-founded formulation of human death, and it avoids legal inconsistency. It promises to generate public education and thinking about death, and it respects a right of self-determination consistent with our societal need for a common principle regarding the declaration of death. Finally, this policy has impact on only a limited number of persistent vegetative state cases, while it leaves our treatment of the brain-dead and of those who fulfill the traditional criteria unchanged. It remains open to improvements in our ability to determine that an individual is irreversibly unconscious, since it allows that any criteria accepted by the medical profession as a basis for determining persistent vegetative status will be acceptable criteria for declaring death.

This book has been a sustained argument for an alternative understanding of the relationship between the brain-death criterion and the traditional criteria for declaring death. I refer to it as an alternative understanding because it is a perspective which is absent from the medical, legal, and philosophical literature. The brain-death criterion commits us to a redefinition of our concept of human death, a redefinition that involves a shift of perspective from the human as organism to the human as person. We ought to be concerned about the death of the person in declaring death. I have developed an ontological argument in the form of a conservative mentalist personal identity theory showing that personal existence ceases with the permanent cessation of consciousness. Since the persistence of consciousness must be considered the sine qua non of human personal life, the brain-death criterion, as well as the neocortical-death criterion or any criterion whose fulfillment is conclusively associated with persistent vegetative existence, is justified.

Contrary to the President's Commission, human death is hardly "the one great certainty" (3). Death has become a great uncertainty for us, at both the conceptual and public policy levels. Some uncertainties are tolerable; others are not. Since dying and death are sources of the deepest, most intractable anguish humans can suffer, uncertainty here is morally intolerable, for it promises only to compound that anguish, not diminish it. The search for conceptual clarity and the definition of adequate concepts may strike some as philosophical game-playing, far removed from the hard choices introduced by medical advances, but I hope I have shown that these choices require hard thinking of a far more abstract and elaborate nature than one might initially expect, and that such thinking will gain for us the strongest purchase on a humane and flexible public policy.

Notes
References
Index

Notes

CHAPTER ONE

1. Morison, 1971, 694.
2. Ibid., 694, 695.
3. President's Commission, 1981, 132–40.
4. See "Against the Stream: Comments on the Definition and Redefinition of Death," in Jonas, 1974, 132–40.
5. Korein, 1978, 7.
6. Veatch, 1976a, 21.
7. Korein, 1978, 7.
8. Ad Hoc Committee, 1968, 337.
9. In a recent article, E. Rodin and others argue that on the basis of clinical tests alone, it is not possible to infer that a patient on life-support systems has undergone cerebral death. They construct a hypothetical case in which a discrete brain hemorrhage may impact on the brainstem such that the patient will fulfill the clinical tests for brain death, yet exhibit a non-isoelectric EEG, indicating ongoing cortical function which they conjecture would be dreamlike (Rodin et al., 1985).
10. Ad Hoc Committee, 1968, 337.
11. Korein, 1978, 7.
12. Ibid., 8.
13. Ibid., 8, 9.
14. Cranford and Smith, 1979, 207.

15. Brierley et al., 1971, 10.

16. Ibid., 13–14.

17. The biological school is represented by such writers as Lawrence Becker (see Becker, 1975) and David Lamb (see Lamb, 1978). The ontological argument is advanced by Michael Green and Daniel Wikler, among others (see Green and Wikler, 1980). Hans Jonas (Jonas, 1974) is among the proponents of the moral school.

CHAPTER TWO

1. Becker, 1975, 334.

2. Lamb, 1978, 144.

3. Green and Wikler, 1980, 106.

4. Ibid.

5. See, for example, chapter 14 of Dennett, 1978.

6. Isaacs, 1978, 7–8.

7. Ibid., 7.

8. *Black's Law Dictionary*, 1968, s.v. "death."

9. Ad Hoc Committee, 1968, 339.

10. Ibid., numbering mine.

11. Stickel, 1979, 183.

12. Schwager, 1978, 39–40. Paul Ramsey holds a similar view; see Ramsey, 1970, 97.

13. Halley and Harvey, 1968, 425.

14. Schwager, 1978, 42.

15. Ibid.

16. President's Commission, 1981, 15.

17. Cranford and Smith, 1979, 201–02.

18. President's Commission, 1981, 16.

19. Ramsey, 1970, 62.

20. Brody, 1981, 79.

21. Korein, 1978, 2.

22. Becker, 1975, 353.

23. Veatch, 1976, 25. For the reader's convenience, page references to this work are given parenthetically in the text for the remainder of the chapter.

24. Engelhardt, 1978, 272. Page references to this work are given parenthetically in the text for the remainder of the chapter.

CHAPTER THREE

1. Becker, 1975, 335. For the remainder of this section, page references to this article are given parenthetically in the text.

2. Lamb, 1978, 151. Lamb points out the same inconsistency in Becker's view.

3. Laing, 1960, 18–21.

4. Lamb, 1978, 144. For the remainder of this section, page references to this article are given parenthetically in the text.

5. Christopher Pallis, for example, writes: "Within three years [of the Harvard Committee Report] . . . two neurosurgeons from Minneapolis made the challenging suggestion that 'in patients with known but irreparable intracranial lesions' irreversible damage to the brain-stem was the 'point of no return.' . . . Their recommendations later became known as the Minnesota criteria and were to influence thinking and practice in the UK considerably" (Pallis, 1982, 1487).

6. Becker, 1975, 335.

7. Green and Wikler, 1977, 112–13. For the remainder of this chapter, page references to this article are given parenthetically in the text.

CHAPTER FOUR

1. Brody, 1981, 80.

2. Hoffman, 1979, 445.

3. Green and Wikler, 1980, 115.

4. Jonas, 1974, 132–40. Further references to this work will be given parenthetically in the text for the remainder of this section.

5. Brody, 1981, 80. Further references to this work will be given parenthetically in the text for the remainder of this section.

6. Veatch, 1976a, 26. Further references to this and other works by Veatch are given parenthetically in the text for the remainder of this section. Because several works by Veatch are cited, in-text citations include a year as well as a page reference.

7. The following articles are relevant to the discussion of posthumous harm: Feinberg, 1974; Feinberg, 1977; Partridge, 1981; and Levenbook, 1984.

8. Hoffman, 1979, 436. Subsequent references to this article are given parenthetically in the text for the remainder of this section.

9. Schwager, 1978, 44.

10. Green and Wikler, 1980, 114. Subsequent references to this article are given parenthetically in the text for the remainder of this chapter.

11. Glover, 1977, 45; quoted in ibid., 116.

CHAPTER FIVE

1. Green and Wikler, 1980, 105.

2. Ibid., 131. The structure of Green and Wikler's argument has had an

undeniable, though subliminal, impact on that of my own argument. In my analysis of the biologists' and moralists' positions, I have shown that Green and Wikler's counterarguments are sometimes unsound. Further, I hope to demonstrate that Green and Wikler fail to address themselves to all the questions they must in order to establish that the death of a person's brain is a sufficient condition for declaring that person's death.

3. Howard Brody (1983) attacks the personal identity approach to justifying the claim that brain death is a person's death. I discuss his argument later in this chapter.

4. Lamb, 1985.

5. In a footnote on page 119, Green and Wikler explain that their mental continuity theory of personal identity is essentially the theory developed by John Perry. Perry argues for a modified version of Locke's memory theory of personal identity. Insofar as Green and Wikler's adaptation of Perry's theory is a fair one, my objections to their view are also objections to Perry's. For me to present and respond to Perry's intricate arguments as part of my treatment of Green and Wikler's argument would carry me too far afield. The reader wishing to consider other personal identity theories should consult Perry, 1975, and Rorty, 1976. Further pursuit of Perry's theory is appropriate for those who are in tentative sympathy with it. Green and Wikler fail to ground their claim that an individual is "essentially an entity with psychological properties" (121); although they build their argument about brain death upon this claim, it remains only an assumption in their argument.

6. Green and Wikler, 1980, 118. Subsequent references to this work are given parenthetically in the text for the remainder of this section.

7. My understanding of this portion of Green and Wikler's argument has been greatly enhanced by my reading of a paper by George J. Agich and Royce P. Jones, entitled "Personal Identity and Brain Death: A Critical Response." Agich and Jones argue that determining the essential characteristics of an entity is a logically distinct process from determining criteria for the reidentification of an individual as the same individual. Further, the basis for reidentifying something as the same need not have anything to do with its essential characteristics; yet Green and Wikler appear to assume that it does.

8. I am indebted to my editor, Channing Hughes, for pointing out this additional complexity.

9. Wikler, 1984a, 172.

10. Brody, 1983, 188.

11. See my objections to this view in chapter 2, pages 34–37.

12. Lamb, 1985, 19. Subsequent references to this work will be given parenthetically in the text for the remainder of this chapter.

13. See also Veatch, 1982, 1102–03.
14. Rodin et al., 1985, 63.
15. Ibid., 67.
16. Pallis, 1983a, 286.
17. Veatch, 1976, 314.

CHAPTER SIX

1. Youngner and Bartlett, 1983, 252–53.
2. Tooley, 1983, 64.
3. Ibid., 65.
4. After I had worked out my application of the contractarian strategy, I was referred to the similar strategy suggested by Thomas C. Schelling, who recommends that features of economic reasoning be used in developing an ethics of policy. Essentially, he claims that we can diffuse troublesome ethical questions if we develop the facility to think disinterestedly about a policy choice. We dissipate the moral issue, he says, if we can "legislate our relation to each other" (Schelling, 1984, 11) in advance. I would argue that we do not dissipate the issue; rather, we render ourselves more capable of reaching a rationally justified ethical response to the question.
5. Dennett, 1978, 285. Subsequent references to this work are given parenthetically in the text for the remainder of this chapter.
6. Tooley, 1983, 51.

CHAPTER SEVEN

1. President's Commission, 1981, 31. Subsequent references to this document are given parenthetically in the text for the remainder of this chapter.
2. Youngner and Bartlett, 1983, 254.
3. See Bernat, Culver, and Gert, 1982a.
4. On the basis of the physiological information presented to it, the commission concludes that "the only proper neurologic basis for declaring death" is "the cessation of the vital functions of the *entire* brain—and not merely portions thereof, such as those responsible for cognitive functions" (President's Commission, 1981, 18; italics mine). The commission holds that the traditional criteria were actually tests for the neurologic failure we associate with the death of the entire brain, a view I refuted in chapter 2.
5. Bernat, Culver, and Gert, 1982a, 7.
6. The Law Reform Commission of Canada, "Criteria for the Determination of Death," quoted in President's Commission, 1981, 149, 150.
7. Skegg, 1984, 220.

References

Ad Hoc Committee of the Harvard Medical School to Examine the Definition of Brain Death. 1968. A definition of irreversible coma. *Journal of the American Medical Association* 205, no. 6 (5 August): 337–40.

Agich, George J. 1976. The concepts of death and embodiment. *Ethics in Science and Medicine* 3:95–105.

Agich, George J., and Jones, Royce P. 1985. Personal identity and brain death: A critical response. Unpublished paper.

_____. 1985. The logical status of brain death criteria. *The Journal of Medicine and Philosophy* 10:387–95.

Annas, George J. 1983. Defining death: There ought to be a law. *The Hastings Center Report* 13, no. 1 (February): 20–21.

Becker, Lawrence C. 1975. Human being: The boundaries of the concept. *Philosophy and Public Affairs* 4, no. 4 (Summer): 335–59.

Bernat, James L., Culver, Charles M., and Gert, Bernard. 1982a. Defining death in theory and practice. *The Hastings Center Report* 12, no. 1 (February): 5–9.

_____. 1982b. Reply to Capron and Lynn. *The Hastings Center Report* 12, no. 12 (February): 5–9.

Black, Peter M. 1978. Definitions of brain death. In *Ethical issues in death and dying*, edited by Tom L. Beauchamp and Seymour Perlin. Englewood Cliffs, N.J.: Prentice-Hall.

Black's law dictionary. 1968, 4th ed. St. Paul, Minn.: West Publishing.

223

Brierley, J. B., et al. 1971. Neocortical death after cardiac arrest. *The Lancet* 2 (11 September): 560–65.

Brody, Howard. 1981. *Ethical decisions in medicine.* 2d ed. Boston: Little, Brown.

———. 1983. Brain death and personal existence: A reply to Green and Wikler. *The Journal of Medicine and Philosophy* 8:187–96.

Browne, Alister. 1983. Whole-brain death reconsidered. *Journal of Medical Ethics* 9:28–31.

Buchanan, James M., and Lomasky, Loren E. 1984. The matrix of contractarian justice. *Social Philosophy and Policy* 2, no. 1 (Autumn): 12–32.

Canadian Government. 1981. Criteria for the determination of death. Ottawa: Law Reform Commission.

Capron, Alexander M. 1973. The purpose of death: A reply to Professor Dworkin. *Indiana Law Journal* 48, no. 4 (Summer): 640–46.

———. 1978. Legal definition of death. *Annals of the New York Academy of Science* 315:349–62.

Capron, Alexander M., and Kass, Leon. 1972. A statutory definition of the standards for determining human death: An appraisal and a proposal. *University of Pennsylvania Law Review* 121:87–118.

Capron, Alexander M., and Lynn, Joanne. 1982. Defining death: Which way? *The Hastings Center Report* 12, no. 2 (April): 43–44.

Care, Norman S. 1969. Contractualism and moral criticism. *The Review of Metaphysics* 23:85–101.

Copp, David, ed. 1984. *Morality, reason and truth.* Totowa, N.J.: Rowman and Allenheld.

Cranford, Ronald E., and Smith, Harmon L. 1979. Some critical distinctions between brain death and the persistent vegetative state. *Ethics in Science and Medicine* 6:199–209.

Dennett, Daniel. 1978. Conditions of personhood. In *Brainstorms.* Montgomery, Vt.: Bradford.

Dworkin, Roger B. 1973. Death in context. *Indiana Law Journal* 48, no. 4 (Summer): 623–39.

Engelhardt, H. T. 1978. Medicine and the concept of person. In *Ethical issues in death and dying*, edited by Tom L. Beauchamp and Seymour Perlin. Englewood Cliffs, N.J.: Prentice-Hall.

Feinberg, Joel. 1974. The rights of animals and unborn generations. In *Philosophy and environmental crisis*, edited by William Blackstone. Athens: University of Georgia Press.

———. 1977. Harm and self-interest. In *Law, morality, and society: Essays in honor of H. L. A. Hart*, edited by P. M. S. Hacker and J. Ray. Oxford: Clarendon.

_____. 1980. *Rights, justice, and the bounds of liberty: Essays in social philosophy*. Princeton: Princeton University Press.

_____. 1984. *Harm to others: The moral limits of the criminal law*. New York: Oxford University Press.

Gauthier, David. 1974. Rational cooperation. *Nous* 8 (March): 53–65.

_____. 1975. Reason and maximization. *Canadian Journal of Philosophy* 4, no. 3 (March): 411–33.

_____. 1977. The social contract as ideology. *Philosophy and Public Affairs* 6, no. 2 (Winter): 130–64.

_____. 1984. Justice as social choice. In *Morality, reason and truth*, edited by David Copp. Totowa, N.J.: Rowman and Allenheld.

Gaylin, Willard. 1984. In defense of the dignity of being human. *The Hastings Center Report* 14, no. 4 (August): 18–22.

Glover, Jonathan. 1977. *Causing death and saving lives*. Middlesex: Penguin.

Green, Michael, and Wikler, Daniel. 1980. Brain death and personal identity. *Philosophy and Public Affairs* 9, no. 2 (Winter): 105–33.

Halley, M. Martin, and Harvey, William F. 1968. Medical and legal definitions of death. *Journal of the American Medical Association* 204, no. 6 (6 March): 423–25.

Harth, Eric. 1982. *Windows on the mind*. Brighton: Harvester.

Held, Virginia. 1984. *Rights and goods: Justifying social action*. New York: Macmillan, Free Press.

High, Dallas M. 1972. Death: Its conceptual elusiveness. *Soundings* 55 (Winter): 438–58.

Hoffman, John C. 1979. Clarifying the debate on death. *Soundings* 62, no. 4 (Winter): 430–47.

Institute of Society, Ethics and the Life Sciences—Task Force on Death and Dying. 1972. Refinements in criteria for the determination of death. *Journal of the American Medical Association* 221:48–53.

Isaacs, Leonard. 1978. Death where is thy distinguishing? *The Hastings Center Report* 8, no. 1 (February): 7–8.

Jonas, Hans. 1974. *Philosophical essays: From ancient creed to technological man*. Englewood Cliffs, N.J.: Prentice-Hall.

Kass, Leon R. 1971. Death as an event: A commentary on Robert Morison. *Science* 173:698–702.

Kennedy, Ian McColl. 1971. The Kansas statute on death—An appraisal. *New England Journal of Medicine* 285, no. 17: 946–50.

Korein, Julius, ed. 1978. *Brain death: Interrelated medical and social issues*. New York: New York Academy of Sciences.

Laing, R. D. 1960. *The divided self*. New York: Pantheon, Random House.

Lamb, David. 1978. Diagnosing death. *Philosophy and Public Affairs* 7, no. 2 (Winter): 144–53.

————. 1983. Review of *Medicine and moral philosophy* (a book edited by Marshall Cohen, Thomas Nagel, and Thomas Scanlon). *Journal of Medical Ethics* 9:175–76.

————. 1984. Reply to Professor Wikler. *Journal of Medical Ethics* 2:102.

————. 1985. *Death, brain death and ethics.* Albany: State University of New York Press.

Levenbook, Barbara Baum. 1984. Harming someone after his death. *Ethics* 94 (April): 407–19.

Lynn, Joanne. 1983. The determination of death. *Annals of Internal Medicine* 99, no. 2 (August): 264–66.

Menzel, Paul T. 1983. *Medical costs, moral choices: A philosophy of health care economics in America.* New Haven: Yale University Press.

Mills, Don Harper. 1971. The Kansas death statute—Bold and innovative. *New England Journal of Medicine* 285, no. 17: 968–69.

Morison, Robert S. 1971. Death: Process or event? *Science,* 173 (20 August): 694–98.

New Jersey Supreme Court. 1976. Opinion in the matter of Karen Quinlan. 70 N.J. 10, 335A 2d, 647.

Pallis, Christopher. 1982–83. ABC of brain stem death. *The British Medical Journal* 285 (20 November): 1487–90; (27 November): 1558–60; (4 December): 1641–44; and 286 (8 January): 123–24; (15 January): 209–10.

————. 1983a. The arguments about the EEG. *British Medical Journal* 286:284–85.

————. 1983b. Whole-brain death reconsidered—Physiological facts and philosophy. *Journal of Medical Ethics* 9:32–37.

————. 1984. Brainstem death: The evolution of a concept. In *Kidney transplantation: Principles and practice,* 2d ed., edited by Peter J. Morris. Orlando, Fla.: Giune and Stratton.

Parfit, Derek. 1984. *Reasons and persons.* Oxford: Clarendon.

Partridge, Ernest. 1981. Posthumous interests and posthumous respect. *Ethics* 91:243–64.

Perry, John, ed. 1975. *Personal identity.* Berkeley: University of California Press.

President's Commission for the Study of Ethical Problems in Medicine and Biomedical and Behavioral Research. 1981. *Defining death: Medical, legal and ethical issues in the determination of death.* July. Washington: U.S. Government Printing Office.

Puccetti, Roland. 1983. The life of a person. In *Abortion and the status of the fetus*, edited by W. B. Bondeson, H. T. Engelhardt, S. F. Spicker, and D. H. Winship. Boston: D. Reidel.

————. 1978. The conquest of death. In *Language, metaphysics, and death*, edited by John Donnelly. New York: Fordham University Press.

Ramsey, Paul. 1970. *The patient as person*. New Haven: Yale University Press.

Rawls, John. 1971. A *theory of justice*. Cambridge: Harvard University Press.

Reilly, Edward L., et al., 1985. Failure of pavulon to consistently provide adequate EMG attenuation for recording electrocerebral inactivity. *Clinical Electroencephalography* 16, no. 2 (April): 72–76.

Rodin, E., et al. 1985. Brainstem death. *Clinical Electroencephalography* 16, no. 2 (April): 63–71.

Rorty, Amelie Okensberg. 1976. *The identities of persons*. Berkeley: University of California Press.

Schelling, Thomas C. 1984. *Choice and consequence*. Cambridge: Harvard University Press.

Schiffer, R. B. 1978. The concept of death: Traditional and alternative. *The Journal of Medicine and Philosophy* 3, no. 1: 24–37.

Schwager, Robert L. 1978. Life, death, and the irreversibly comatose. In *Ethical issues in death and dying*, edited by Tom L. Beauchamp and Seymour Perlin. Englewood Cliffs, N.J.: Prentice-Hall.

Skegg, P. D. G. 1984. *Law, ethics, and medicine*. Oxford: Clarendon.

Stickel, Delford L. 1979. The brain death criterion of human death. *Ethics in Science and Medicine* 6:177–97.

Tomlinson, Tom. 1984. The conservative use of the brain death criterion— A critique. *The Journal of Medicine* 9:377–93.

Tooley, Michael. 1983. *Abortion and infanticide*. Oxford: Clarendon.

Veatch, Robert M. 1972. Brain death: Welcome definition or dangerous judgment? *The Hastings Center Report* 2 (November): 10–13.

————. 1975. The whole-brain-oriented concept of death: An outmoded philosophical foundation. *Journal of Thanatology* 3:13–30.

————. 1976a. *Death, dying, and the biological revolution*. New Haven: Yale University Press.

————. 1976b. The definition of death: Ethical, philosophical, and policy confusion. Paper delivered at Illinois Wesleyan University Symposium on Brain Death.

————. 1982. Maternal brain death: An ethicist's thoughts. *Journal of the American Medical Association* 248, no. 9 (3 September): 1102–03.

Veith, Frank J., et al. 1977. Brain death: Part 1, A status report of medical and ethical consideration; Part 2, A status report of legal considerations. *Journal of the American Medical Association* 238 (17 October): 1744–48.

Walker, A. Earl. 1981. *Cerebral death*. 2d ed. Baltimore: Urban and Schwartzenberg.

Walton, Douglas N. 1980. *Brain death: Ethical considerations*. West Lafayette, Ind.: Purdue University Press.

Wikler, Daniel. 1984a. Correspondence: Brain death. *Journal of Medical Ethics* 10:101–02.

———. 1984b. Conceptual issues in the definition of death: A guide for public policy. *Theoretical Medicine* 5 (June): 167–80.

Youngner, Stuart J. and Bartlett, Edward T. 1983. Human death and high technology: The failure of the whole-brain formulations. *Annals of Internal Medicine* 99 (August): 252–58.

Index

Anencephaly, 137–41
Apallic syndrome, 12

Biological arguments: Lawrence Becker's support of traditional criteria, 46–61; objections to, 56–58, 60–61, 63–66, 70, 71–74; David Lamb's support of brain-death criterion, 144–55
Brain: as central vital agency, 34–37; body's regulatory center, 71–74, 123–25, 186–90; person-body transfer, 120–23; substrate/process distinction, 125–27
Brain death: definition of, 6–8; contrasted with persistent vegetative state, 12–13; and death of person, 111, 119; similarity to brain removal, 127–28; in pregnant women, 146–47
Brain-death criterion: divergent conceptual bases for, 10, 12, 24–25; relationship to traditional criteria, 18–19; consciousness-based, 42–44; objections to, 52–56, 79–84, 80–

81; defenses of, 62–66, 68–73, 84–91
Brain stem: role in systemic functioning, 72–73
Brain-stem criterion: Lamb's argument for, 145–55; prognostic significance of, 147–48; diagnostic significance for brain-death denied, 148–49

Canadian Law Reform model statute, 203–05
Cerebral death, 11
Chronic vegetative state. See Persistent vegetative state
Computer-tape thought experiment, 97–99, 129–32
Conceptual problem: nature of, 21–23
Conscience clause: in public policy for declaring death, 210–12 passim; defects with, 212–15 passim
Consciousness: permanent absence of, and death, 32–33, 38, 134–37; distinguished from psychological con-

Consciousness (*continued*)
tinuity, 133–34; as a policy con-
concern, 207–08
Consensual strategy. *See* President's
Commission
Consensus: departure from, 214
Contractarian methodology, 166–69
Criteria for declaring death: related to
conceptual framework, 1–2, 10, 18;
a medical-scientific matter, 7; presuppose different concepts of death,
19, 42–44; moral and ontological
arguments required to support, 91–
92

Death: distinguished from biologic
cessation, 2–3, 5; process or event,
3–4; *Black's Law Dictionary* definition of, 24–25; formal definition of,
38–39, 95
Death of organism, 37–38, 42–44,
46–47, 52–56, 62, 95–98, 145–46,
161, 164–66
Death of person, 43–44, 114–15,
116–17, 160–62, 164–77, 181–82
Declaring death: technology's impact
on, 2, 7, 68–70, 95, 144–45; presupposes decision of significance,
2–3, 5
Dignity: affront of treating dead as
alive, 92–94

Euthanasia, 70, 79, 142, 174

Harms and losses: legally equivalent,
171–73, 211, 214
Harvard committee report, 6–14, 19,
23–25
Heart: as central vital agency, 25–33;
spontaneity of in brain-death cases,
27–32; nonspontaneity of in brain-
death cases, 29–32
Human death: problem of concep-
tualizing, 5, 19, 20, 21–22; different concepts of, 39–41; loci of, 41–

42; biological definition of, 46; essentially significant characteristics
lost at, 95–97; conceived of as organismic or personal, 99, 101–03,
156–58

Individual essentialism, 109, 111–12,
115, 116, 119–20, 161
Irreversible coma, 9–10, 69

Kind-essentialism, 109, 111–12, 115,
119–20, 161

Life: Lawrence Becker's metamorphic
definition of, 47–52; differing concepts of, 101

Moral arguments: objections to, 58–
60, 66–68, 105–10; nature of, 75–
76; divergent arguments about declaring death, 75–79; John Hoffman's primary and secondary levels
of moral debate, 99–105; role in
redefinition debate, 112

Neocortical death: definition of, 11–
12; a variant of persistent vegetative
state, 13, 14; compared with brain
death, 13–14; morally problematic
nature of, 163–64
Neocortical-death criterion: as basis
for declaring death, 14; Howard
Brody's argument rejecting, 85–87,
89–91; reply to Brody on, 87–91;
Robert Veatch's defense of, 91–99;
Green and Wikler's defense of,
132–34, 155–58; David Lamb's rejection of, 150–54; President's
Commission's rejection of, 190–95;
policy recommendation based on,
207–10, 213–15
Nonspontaneity, 81–82, 159

Ontological arguments: nature of,
111, 117; role in redefinition de-

bate, 112, 141–42; connection with human death as brain death, 132–34, 141–42

Persistent vegetative state: definition of, 11–12; problems posed by, 14, 85; nonperson status of patient, 85–87; rights of patient, 85–88; interests of patient, 86–88; quality of life assessments inappropriate for patient, 162–64; declaring patient dead, 169–77; American Medical Association's 1986 ruling on, 175; management of patient after declaring death, 176; organ donation after declaring death, 176

Person: concept of, 161; normative conception of, 177–81; descriptive conception of, 180–81

Personal identity theory: Hans Jonas's theory, 81–83; John Hoffman's theory, 103–05; loss of personal identity and death, 112–13; Green and Wikler's psychological continuity theory, 112–32; counterexamples to psychological continuity theory, 117–19, 123–32 passim; objections to as basis for declaring death, 149–55, 191–92

Posthumous harm, 93–94

President's Commission: on whole-brain formulations, 183–90; on higher-brain formulations, 190–98;

on nonbrain formulations, 195; consensual strategy used by, 195–96

Public policy: role of moral argument in, 141; contractarian reasoning in, 166–69; argument for person-centered policy, 169–77; alternative policies, 205–15

Quality of life, 78–79, 99–100, 108–09

Redefinition debate: history of, 6–14; empirical and philosophical issues, 18; biological arguments in, 19–20; moral arguments in, 20; ontological arguments in, 20; role of moral argument in, 76–77, 84, 105, 110

Slippery slope arguments: and brain-death criterion, 142–44; and consciousness-based criterion, 153–55; and higher-brain formulation, 208

Toleration, 206–07, 210

Traditional criteria: presuppose view of human as organism, 1–2, 5

Uniform Declaration of Death Act: legal role of, 6, 25; and brain-death criterion, 111; assessment of, 198–206